The Codasyl Approach
to
Data Base Management

WILEY SERIES IN COMPUTING

Consulting Editor
Professor D. W. Barron, *Department of Mathematics, Southampton University*

Numerical Control—Mathematics and Applications

P. Bézier
Professeur au Conservatoire National des Arts et Métiers
and
Technological Development Manager, Renault, France

Communication Networks for Computers

D. W. Davies and D. L. A. Barber
National Physical Laboratory, Teddington

Macro Processors
and Techniques for Portable Software

P. J. Brown
University of Kent at Canterbury

A Practical Guide to Algol 68

Frank G. Pagan
Memorial University of Newfoundland

Programs and Machines

Richard Bird
University of Reading

The Codasyl Approach to Data Base Management

T. William Olle
Independent Consultant and Lecturer
Data Base Management Systems and Techniques

The Codasyl Approach
to
Data Base Management

T. William Olle

Independent Consultant and Lecturer
Data Base Management Systems and Techniques

A Wiley–Interscience Publication

JOHN WILEY & SONS

Chichester · New York · Brisbane · Toronto

Library of Congress Cataloging in Publication Data:

Olle, T. William.
 The CODASYL approach to data base management.

 'A Wiley–Interscience publication.'
 Includes index.
 1. Data base management. I. Title.
QA76.9.D3044   001.6'425   77–12375

ISBN 0 471 99579 7

Text set in 11/12 pt Photon Times, printed by photolithography, and bound in Great Britain at The Pitman Press, Bath

This, my first book, is dedicated to my mother Mrs. Kathleen Olle and to the memory of my father Thomas Cecil Olle.

Acknowledgement

During the course of preparation of this text, drafts of the whole text and of specific chapters have been reviewed by the following—Martin Anderson (Logica Ltd.), Geoff Baker (CACI, Ltd.), Emile Broadwin (Computer Sciences, Inc.), Gordon Everest (University of Michigan), and John Hale (Cincom, Ltd.). Their comments have been valuable and their efforts are much appreciated.

Many authors in their acknowledgement give thanks to a wife who has lived through the period of the book with understanding. Some can go further and thank their wife for her skill and patience in typing the manuscript. It is my pleasure to acknowledge the help of my wife, Greta, for producing a neat typescript from my execrable handwritten manuscript, but also for using her skills as an editor in checking the consistency and accuracy of the text.

T. W. OLLE
West Byfleet, Surrey
England

November 1977

Contents

Preface

This book is intended as a tutorial text on one approach to data base management, namely that espoused by the CODASYL Organization between 1967 and 1971 and perpetuated in the numerous reports published by CODASYL between 1968 and 1975. There are several commercial implementations of this approach available, best known of which are Univac's DMS 1100, Honeywell's IDS/2, Cullinane's IDMS (availabe on IBM machines and also on ICL machines), and Siemens' UDS. This text is in no way intended to replace the manuals of these systems, but hopefully it will serve as a valuable explanatory text to users of any implementation of the CODASYL approach.

In addition, the book is intended as a basis for teaching students in universities, colleges, and polytechnics. I am convinced that most of the information systems of the nineteen eighties will be built using data base management techniques rather than the conventional techniques which evolved during the first decade of data processing and have been heavily influenced by the early widespread use of magnetic tape as a storage medium.

Many readers will be aware that there has been considerable debate among both practitioners and researchers on the relative merits of the different approaches to data base management. The practitioner has a choice in the market place and indeed it is fitting that he should. It would be a sad world if we all had to live in the same kind of house or drive the same kind of car. Nevertheless, choosing a DBMS to live with requires a very different decision process from that involved in choosing a house or a car. In the hope of making this decision process easier, chapters have been included in this book explaining other approaches, namely TOTAL, IMS, and ADABAS. A chapter has also been included comparing relational theory with the CODASYL approach.

When I started this text in 1974, I thought I would have an advantage over the many authors from universities whose time for writing is restricted by the demands of lecturing, tutorials, research students, and the like. Indeed, most of this book was completed fairly quickly as I was able to put aside blocks of days which were free from consulting and lecturing commitments around the world. However, the demands on my time built up and, as a result, the book has followed the golden rule which one can use with computer programs—namely that the last 10% of the predicted work took 90% of the total elapsed time.

The time factor is in itself a problem because the CODASYL specifications are changing inexorably as the years go by. The book reflects as accurately as possible the most recently published specifications available at time of writing. The capabilities defined are provided in the commercial implementations in use worldwide. However, the aim of the text is also to give a tutorial expose of the principles and the ideas which dominate the commercially available implementations of the CODASYL approach. These will change more slowly and hence the ideas explained in this text will hopefully continue to be of value to student and practitioner alike.

Chapter 1

Historical Perspective

1.1 Introduction

The formal historical background to the CODASYL work on data base management can be read in Section 1.2 of the Data Description Language Committee's June 1973 Journal of Development.[1] This history will be summarized in this chapter with a few personal comments on the relevant events which have taken place over the past 15 years.

1.2 Origin of Terms

It is not completely clear where the terms *data base* and *data base management* originated, although it can be stated that these are not originally CODASYL terms. It is important to distinguish between the origin of the capabilities and the origin of the terminology.

Charles W. Bachman is widely recognized as one of the early pioneers in the field of what we today call data base management. Yet, if one reads his early papers[2,3] the term *data base* is not used. Bachman's main concerns are reflected in the titles of his papers—'A General Purpose Programming System for Random Access Memories', and 'Software for Random Access Processing'.

In other words, his aim was to make more effective use of what we now call direct access storage devices. The cornerstone of his thinking was a flexible scheme for linking together records of different types, using what is still referred to as a chain structure. In the first of his papers,[2] Bachman refers to the fact that his software system, Integrated Data Store or IDS, was running in early 1963 and he references an internal GE publication which was the initial specification for that system with a date of January 1962. To trace the origin of the term *data base* it is necessary to refer to the work sponsored by the military in the early nineteen sixties. In June 1963, System Development Corporation sponsored a symposium in Santa Monica with the title 'Development and Management of a Computer-centered Data Base'. Seven papers were presented, all of which were connected with defence work.[4] The titles of some of these contained the term *data base* as follows:

J. H. Bryant, 'AIDS Experience in Managing Data Base Operations'.

A. K. Swanson, 'A Computer-centered Data Base Serving USAF Personnel Managers'.

R. L. Patrick, 'Adapting Mass Storage Equipment for the Handling of a Data Base'.

AIDS is an acronym for Aerospace Intelligence Data Systems. Two of the other papers dealt with very early DBMS, namely ADAM, Automated Data Management, and LUCID, Language Used to Communicate Information System Design.

In addition to the seven papers, there were four working sessions held at the symposium. Their titles are of more than passing interest, simply because they could equally well be used as titles for working sessions at a conference today. The titles were:

A. Factors determining data base content requirements.

B. Criteria influencing data base organization or design.

C. Methodology of collecting data and maintaining a data base.

D. Economic considerations relevant to data base management.

In the second session, it appears that a definition of the term data base was proposed. It read:

1. A data base is a set of files.
2. A file is an ordered collection of entries.
3. An entry consists of a key or keys and data.

The report on the session goes on to state that the definition was not universally accepted! However, it is the earliest definition of the term on record.

The papers in the proceedings of this symposium were clearly very concerned with the problem of retrieving information easily from files of data and some used the term *data base* to refer to the stored files from which they were trying to retrieve the information. In most cases, the storage medium was magnetic tape. This implies some very different objectives from those with which Bachman's early work was associated.

In September 1965, the System Development Corporation (together with ARPA and the Air Force Systems Command) sponsored the second symposium on Compter-centered Data Base Systems. The format of this symposium was interesting in that a fairly complex problem was presented and a number of companies illustrated how their system would tackle the problem. One of the people attempting to solve the problem was Charles Bachman with IDS. The proceedings of this symposium[5] contain a full description of the problem and the five historic approaches to it.

All in all, 1965 could be viewed as the year the data base baby began to toddle. It was also the year in which CODASYL grasped the nettle.

1.3 Early CODASYL Work

One of the central figures in the early CODASYL moves into data base management was Warren Simmons from US Steel in Pittsburgh. In the course of finding out about the hardware and software available in 1965, he was exposed to General Electric's IDS.

US Steel was one of the early supporters of COBOL and as such was active on the various CODASYL committees which were working on maintaining the language. Warren Simmons was their representative on a COBOL Programming Language Committee, and it was thanks to his perception and insight that the List Processing Task Force was formed.

The use of the term list processing calls for some explanation. The chain concept in IDS provided for a number of records to be linked together in direct access storage. This *chain* could also well be thought of as a list and list processing was a widely used term in the early and mid sixties.

The first meeting of the List Processing Task Force was held in Atlanta, Georgia, in October 1965. A number of meetings were held under the umbrella of this title. However, in May 1967 a meeting was held in Minneapolis at which by some strange coincidence about half of the attendees were new to the group. I was one of the new members, representing the company then known as Radio Corporation of America.

The meetings throughout 1967 were regular, lasting approximately one week every four to six weeks. The discussions were often very heated. The main technical input into the deliberations came from Charles Bachman and George Dodd. The latter was also a new member at the Minneapolis meeting. He had developed a system at the General Motors Research Laboratory called APL or Associative Programming Language,[6] which was very similar to IDS except that it was an extension to PL/1 and not to COBOL. (It must be noted that Dodd's APL and Iverson's APL–360 are completely unrelated.)

At the historic May 1967 meeting it was decided that the term *list processing* had to go. The reasons for this were that somehow it did not fit with the down to earth practical aspects of COBOL which the group was trying to extend. Similarly, the term *task force* was found to be too strong. It was probably a term used in military circles. After much deliberation the group decided to call themselves the *Data Base Task Group*, and this name was retained until they were formally disbanded in 1971.

The arguments which were raging during the years 1967 and 1968 reflected the two principal types of background from which contributors to the data base field came. People like Bachman, Dodd and Simmons epitomized the manufacturing environment and they saw the need for the more powerful structures which IDS and APL (Dodd's) offered. Others, such as those who had spoken at the early 1963 SDC symposium, and indeed myself had seen the need for easy to use retrieval languages which would enable easy access to data by non-programmers.

This issue crystallized into the form host language versus self-contained, and I had the honour to chair a structured debate on the topic in August 1968.[7] One sentence by Bachman sums up what in retrospect could be the only conclusion with respect to the two approaches. 'Each has its place; both are needed.'

Fortunately, DBTG pressed on with its work on a host language approach. Progress was not easy in the early days. Some members (including myself) were not convinced that the IDS approach was the right one for the long term. Some members representing competitive hardware vendors suspected General Electric of trying to get its approach standardized as part of COBOL in order to achieve a competitive edge in the market place.

The first report from the DBTG came out in January 1968[8] and was entitled 'COBOL extensions to handle data bases'. Some quotations from the one page summary of recommendations show the thinking of the era. It was recommended to

'Add a facility for declaring master and detail record relationships which use circular chains as a means to provide the widest possible file structuring cabability.

'The report supports the recommendation by first considering the several modes of interaction with a data base, and then discussing the data management techniques currently used to solve the programming problem. After a comparison of known data organization and accessing techniques, the conclusions in favour of the circular chain or ring structure are presented.'

Shortly after the release of this January 1968 report, Warren Simmons retired from the chairmanship of the DBTG for personal reasons. The DDLC report states that G. Durand of Southern Railway System replaced Warren Simmons as chairman, but in fact the person who chaired the meetings during 1968 was D. L. Rapp, at that time with Traveller's Insurance. This was a difficult year for the DBTG as the January 1968 report had drawn attention to their work and what the group was trying to achieve became better understood by a wider spectrum of people. At the end of 1968, Don Rapp left Traveller's Insurance and at the same time gave up his participation in the DBTG.

Tax Metaxides of Bell Laboratories had joined the DBTG in the autumn of 1967 and on Don Rapp's departure he took over as chairman. He was a forceful and effective chairman and it must be stated that while most of the early ideas came from Bachman and Dodd, and Simmons had the insight to get the endeavour started, Metaxides must take the credit for getting it finished.

In October 1969, the first set of language specifications emerged. The concept of the sub-schema made its appearance together with the idea that the approach was not only aimed at COBOL. Between 1965 and 1969, PL/1 had made some modest inroads into COBOL and it was recognized that programmers using FORTRAN and PL/1 would also want to process the data in a data base. Nevertheless, the October 1969 report caused quite a flurry when it was presented to its parent committee. The main problems came from IBM who released a self styled minority report stating that they were opposed to the DBTG's approach and suggesting alternatives. Some of their arguments stemmed from the fact that IBM was at that time very actively promoting PL/1 as a replacement for COBOL. This probably stimulated the emergence of the sub-schema concept, but IBM was not satisfied. They claimed that the approach was still too COBOL oriented and that the DBTG could not claim to interface with all programming languages equally well.

It is indeed true that the data base record types in the October 1969 report looked very much like COBOL record types. PL/1 record types were much more complex and one of the steps which DBTG took prior to its final release in April 1971 was to change the schema record types to PL/1 record types. The COBOL sub-schema record types were, of course, unchanged.

1.4 More Recent CODASYL Work

1971 contained two major milestones in the life of CODASYL data base specifications. The DBTG's April 1971 report was accepted by the parent committee, by then called the Programming Language Committee, at a historic meeting in Washington in May 1971. The acceptance was not entirely unanimous and yet again IBM voiced objections. These are documented in a paper authored by Engles[9] which apparently represented the combined efforts of many people inside IBM. It must be recalled that by 1971, IBM had a fairly major investment in their own system (IMS) and it was clearly not in their best commercial interests to see a radically different approach moving along the slow path to standardization.

In May 1971, CODASYL took a step which in retrospect has had some unfortunate technical repercussions. It was decided that the Schema DDL, which is to be used by a data administrator for defining a data base, was not a part of COBOL. Therefore a separate standing committee, called the Data Description Language Committee (DDLC), was created to study the problems of data base description. The language for specifying the part of a data base to be processed by a COBOL program, called the COBOL Sub-schema DDL, and the statements to be added to the COBOL Procedure Division in order to allow a programmer to manipulate the data in a data base, called the COBOL Data Manipulation Language, DML, were both formally referred to the Programming Language Committee for consideration as extensions to COBOL.

The Programming Language Committee immediately formed a small task group called the Data Base Language Task Group, or DBLTG. Their assignment was to take the DBTG's work and mould it into a form which was suitable for inclusion in the CODASYL COBOL Journal of Development. This they did and their first report[10] was widely distributed in order to obtain feedback from the COBOL community. In 1976 it was approved for inclusion as part of CODASYL COBOL and was published in the 1976 CODASYL COBOL Journal of Development.[11] In the present text, I have attempted to reflect the thinking of the DDLC and the DBLTG, referring back to the 1971 report of the DBTG where it is felt important to convey one of their ideas which will be found in commercially available systems even though it has fallen out of favour in the work of subsequent committees.

1.5 Current Events

The history of data base specification in CODASYL has not ended. In fact, if CODASYL is to play a continuing role in the further development of data processing technology, then one can assert that work has only just begun. Action has moved to the formal standardization bodies such as ANSI. ANSI X3J4, the ANSI committee responsible for COBOL standardization, is at the present time studying the inclusion of the CODASYL COBOL Data Base Facility in ANSI COBOL. An ISO study group reporting to the TC97/SC5 committee is holding meetings to probe some of the broader issues connected with data base standardization work.

References

1. CODASYL Data Description Language Committee. Journal of Development June 1973. Available from British Computer Society, London, IFIP Applied Information Processing Group (IAG) HQ, Amsterdam, and ACM HQ, New York.
2. C. W. Bachman, S. B. Williams, 'A general purpose programming system for random access memories', *Proc. Fall Joint Computer Conference*, October 1964, 26 411–422.
3. C. W. Bachman, 'Software for random access processing', *Datamation*, April 1965.
4. Proceedings of the Symposium on Development and Management of a Computer-centered Data Base, held June 1963. Published January 1964 by System Development Corporation, Santa Monica, California.
5. Proceedings of the Second Symposium on Computer-centered Data Base Systems, held September 1965. Published December 1965 by System Development Corporation as TM—2624/100/00.
6. G. G. Dodd, 'APL—a language for associative data handling in PL/1', *Proc. Fall Joint Computer Conference* 1966, 29 677–684.
7. The Large Data Base: its organization and user interface. Transcript of a Panel Session at ACM Conference August 1968. Published in DATA BASE (Newsletter of ACM's Special Interest Group in Business Data Processing), Vol. 1, No. 3, Fall 1969.
8. Report to the CODASYL COBOL Committee. COBOL extensions to handle data bases. Published as April 1968 Newsletter of ACM Special Interest Group in Business Data Processing.
9. R. W. Engles, 'An analysis of the April 1971 DBTG report', A position paper presented to the Programming Language Committee by the IBM Representative to the Data Base Task Group. Published as an Appendix in Proceedings of BCS Symposium on CODASYL DBTG report, held October 1971. Published in Proceedings of ACM SIGFIDET Workshop on Data Description Access and Control, held November 1971, 68–91.
10. CODASYL Data Base Language Task Group. Proposal for a data base facility in COBOL. January 1973. Avilable from Technical Services Branch, Dept. of Supply and Services, Ottawa, Canada.
11. CODASYL COBOL Journal of Development 1976. Available from Technical Services Branch, Dept. of Supply and Services, Ottawa, Canada at $7.50 per copy or $20.00 including updating service.

Chapter 2

Components of a DBMS

2.1 Introduction

How a DBMS based in the CODASYL approach is broken down into components varies from one implementation to another. In some cases, the difference is merely one of terminology; in others it is more fundamental. For subsequent reference, the five major components are identified as:

1. Schema Data Description Language
2. Sub-schema Data Description Language
3. Data Manipulation Language
4. Data Base Control System
5. Device Media Control Language

Each will be discussed in turn.

2.2 Concept of a Schema

The word *schema* exists in the English language but is not widely used and has not been given meaning in data processing terminology prior to the efforts of the CODASYL Systems Committee and the DBTG during the late sixties. The Concise Oxford Dictionary defines *schema* as a noun with the following meanings:

Synopsis, outline, diagram; (Logic) syllogistic figure; (Grammatical Rhetoric) figure of speech; (Kantian Philosophy) general type, essential form, conception of what is common to all members of a class.

It is the last of these meanings which is most relevant in the present context. To the DBTG, it is clear that *schema* may be defined as *the description of a data base*.

Strictly speaking, there could be more than one data base conforming to a given schema, but in practice here there is only one. Furthermore, there is normally only one schema for each data base.

2.2.1 Concept of a Data Base

Having defined a schema as a description of a data base, we are precluded from defining a data base as *that which is defined in a schema*, although this is tempting. It is desirable to define *data base* in such a way that it excludes the older and well understood concept of a file. The essential difference between a data base and a file should be that the former contains cross referencing from one part of the data base to the other. This should exclude an indexed file, in which each part of the file is equally accessible from outside.

To avoid getting into too much deep water on this issue, it is proposed to define a data base as *a cross referenced collection of data records of different types* and a file as *a collection of records which is not cross referenced and in which the records are normally all of the same type*.

Hopefully, this conveys the impression of allowing for the existence of the COBOL multi-record type file which should certainly never be regarded as a data base.

It is important to emphasize that by introducing the concept of a data base into data processing, nobody is attempting to remove the concept of a file, but merely supplementing it with that of a data base. The data base will normally replace the master file, but not the input file, output file, print file, transaction file, archive file and so on. To be precise, a data base should replace *several* master files. It is indeed unfortunate that the word *file* has often replaced the word *data base* in situations where clearly only a file is implied.

2.3 Schema Data Description Language, Schema DDL

The Schema Data Description Language is a free standing declarative language which is used to define the structure of a data base (now called a schema). With one significant exception to be discussed much later in this book, the Schema DDL does not define the processing to be performed on the data. It does not even allow statements to be made concerning the amount of data to be stored in the data base and how much space is to be reserved for the data. The data base is regarded as being stored on direct access storage—hence the emphasis on cross referencing which would not be feasible if the data were stored on a sequential access medium such as magnetic tape.

To return to the Schema DDL, it is used to define a schema. One successful use of the language produces one schema which is a number of English-like statements written on paper or possibly displayed on a video terminal. Using the Schema DDL does *not* produce a data base, merely a description of what one looks like.

In order to produce a data base, a number of further actions are necessary. The schema must be converted into a computer readable form if it is not in such a form already. It must then be translated into an object form which the DBTG refers to as the *object schema*. In case of ambiguity, the form prepared by human hand is called a *source* schema (cf. source program and object program). Finally, programs must be written to enter data into the data base.

The CODASYL groups (DBTG and DDLC) appear to have avoided giving a name to the process by which a source schema is converted into an object schema. As a result, several implementors have chosen to refer to a 'Schema (DDL) Compiler' while others use 'Schema (DDL) Translator'. In view of the fact that no executable code is generated (i.e. compiled) by this process, it is proposed in this book to prefer the term Schema Translator.

2.4 Concept of a Sub-schema

The origin of the sub-schema concept is not clear. It was certainly not mentioned in the January 1968 report of the DBTG, but by October 1969, it was quite fully defined.

A sub-schema is best defined as *a part of a schema*. It is better to avoid thinking of it as *part of a data base* because it is the way in which the part is identified which is important. For instance, if there are seven types of records in a data base, then a sub-schema may include three of them, but not some records of a given type. (This is a simplified view of the capability and a full elaboration will be given in a later chapter.)

For a given schema, there may exist several sub-schemas. These sub-schemas may overlap, which means that one record type may be included in two or more sub-schemas. Furthermore, a sub-schema may consist of the whole data base or it may be restricted to one record type.

A useful way to think about the schema and sub-schema is the following. The schema is the overall view of the logical structure of the data base as seen by the central authority responsible for the data base. This authority is usually referred to as a Data Administrator (or Data Base Administrator). The sub-schema is the view of the data base as seen by the Applications Programmer (herein simply to be called the programmer). Hence, one reason for the sub-schema concept is to make life easier for the programmer.

The sub-schema concept allows the programmer's view of the data base to be restricted, so that he need not bother about parts of the data base which his program does not need to process. This also means that he cannot inadvertently change parts of the data base outside his domain of interest.

2.4.1 Sub-schema Data Description Language, Sub-schema DDL

A sub-schema is defined using a Sub-schema DDL. An object sub-schema is produced from a sub-schema in the same way as an object schema is produced from a schema, namely by translation. However, an object sub-schema cannot be produced until an object schema has been produced, and the sub-schema necessarily belongs to that one schema. There is no way of taking part of one schema (say two record types) and part of some other schema (say three record types) and making up a sub-schema of the two schemas.

For various reasons which will hopefully become apparent, a Sub-schema DDL is regarded as belonging to a programming language. For example, one can talk of a COBOL Sub-schema DDL or a FORTRAN Sub-schema DDL. However, a Schema DDL is explicitly not regarded as belonging to any programming language.

However, the processor which handles a number of declarations written using, say a COBOL Sub-schema DDL, should not be regarded as part of the COBOL Compiler. It is preferable to refer to the COBOL Sub-schema DDL Translator which must be used after the Schema DDL Translator and prior to the enhanced COBOL Compiler which compiles the programs to process the data in the data base.

The question arises as to who in fact uses the Sub-schema DDL. The DBTG was curiously ambivalent on this issue and commented that 'the Data Administrator may be responsible for defining the sub-schemas'. It is better to suggest that he normally is responsible for this task, bearing in mind that in order to do this he has to be aware of the function to be performed by the programs using the sub-schema.

Before leaving the sub-schema, it is important to note that several programs may use any one sub-schema—even concurrently. This means that two programs may be in executing status at the same time and both processing data in the same part of the data base, that is to say using the same sub-schema. Furthermore, a program may not use more than one sub-schema and it must use one sub-schema in order to be able to process the data base data. Whether a non data base program may be executing at the same time as data base programs is usually a property of the operating system. Normally it should be possible.

2.5 Data Manipulation Language, DML

Data Manipulation Language is the name given by the DBTG to the collection of statement types which must be added to an existing programming language to enable the programming language to be used to process the data in a data base which has been defined using the Schema DDL. In a sense, the choice of the phrase *data manipulation language* was confusingly grandiose. The DML is not and indeed cannot be a complete language in its own right. It is normally an extension of two or three existing statements plus about 15 new ones. It does not duplicate any of the facilities already found in the programming language.

The term *host language* was probably first used by the present author in 1969[1] to identify a class of DBMS, although Fry and Gosden recognized the significant difference of this class in 1968[2] when they talked about *POL embedded systems*. (POL, meaning (according to the authors) Procedure Oriented Language, is one of those terms which seems to have fallen into disuse.)

The DBTG approach to data base management is clearly that of a host language DBMS. There are several DBMS in this category and there have been others over the years which have fallen by the wayside. Since, as indicated in the first chapter, the DBTG's original charter was to 'extend COBOL', it is quite reasonable that their approach is that of a host language DBMS. The difference between DBTG-based DBMS and the other host language DBMS is that, in the former, the actual language of COBOL is modified from the programmer's point of view, whereas in the latter, the programmer has to communicate with the execution time module of the DBMS through CALL statements.

2.5.1 Implementation Approaches to DML

In practice, the difference between the two sub-classes of host language DBMS is not so significant from this point of view. It is of course the intent that the COBOL Sub-schema DDL and the COBOL DML should become part of COBOL. At time of writing, the two capabilities are in CODASYL COBOL and being considered for inclusion in ANSI COBOL. In the future, the difference between the existing COBOL statements and the 'new' DML statements will become merely a historical one.

An implementor of COBOL may look on the DML statements in much the same way as he looks on the SORT verb or the Communications Facility statements. Present day implementors of the DBTG proposals are being more cautious and more economical. They choose not to modify the existing COBOL Compiler, but rather to provide what is generally referred to as a DML to COBOL Pre-processor.

A DML/COBOL Pre-processor takes a source program written by a programmer using COBOL statements interspersed with DML statements. It recognizes each DML statement and converts it into a CALL statement producing a second source program which the unmodified COBOL Compiler can then compile.

2.5.2 Multiple Host Languages

The above emphasis on COBOL, while fully justified, is perhaps misleading. The initial impetus to the work of the DBTG came from COBOL sources. As a result of the meeting to review the October 1969 report, it was recognized that it would be expedient to de-emphasize COBOL somewhat. To this end, the Schema DDL was modified to cater for PL/1 infra-record structures (to be discussed later), and the Sub-schema DDL and DML were recognized as indeed COBOL oriented but also prototypes from which corresponding facilities for other languages could relatively easily be developed. Since April 1971, DBMS activity for other programming languages has been slow in getting started. There has been some published work from university environments,[3] and in 1975 the CODASYL Executive Committee established a FORTRAN Data Base Manipulation Language Committee whose first Journal of Development was published in 1976.[4]

The DBTG's idea as expressed in 1971 was that a data base defined using the Schema DDL could be processed by programs written in COBOL, FORTRAN, PL/1, ALGOL. Each program could use a sub-schema written in the appropriate Sub-schema DDL for that language.

In practice, most commercial implementors have restricted their attentions to COBOL as a host language although experimental implementations using

FORTRAN have been made. The commercial viability of the multi-processing language interface still lies in the future.

2.6 Data Base Control System

Before proceeding to discuss the various structuring capabilities in the Schema DDL, it is important for the reader to understand completely the situation at execution time. A user of a DBMS has at his disposal a number of languages (or sub-languages), namely the Schema DDL, a COBOL Sub-schema DDL, a COBOL DML and possibly a Schema DDL and a DML for other programming languages.

An implementor may build at least the following visible components:

Schema DDL Translator
Sub-schema DDL Translator
DML/COBOL Pre-processor (or modified COBOL Compiler)

The major part of his effort will go into the execution time component which the DBLTG calls the Data Base Control System, DBCS. The DBTG in its report frequently referred to it as *the DBMS* which caused a conflict with whatever one should call the whole system including the translators. This shortcoming was recognized by the early implementors who referred to the DBCS as a Data Management Routine or Data Base Module. For the remainder of this book, the term DBCS will be used to refer to the execution time component and DBMS to the whole system (which includes the DBCS).

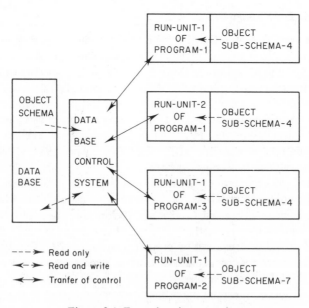

Figure 2.1 Execution time overview

2.6.1 Execution Time Overview

A possible execution time overview is depicted in Figure 2.1. It can be seen that all accesses to the data base are channelled through the DBCS. Since the DBCS is used by several executing programs concurrently, it should be written in re-entrant code.

The DBCS includes system buffers where physical blocks of data are stored en route between the data base and an executing program. Each executing program (which the DBTG has chosen to call a run unit) must have a working area for each record type in the sub-schema it uses. Details concerning this area will be discussed later, but for the time being it is important to note that the DML employs what has been described as a 'one record at a time logic'. As each DML statement is executed, no more than one data base record is moved between the record area in the program and the system buffer, because there is room in the program for only one record of each type. It is possible that a DML statement might cause accesses to several (even several thousand) records in the data base, but the flow of data in and out of the program's record area is limited to single records.

2.7 Device Media Control Language, DMCL

The DMCL is a component of the DBMS which each implementor must specify for himself. It fulfils a number of possible roles as follows:

1. Interface with host operating system
2. Mapping parts of the data base to different types of direct access device
3. Record packing within the data base
4. Recovery provisions

In a sense, the DMCL is a second stage of the data definition process which is stated in the Schema DDL. Some implementors have chosen to interweave the DMCL statements into the Schema DDL. In theory, the programmer does not need to be cognizant of the DMCL declarations made by the data administrator in order to be able to write his program. However, if machine performance is a major objective, then the DML is specified in such a way that he can indeed achieve better performance by utilizing knowledge of the DMCL declarations.

References

1. T. W. Olle, 'An Analysis of Generalized Data Base Management Systems, *Proceedings of Founding Conference of Society for Management Information Systems*, Minneapolis, September 1969.
2. J. P. Fry and J. A. Gosden, 'Survey of Management Information Systems and other Languages', in *Critical Factors in Data Management* (Ed. F. Gruenberger), Prentice Hall, 1969.
3. G. M. Stacey, 'A FORTRAN Interface to the CODASYL DBTG Specifications', *The Computer Journal*, **17**, No. 2, May 1974, 124–129.
4. FORTRAN Data Base Facility Journal of Development 1976. Available from Dr. Chester M. Smith, Pennsylvania State University, University Park, PA 16802.

Chapter 3

Basic Structuring Concepts

3.1 Record Type

To any COBOL programmer, the record type is a very basic and well understood concept. Each record type used in a program has to be described in the Data Division of a program. The programmer may define record types as being part of a file stored in some kind of secondary storage media or he may define a record type as part of his working storage which means that an area is reserved in core where records of the type described may be stored.

The COBOL concept of a record type was taken over into PL/1 and extended somewhat so that any PL/1 programmer will also be fully aware of what is meant by the term *record type*. The FORTRAN or ALGOL programmer may have some difficulty. To overcome this, the following short explanation is given.

3.2 Record Type for Scientific Programmers

The smallest nameable quantity in COBOL is called an *elementary item* or more briefly an *item*. This corresponds approximately to the FORTRAN concept of an undimensioned variable or an ALGOL simple variable. Each item has an item name (cf. variable name and variable identifier), and each item may take several values.

Several items which are related in some way to each other may be defined as belonging to the same record type where a record is conceptually similar to a row in a two-dimensional FORTRAN array. Commercial data processing places much more emphasis on handling alphanumeric data.

If a record type is included in that part of the data description (Data Division) called the File Section, then the implication is that there will be several occurrences of the record type stored in the file. Just how the individual records are stored in the file may or may not concern the programmer. A given file may contain records all of the same type or else of several different types, the former being single record type files and the latter multiple record type files.

When the programmer includes a READ statement in his program, he knows that the effect of executing that READ is to cause one record to be read from the file into core, where he can perform further actions on it. In the case of a multiple record type, he possibly does not know which type of record his READ will produce and hence the syntax of the READ statement is

READ file-name RECORD.

When he writes to an output file, he names the record type because that in turn designates the file to which the record will be written. This approach should be contrasted with FORTRAN in which execution of both the READ and WRITE statements can act on a whole array of data items.

Bearing in mind the emphasis on handling alphanumeric strings in COBOL, one of the important statements in COBOL is the MOVE, which a programmer may use to move the value of an item or items from one position in core to another. (In addition, he may also use a MOVE statement to cause a format change.) Quite a lot of moving takes place in a typical COBOL program, but it is handled differently from FORTRAN. In FORTRAN one would write

$$X = Y$$

in order to take whatever value was in location Y and put it in the location X, at the same time leaving Y containing the same value. In COBOL one writes

MOVE Y TO X.

3.2.1 Group Items

A shorthand is needed for referring to several items in one MOVE statement, and this problem is tackled by allowing an intra-record naming structure to be declared as part of the record description. Two or more contiguous elementary items may be grouped together to form a *group item*. A group item may consist not only of elementary items but also of other group items, hence allowing the user to build up a naming structure. To avoid confusion, the levels in this structure must be numbered downwards from the top as illustrated in Figure 3.1.

```
01  CUSTOMER.
    02  CUSTOMER-NUMBER.
        03 CUSTOMER-ID; PICTURE IS 99.
        03 CUSTOMER-SEQ-NO; PICTURE IS 9(6).
    02  CUSTOMER-NAME; PICTURE IS X(24).
    02  CUSTOMER-TOWN; PICTURE IS X(24).
```

Figure 3.1 COBOL record description

In this example, CUSTOMER on the 01 level is the name of the record type, CUSTOMER-NUMBER is the name of a group item containing two elementary items and CUSTOMER-NAME and CUSTOMER-TOWN are two other elementary items. Whether or not an item is elementary is independent of its level.

It is necessary to declare either an item type or a picture for each elementary item. In a program, it is possible to write

MOVE CUSTOMER TO X1

or

MOVE CUSTOMER-NUMBER TO X2

or

MOVE CUSTOMER-ID TO Z.

From this it is clear hopefully not only what a record type is, but also what the concepts of levels and group items within a record type are all about.

The intra-record type structure can be more complex in that it is possible to define tables and variable length records.

3.2.2 Table Handling

A table is something like a FORTRAN array in that it may have 1, 2 or 3 dimensions and in that the programmer references the elements in the table using subscripting as in FORTRAN. However, one important difference is that the COBOL table is an intra-record type structure, where the maximum permitted length of a record is usually limited and there are, of course, potentially several occurrences of any record type defined as belonging to a file. The table can be an in core table if the record type is defined as part of the programmer's working storage. In FORTRAN, arrays have nothing to do with records simply because FORTRAN has no records in the COBOL sense. Also, the elements in a FORTRAN array are all the same type of variable.

The definition of a simple one dimensional table is illustrated in Figure 3.2.

```
01 CUSTOMER
   02 CUSTOMER-NO.
      03 CUSTOMER-ID ... ;
      03 CUSTOMER-SEQ-NO ... ;
   02 CUSTOMER-NAME ... ;
   02 CUSTOMER-TOWN ... ;
   02 PRODUCT-ORDERED ... ;
   02 MONTHLY-ORDERS; OCCURS 12 TIMES.
      03 MONTHS-ORDER-QUANTITY ...
```

Figure 3.2 One-dimensional table

This is an example of a simple one dimensional table of fixed dimensions. Space is allowed in each record for exactly 12 occurrences of the item value MONTHS-ORDER-QUANTITY. What each of the 12 values means is a matter to be interpreted by the programmer.

It is also possible in COBOL to allow one dimension of the table (irrespective of whether it is a one, two or three dimensional table) to be of variable length. In the above example of a one dimensional table, this implies that the number of monthly order quantities stored in the record could vary from one customer record to another. A new customer for example might have only one or two items of monthly data whereas a long standing customer might have 30 or 40. The exact number of repetitions must be stored in the record, and the record description would probably be written as shown in Figure 3.3.

```
01 CUSTOMER.
    02 CUSTOMER-NO.
        03 CUSTOMER-ID ...
        03 CUSTOMER-SEQ-NO ...
    02 CUSTOMER-NAME ...
    02 CUSTOMER-TOWN ...
    02 PRODUCT-ORDERED ...
    02 NO-OF-MONTHS ...
    02 MONTHLY-ORDERS; OCCURS 1 TO 60 TIMES
        DEPENDING ON NO-OF-MONTHS.
        03 MONTHS-ORDER-QUANTITY... .
```

Figure 3.3 Variable length one-dimensional table

It must be noted that the programmer is expected to estimate a maximum size for the record by estimating the maximum number of occurences of MONTHS-ORDER-QUANTITY which can occur in the file. Hence, the length of the different records varies, depending on how many values are in each record.

The programmer may reference the separate values of MONTHS-ORDER-QUANTITY in his program by using subscripting in much the same way as in FORTRAN. The same applies to the two and three dimensioned tables.

3.2.3 Qualification

One important concept found in COBOL but not in FORTRAN is that of *qualification*. In a given program, there may be two or more record types each containing several items. For the sake of illustration, assume the two record types shown in Figure 3.4.

In his program, the programmer needs to refer to QUANTITY which is an item in both record types. In order to distinguish one from the other, he must write QUANTITY IN ORDER-RECORD or QUANTITY OF ORDER-RECORD as opposed to QUANTITY OF BACK-ORDER-RECORD. In these examples, the item name QUANTITY is qualified by the name of the record type.

The qualification concept in fact carries through all levels of naming within a record type and up to the name of the file in which the records are stored. Hence, an item name could be qualified by the name of a group item in which it participates and further by a record name and a file name.

```
01 ORDER-RECORD
   02 ORDER-SEQ-NO ... ;
   02 PRODUCT-CODE ... ;
   02 DATE-RECEIVED ... ;
   02 QUANTITY ...
01 BACK-ORDER-RECORD
   02 ORDER-SEQ-NO ... ;
   02 PRODUCT-CODE ... ;
   02 DATE-ON-BACK-ORDER ... ;
   02 QUANTITY ....
```

Figure 3.4 Illustration of name qualification

3.2.4 Summary

The concepts of group items, intra-record tables, and qualification are all COBOL record structuring concepts which were carried over into PL/1 and which the DBTG chose to perpetuate in their proposals for a DBMS. In fact, the intra-record structure of the Schema DDL as proposed is closer to PL/1 than to COBOL. However, most implementors have chosen for various reasons to restrict the intra-record structures to those of COBOL. In some cases, even the facility for handling variable length tables has been omitted so that all record types defined in the Schema DDL are fixed length.

3.3 Comparison of Intra-record and Inter-record Structuring

One important facet of the CODASYL approach is the perpetuation of the historical intra-record structures. However, the cornerstone of the proposals is for new inter-record structures which will now be discussed in more detail.

The important structuring concept which the DBTG adopted from Honeywell's IDS (as developed by Bachman at GE in the early sixties) is that of the *set type* relationship. This terminology is a little unfortunate in view of the mathematical implication of the word 'set'.

A set type is best described as *an association among two or more record types*. For instance, if one considers two record types, the first containing employee basic data and the other containing data on his educational background, then there is a fairly obvious relationship between the two record types. The educational data for one employee could all be stored in one record, but more likely it would be spread across several records depending on how much education the employee has. In other words, the number of education records associated with an employee record will vary from one employee to the next. This is an example of a *one to many relationship* on which the CODASYL approach has been based.

It is interesting to compare the inter-record approach with the conventional intra-record one. Using the conventional approach, the education data would probably be included in the employee record type because, although the amount of education may vary from one employee to another, it is unlikely to vary by a very high factor. The most highly educated employee may need five times as much space as the least educated, but the factor of five would never become ten or fifteen. Using a conventional approach, the program might handle this modest variation by using variable length records or he might use fixed length records but allow sufficient space in each record for the maximum.

Figure 3.5 represents the two situations.

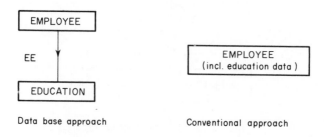

Figure 3.5 Comparison of inter-record and intra-record

Each rectangle represents a record type. The arrow between EMPLOYEE and EDUCATION implies that a set type relationship has been defined between these two record types, that the relationship has been named EE and that the relationship means that each employee may have zero, one or more pieces of education. Furthermore, each education record belongs to one and only one employee.

It was unfortunate that the DBTG in 1971 referred to the set type as a set. This has lead to considerable confusion in the minds of those attempting to learn about this kind of structuring for the first time. In 1973, DBLTG carefully moved to make *set type* and *set* replace *set occurrence*. This lead was followed by the DDLC in their 1973 report. The newer terminology is consistent with *record type* and *record* as well as being less cumbersome. The phrases *set occurrence* and *record occurrence* are used occasionally in this book for emphasis. Numerous implementors who followed the DBTG 1971 report use *set* to mean *set type*. Once the concepts have been firmly grasped from this book, the meaning of the implementor's specification is usually clear from the context.

3.4 Set Types

The preceding example of a set type relationship illustrated the fairly common situation where a set type can be used instead of a variable length record approach. It is hopefully fairly clear that the EMPLOYEE record type plays a different role in the relationship from that played by the EDUCATION record type. In CODASYL terminology, the EMPLOYEE is regarded as *the owner* record type of the set and the EDUCATION record type is *a member*. This set type falls into the most useful class of set type which is referred to as a single member set type.

In addition, it is possible to define multi-member set types which means that three or more record types are involved, one of which is the owner and the others are all members. An example of a multimember set type is depicted in Figure 3.6.

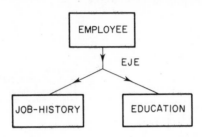

Figure 3.6 Multi-member set type

Again, each rectangle in the figure represents a record type and the arrows point to each member indicating that the unidirectionality of the relationship is from owner to members.

Finally, the third class of set type is referred to as a *system owned set type*, or *singular set type*. One can think of it as an ownerless set type and it can be illustrated as shown in Figure 3.7.

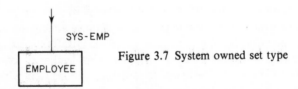

Figure 3.7 System owned set type

The exact role of a system-owned set type will become clear in Chapter 5 when the mappings of a set type to storage are discussed.

For the present, it is important to note that each set type must be given a name which follows the rules for names as given in the specifications. There are three conceivable ways of deciding on what to call a set type. The first is to make up a name using the initial letter or letters of the owner record and member record. It will be clear from a glance at Figures 3.5, 3.6, and 3.7 that this approach is often used in this book.

The second is to try to find a name which conveys to the reader something about the relationship which the set type represents. For instance in Figure 3.8, the relationship between a PRODUCT record and the PART record which com-

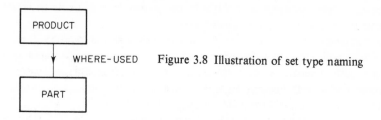

Figure 3.8 Illustration of set type naming

pose each product is called a WHERE-USED relationship. One weakness with this approach is that all too often the name becomes fairly long, or else the only name which would be meaningful is something like HAS, OWNS, USES.

The third alternative is included for completeness, and that is to choose any name as X, Y, P or Q. This is discouraged for the same reason as it is discouraged in naming record types. Programs should be written so that they can be easily read. The scientific habit of using short non-meaningful names is widely discouraged by many commentators on recommended practice in commercial programming.

3.4.1 Sets (Set Occurences)

Although the mapping of a set type to storage will be discussed in full later, it is necessary here to mention a few facts about the sets of a given set type.

For each set type (other than system owned) there may be several sets represented in storage. The precise number depends entirely on the number of owner records in the data base. If there are three records in the data base which correspond to the owner record type, then there are three occurrences of the set type. If there are 2,743 owner occurrences, then there are 2,743 sets.

Each set may be *empty* or not, where the word *empty* must not be interpreted in the mathematical sense. If a set is empty, then no member record occurrence is associated in the data base with the owner. Invariably, however, there are several records (as few as one or as many as several thousand) which are 'connected' to the owner. Exactly how they are connected and how the decision is made to which of the several sets a member shall be connected, are both problems for subsequent discussions.

It is important that a record may only be connected to one set of a given set type, but it may be connected to two (or more) sets which are of different types.

3.5 Role of the Set Type

The set type has been identified as a one to many relationship between two or more record types, where each record type contains data items which collectively represent some 'real world type of entity'. In the so-called real world, numerous relationships exist between such entity types and it is reasonable to attempt to represent them in computerized data bases.

Such representation of real world relationships was not possible (or at least very difficult) with the data records stored on sequential storage media, typically magnetic tape. The arrival of large direct access storage devices removed that restriction and it has become possible, with the extra dimension provided, to represent networks of relationships among entities.

Many of the proponents of the data base concept have been somewhat carried away by this question of representing relationships and a newcomer might gain the impression that data base design is merely a matter of recognizing real world relationships and identifying each as a set type using the Schema DDL. Unfortunately, other considerations must be taken into account and a conscious decision must be taken on whether the set type is needed or not. This decision calls for a study of the programs which are to be written to process the data base.

In practical terms, a set type is never without cost. As will be explained, it requires a certain amount of extra storage space and it can cost processing time when the data base is being updated. On the credit side, a set type provides an access path to the records in the data base. Whether or not one needs the set type depends entirely on whether or not one needs the access path in the data base.

3.6 Building Structures Using the Set Type

The set type must be regarded as a building block, using which it is possible to design a complete data base. There are essentially no restrictions on the way in which a set type may be used in building up a data base. The various possibilities are best illustrated by Figures 3.9 to 3.13.

The following rules for building up data base structures apply.

1. A record type may be an owner in one set type and a member in other set types.
2. A record type may be a member in more than one set type.
3. There is no limit on the number of set types which may be defined between any two record types.

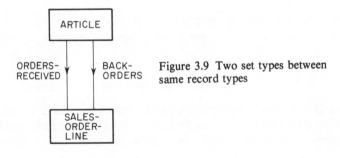

Figure 3.9 Two set types between same record types

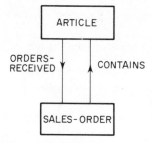

Figure 3.10 Mini-cycle between
two record types

Figure 3.11 Hierarchical
structure

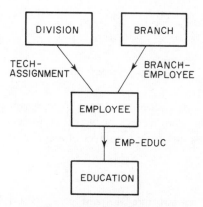

Figure 3.12 Y-structure

4. A data base may contain any number of record types and any number of set types.
5. Cyclic structuring is permitted (see Figures 3.10 and 3.13).

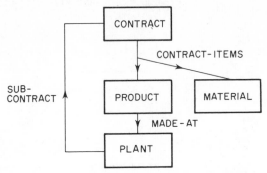

Figure 3.13 Data base structure including cycle and multi-member record type

Figures 3.9 to 3.13 are often called Bachman diagrams.[1] This is a graphic technique for illustrating the structure of a data base. Each rectangle represents a record type and each arrow represents a set type.

Both the record type and the set type have to be mapped to storage in some way and these topics will be discussed in the following chapters. Since the record type is more fundamental, it will be discussed first.

In conclusion, an extension to the Bachman diagram useful for depicting set occurrences must be introduced. Three occurrences of the single member set type of Figure 3.5 are given in Figure 3.14.

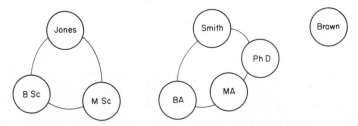

Figure 3.14 Three occurrences of single member set type

It must be noted that circles are chosen to represent record occurrences. The lines drawn between the record occurrences indicate that the records are 'connected' into the set in one of a number of ways to be discussed in Chapter 5.

References

1. C. W. Bachman, 'Data Structure Diagrams', *Data Base*, **1**, No. 2 (1969). (Publication of ACM Special Interest Group on Business Data Processing.)

Chapter 4

Mapping Record Types to Storage

4.1 Overview

There are several facets of the mapping of record types to storage, most of which can well be presented without an in depth understanding of how a set type is mapped to storage.

The two main parameters of this mapping process are the specification for each record type of a *location mode* and of a realm or realms in which records of the type are to be stored. Before discussing these two concepts in detail, the idea of a data base key should be clearly understood.

4.2 Data Base Key

The data base key is conceptually a data item, a value of which is associated with each stored record in the data base. One could think of it as a unique internal record identifier used inside the DBMS to distinguish one record from another.

It is not an item which the data administrator *must* define in the Schema DDL, although it is possible for him to define an item of type data base key in any record type. The data base key is a concept which is traditionally very intrinsic to the CODASYL approach, and it appears to be impossible to perform as either a data administrator or indeed as an applications programmer without some level of understanding of the role of these.

Each record is assigned a data base key value at the time it is first stored in the data base. It retains that value even if the record is modified until the record is finally deleted from the data base. In some ways, the data base key for the record is like a social security number of personal identification number for an individual.

Although the programmer has to be aware of the data base key concept, there are levels of involvement for him, each with an appropriate trade-off.

It is possible for him to avoid the concept as much as possible and still write reasonably efficient programs. If he needs to cut the response time in a translation program to an absolute minimum, there are ways in which he can get heavily involved in manipulating data base keys and squeeze extra machine efficiency out of the system. These options will be indicated in the course of this book at the appropriate places. Finally, it is useful, although not strictly necessary, to consider what a data base key looks like. In theory it could be a simple integer starting with 1 for the earliest record to be stored in the data base and running up to N where there are N records in the data base after the initial loading is complete. However, in practice, the system has to be able to find a record from its data base and if this kind of scheme were used, a fairly lengthy table of key values and addresses would need to be stored and the time taken to access this table could also be meaningful.

Most, if not all, implementors provide the data base key in such a way that it is associated with the physical location in the data base where the record is stored. This does not mean that the data base key is a cylinder and track address in the disc. Rather, it implies that the data base key value consists of several components (usually three or four), and that these parts allow the DBCS to associate a location in the data base with a given record with a minimum of computation and table look-up.

4.3 Location Mode

Experience in teaching this concept has indicated that this concept is somewhat ill named. The word *locate* in both English and American connotes both the idea of finding and the idea of placing, e.g. 'I cannot locate may address book, where is it?', and 'A new supermarket has recently been located in the main street of the town'.

The reason for this choice of the term *location mode* is historical. In IDS/1, there was a concept called *storage mode* and another called *retrieval mode*. The DBTG decided, reasonably enough, that one did not need both, and what they did effectively was to remove the concept of retrieval mode. As a result, the DBTG's concept of *location mode* is best thought of as a *storage mode*, although we shall continue to call it *location mode*.

Some observers with a background in conventional data processing have gained the impression that *location mode* is some kind of newfangled term for *access method*, but that would be a dangerous misrepresentation of the situation.

The data administrator has a number of location mode options available to him. He must choose one for each record type. DBTG identified the following three:

CALC
DIRECT
VIA SET

and allowed for the situation where the data administrator could legally omit to select a location mode for a record type. Hence, the relevant DBTG syntax was as follows:

RECORD NAME IS record-name

$$
\left[\text{LOCATION MODE IS}\left\{\begin{array}{l}\underline{\text{DIRECT}}\left\{\begin{array}{l}\text{db-name-1}\\\text{db-id-1}\end{array}\right\}\\[2ex]\underline{\text{CALC}}\ [\text{db-proc-1}]\ \underline{\text{USING}}\ \text{db-id-2}\\\quad[,\ \text{db-id-3}]\dots\underline{\text{DUPLICATES}}\ \text{ARE}\\\quad[\underline{\text{NOT}}]\ \text{ALLOWED}\\[2ex]\underline{\text{VIA}}\ \text{set-name-1 SET}\end{array}\right\}\right]
$$

The DDLC simply removed the square brackets and added a fourth option, called SYSTEM.

4.3.1 Note on Syntax Formalism

Since the above is the first occurrence in this book of a piece of syntax, it will be useful for some readers who have not previously encountered this formalism to be given a brief review. The formalism follows that developed for COBOL, although the DBTG did expand it slightly. The COBOL programmer will understand the syntax of the LOCATION MODE clause without further explanation and may omit the rest of this section.

The conventions are as follows:

1. Parts of the language are written in capital letters; names to be provided by the user are written in lower case.
2. Required words are underlined. Words not underlined are so-called noise words which may be included to enhance the readability of the schema declaration (as long as they are spelled correctly!). They may be omitted without loss of meaning.
3. When a word, name, phrase or whole clause is surrounded by square brackets, this means that it is legal to omit that word, name, phrase or whole clause. The example of the DBTG's location mode illustrates this rather well. The word NOT, the user provided name db-id-3 and even the whole LOCATION MODE clause may be omitted. Needless to say, in this case the meaning changes depending on the inclusion or exclusion of the part in question.
4. The curly brackets (braces) imply that a choice of one of the options has to be made from the two or more listed columnwise within these brackets. There are two examples of this here, the one nested within the other. The better example is the outer one which in abbreviated form is

$$
\text{LOCATION MODE IS}\left\{\begin{array}{l}\text{CALC}\\\text{DIRECT}\\\text{VIA SET}\end{array}\right\}
$$

The data administrator must write either

LOCATION MODE IS CALC

or

LOCATION MODE IS DIRECT

or

LOCATION MODE IS VIA SET.

5. The three dots, which the DBTG called an *ellipsis* (Concise Oxford Dictionary; *omission from sentence of words needed to complete construction or sense*) is a useful syntactic device adopted to convey the following idea of repetition. Extracting from the CALC option

LOCATION MODE IS CALC USING db-id-2 [, db-id-3] ...

it is hopefully clear that the clause could be finished in any of the following ways

USING db-id-2
USING db-id-3, db-id-4
USING db-id-3, db-id-4, db-id-5

and there could, in theory, be hundreds of data base identifiers listed.
The general form

db-id-2 [, db-id 3] ...

is quite common in the DBTG proposal. It must be noted that the comma is inside the square brackets because it may only be repeated for each extra data base identifier.

4.3.2 Data Base Identifiers and Data Base Names

Even the experienced COBCL programmer will need an explanation of two frequently occurring tokens (PL/1 term) in the syntax statements presented in the DBTG report and here. Examples of these are

db-data-name-1

and

db-id-4.

Both refer to either an elementary item or a group item declared somewhere in the schema. However, the difference between the two is that a data-base-data-name may not be subscripted and qualified, but the other not only may be, but should be if this is necessary to achieve a unique name in the data base.

The various CODASYL reports all wrote 'data-base-data-name' and 'data-base-identifier' out in full all the time—a somewhat time and space consuming practice. In this book, we shall abbreviate the two by 'dbd-name, and 'db-id'.

The simple relationship between the two may then be stated in the following

$$db\text{-}id = dbd\text{-}name \left[\left(\text{integer-1} \left[, \text{integer-2} \right] \ldots \right) \right] \left[\left\{ \frac{ON}{ON} \right\} \text{record-name} \right]$$

The example of location mode clause to illustrate the difference between a db-id and a dbd-name is unfortunate because this provided the one example of where the two are included in the same curly brackets to indicate that a choice must be made between one and the other. This should not confuse the reader and the explanation will be given when the option is discussed. When dbd-name is written, this indicates that qualification and subscription are prohibited. When db-id is used, this means that qualification and subscription should be included if necessary to establish a name unique within the data base.

The trailing integer which always appears after both 'db-id' and 'dbd-name' (for example db-id-2, dbd-name-7) is merely there to allow reference to that particular db-id or dbd-name in the various rules which follow each syntax form. Also, if the integer were not used, there is some danger that a user might think that the same db-id could (or must) be used in two or three places in the statement.

4.4 Discussion of Location Modes

After that lengthy but necessary discourse on the syntax formalism, we can return to the main thread of the presentation to consider each location mode option in turn. Before doing that, however, it is useful to review when and why such a declaration is necessary. It is always examined each time a record of a given type is initially stored in the data base.

As will be seen, in the case of only one of the three options (namely CALC), a prime key is declared which *may* also be used for retrieval purposes. No prime key is defined in the case of the other location modes. There is no implication that the prime key *has* to be used when retrieving a record with a location mode of CALC. While it is premature to launch into a detailed discussion of how records are retrieved from the data base, it is not too early to state one of the basic features of any CODASYL DBTG-based system. This is *there are several different ways of retrieving any individual record in the data base.*

As a corollary to this, it should be noted that defining the location mode for a record type as CALC merely adds to the number of ways.

4.5 Location Mode of CALC

The word CALC is an abbreviation for *calculation* and the implication here is that, when a record is stored in the data base, its data base key (and hence where it is stored) is *calculated* from the concatenated value of one or more items named after USING in the LOCATION mode clause.

There is a sense of understanding from the DBTG report that CALC is the same as randomizing. In fact, this is never stated explicitly. However, all implementations interpret CALC as meaning a randomizing (or hashing) algorithm and in IDS/1 the only CALC algorithm used was (and still is) a randomizing one.

Accepting for the time being this restriction in concept, some explanation of randomizing is called for. The classical treatise on this topic is a paper in 1970 by Lum, Yuen and Dodd,[1] which reports on an empirical study of eight different so-called *key transformation* methods. It concluded that the division method gave the best overall performance. It will frequently be encountered in practice, therefore some explanation is in order.

The value of the key, whether it is numeric, alphanumeric or some combination of items of both types, is treated as one long bit string, effectively as an integer. It is then divided by another integer and the remainder after the division is then the data base key (or at least part of it). The divisor should be some prime number close to the number of addresses available. Back in 1963, Buchholz[2] suggested that the divisor be the largest prime number which is less than the number of available addresses. Lum and his colleagues felt that any number close to the number of addresses was just as good.

To understand the way a randomizing or CALC algorithm works in practice, it is necessary to jump ahead a little and to introduce the concept of a *realm* (admittedly more often referred to as *area* because that was the term used by both DBTG and DDLC). A realm is a named subdivision of a data base and each record type is assigned to one or more of these realms. Furthermore, each realm is usually divided into a number of equal-sized *pages*. The programmer should not in theory be concerned with this breakdown into pages, but it does no harm for him to know.

A typical approach for a CALC algorithm is for the algorithm to generate a page number within the realm, rather than the whole data base key value. The record is then stored somewhere in that page if there is space for it. Otherwise a pointer to some other overflow page is stored and the actual record is stored in the overflow page.

4.5.1 Duplicate Key Values

When the data administrator decides to select a location mode of CALC for a given record type, then he must also make a decision with respect to duplicate values of the prime key. More specifically, he must decide whether to allow or prohibit duplicate values of the prime key. Both situations can occur in practice and need to be considered. If the prime key is the last name of a person, then normally the decision would be to allow duplicate values of the key. It is hard to think of an example where it would be desirable to omit all but one individuals named Smith, Brown, Jones, etc. In this case of 'duplicates allowed', the prime key is not a unique identifier.

To consider the other alternative, if the CALC key is chosen as a product number or a social security number or a personal identification number, then the data administrator would want the key to be a unique one and would in this situation prohibit duplicate values of the key.

The preceding discussion of duplicate key values is relevant whatever means is used to decide on a storage location in terms of a prime key value. As indicated earlier, there has developed a rather unfortunate tendency to equate CALC with randomizing techniques. It could equally well use an ISAM approach instead and the discussion on whether or not to allow duplicate values of the key would be equally pertinent.

4.5.2 Collisons (Synonyms)

The question of *collisions* is one which is only appropriate to a randomization interpretation of CALC. A collision (which some people refer to as a *synonym*) occurs when two different key values randomize to the same internal value. The system is expected to handle this problem. In fact, the possible approach discussed above, where the randomization selects a page in the realm and many records are stored on that page with possible overflow pointers, avoids the collision problem. It is mentioned here only to clarify that it is quite a different problem from the 'duplicate value' problem. The latter is one which concerns both the data administrator and the programmer. The collision problem concerns the implementor only.

4.5.3 Alternative Algorithms

So far most aspects of the CALC location mode have been covered. The syntax on its own is

LOCATION MODE IS CALC [db-proc-1]
    USING db-id-2 [, db-id-3] . . .
    DUPLICATES ARE [NOT] ALLOWED

The reference to 'db-proc-1' calls for explanation. If it is omitted, then the CALC algorithm used is the one provided by the implementor. However, the DBTG's idea is that the data administrator should be able to replace or override the implementor's standard one by the data administrator's own. In practice, the facility to define data base procedures has not yet been implemented, and hence discussion of this powerful concept has been deferred until later in the book. However, many implementations in fact allow the data administrator a choice of algorithms or even a way of defining his own.

4.5.4 Choice of Keys

In the syntax displayed in the previous section, the second line reads

USING db-id-2 [, db-id-3] . . .

To the reader familiar with COBOL this will be self-explanatory. To others it must be explained that USING is the COBOL-like way of identifying parameters and is used here rather than the more scientific approach of enclosing them in parentheses. In this case there must be at least one item comprising the CALC key, but there may be more. Each item may be an elementary item or a group item, qualified or subscripted as necessary.

There is one fairly obvious rule on the choice of the CALC key items. They must be items which are in the record type for which the declaration is being made.

4.6 Location Mode of DIRECT

A careful study of this location mode shows that it has been somewhat ill conceived and possibly also misnamed. The fact that the DDLC removed it from the Schema DDL bears out this assertion, but since it is found in implementations it must be explained.

The word *direct* tends to convey some kind of association with *direct access storage*, but all records of all types, irrespective of location mode, are stored in direct access storage. Giving the record type a location mode of DIRECT does *not* mean that there is a specific way of retrieving it—as is the case with CALC.

The best justification for the choice of the word *direct* is that when a record of this type is stored, the process is a fast and 'direct' one. There is no attempt to decide on where would be a good location with an eye to subsequent retrieval. In fact, location mode DIRECT can imply one of two quite different options depending on the programmer, as will be discussed.

The syntax is very simple

$$\text{LOCATION MODE IS DIRECT } \begin{Bmatrix} \text{dbd-name-1} \\ \text{db-id-1} \end{Bmatrix}$$

and it is significant that the syntax is the same in the DDLC report as in the DBTG. However, the DDLC clearly recognized some kind of problem as they made a number of changes to the semantics of this location mode.

The spirit of location mode DIRECT is that the programmer is allowed to get involved with how the records of a given type are stored. He must do this on an individual record level, and therefore he may have to get deeply involved with *how* data base keys are assigned. Whether or not he is 'deeply involved', he has to have some way of passing data base key values to the system.

4.6.1 Role of Data Base Key Items

Largely for this reason, the DBTG introduced a new schema item type, namely

TYPE IS DATA-BASE-KEY

This is a new in the sense that it is not in PL/1 or in COBOL. If a programmer is to be allowed to 'play with' data base key values, then he has to have a way of storing them in his working location and a way of passing them to the DBCS (the execution time module). One DBTG approach to this problem is to allow the data administrator to define items of type data base key in the schema record types.

This means that data base key values can indeed be stored in the data base—a capability which has rightly been criticized by many observers. However, there is another approach, but to explain that, we must look at the syntax again

$$\text{LOCATION MODE IS DIRECT} \begin{Bmatrix} \text{dbd-name-1} \\ \text{db-id-1} \end{Bmatrix}$$

and explain carefully the difference between dbd-name-1 and db-id-1.

The lower option 'db-id-1' implies that an elementary item of type DATA-BASE-KEY has been defined in *some* schema record type. It need not be the one to which we are in the process of assigning a location mode of DIRECT. However, this item is the one which the programmer will use when he communicates to the system that he has somehow generated a data base key value which is not already used in the data base, and he would like it assigned to a record he is storing therein.

There is no implication here that the data base key value need actually itself be stored in the data base, although this is clearly a possibility. What the data administrator may do is to define a dummy record type containing only the item of type data base key. No occurrences of this record type may be stored in the data base, but if the record type is included in the sub-schema used by the program, then the data base key item is there for use by the programmer.

The other alternative in the syntax, namely dbd-name-1, is a way of achieving the same objective without going through the artificial process of defining a dummy record type. The wording in the DDLC report is interesting (page 3.3.5, Section 3.3.4): 'By its appearance in a LOCATION clause, data-base-data-name-1 is treated as a data base key and is not part of a record.'

In effect, the dbd-name-1 is a schema-declared item which is automatically present in the working storage section of every program processing the record type. The approach is devious and motivated by the reluctance of DBTG and DDLC to propose changes to existing host languages.

Having established the basic concepts of programmer involvement with 'where stored' for a record type with location mode DIRECT, and also the requirement for an item of type data base key which the programmer uses to communicate with the system, it is time to look at the implications of choosing this location mode.

4.6.2 Ways of Using Location Mode DIRECT

In order to appreciate what happens when a record of a type with location mode DIRECT is stored, it is necessary to jump ahead to the DML STORE statement and its highly complex semantics, although only one aspect of it need concern us here.

What happens when a record with a location mode of DIRECT is stored depends on the value of the data base key item which must be initialized by the programmer prior to the execution of the STORE statement. There are three situations which may arise with respect to the value of this item.

1. Valid, i.e. usable because not already in use.
2. Invalid, possibly because already in use.
3. Null.

The first two situations reflect that the programmer is trying to control the exact placement of the record in the data base, and he is either successful or he fails. The third situation is different in that he is probably not trying, but he is saying he does not care where the system stores the record.

The case where the programmer tries and the case where he does not care really ought to be completely separate under data administrator control. In other words, there ought to be two separate location modes. The case where the programmer is genuinely involved with data base keys is one which is frequently condemned by the purists. One can surely obtain improved performance working on this very physical level, but one can just as surely get into trouble. The situation should be allowed, but as a data administrator option, not as a programmer option.

If the programmer feeds only null values for the data base key to the DBCS, then the DBLTG's semantics for the STORE statement indicate that the DBCS does whatever it feels is appropriate to assign a data base key value and store the record. In other words, in this situation it is up to the implementor. It should be noted that this situation then becomes equivalent to the DBTG's idea of not assigning a location mode at all for a record type, which in turn is the same as the DDLC's fourth option

LOCATION MODE IS SYSTEM.

The choice of the word SYSTEM here is marginally cryptic. There is indeed a use for the case where the data administrator does *not* want a prime key (as in CALC) or control over physical contiguity (as in VIA SET to be discussed) or programmer control over physical placement (as in DIRECT if, and only if, the programmer specifies a non-null data base key value). What the data administrator probably does want is for the record to be stored as quickly as possible with no involvement on the programmer's part. This could be called

LOCATION MODE IS FAST.

Furthermore, it should be a requirement in location mode DIRECT that the programmer gives a *non-null* data base key value.

4.6.3 Retrieval when Location Mode DIRECT

A General Rule in the DBTG report (page 104, Section 3.3.6) must surely have caused considerable confusion to readers trying to understand the proposals. The rule reads:

'If a LOCATION MODE DIRECT clause is specified, then the data item specified in the clause must be initialized with a data base key prior to the execution of a command which selects the record on the basis of its LOCATION MODE clause. For a STORE command, however, the data item specified must be initialized either with a data base-key or with a null-value.'

It is the first sentence which is of interest here. In point of fact, there is only one 'command which selects the record on the basis of its location mode clause', and that so-called command states quite clearly that the location mode must be CALC. Hence, the first sentence of the rule is quite meaningless—worse, it is confusing. Fortunately, DDLC recognized the problem and removed the offending sentence.

(As a historical note, readers familiar with IDS/1 will realize that the DBTG's confusion came from the fact that IDS/1 had a storage mode and a retrieval mode. DBTG thought they were combining the two into the ambiguously named location mode. In fact, they removed the retrieval mode concept completely and renamed the storage mode as location mode.)

How does one retrieve a record whose type has a location mode of DIRECT? The answer to this is that it may be retrieved in the same way as a record type with any other location mode, with the important exception that the retrieval specially designed for CALC record types is *not* allowed. A record may be almost retrieved if the data base key value is available, but that capability is quite independent of the location mode. It must be reiterated that there are always several ways of retrieving a record and the whole subject will be elaborated in Chapter 15 which is dedicated to the FIND statement.

4.7 Location Mode VIA SET

To understand this location mode, the reader must be quite clear what a set type is. If there are any doubts, a quick reread of Section 3.4 is suggested.

In order to be able to use this location mode at all, the record type to which the location mode is being assigned must be a member in some set type. The syntax of the option reads

LOCATION MODE IS VIA set-name-1 SET.

The record must in fact be a member in the set type identified by set-name-1. This set type may have other members. The record type may be a member in other set types, but it is the membership in the set type named which dictates the meaning of the location mode option.

The essence of choosing a location mode of VIA SET is to cause a record to be stored physically close to the other members of the set. The DBTG go a little further in their definition of the semantics of the STORE statement (page 262, line 5) and assert

'. . . the record being stored will be placed . . . as close as is possible to the actual or probable logical insert point in the selected set occurrence.'

(The omissions from this quotation do not detract from the sense of the point under discussion.)

Unfortunately, present discussion raises the major issue of 'set selection'. Each record when it is stored may be connected into one of the sets (see Section 3.4.1) of the type named. Since there will normally be several occurrences of the set type, by some mystical process one of these must be selected for the new record to be close to and possibly connected into. This whole process is to be covered later in Chapter 7.

The DDLC's wording on the location mode option is more cautious and is to be found as a semantic rule for the location mode clause (page 3.36, Rule 9). It reads

'If VIA set-name-1 SET is specified, the DBMS (i.e. DBCS) assigns a data base key to the object record as though it were to become a member of an occurrence of the set type named in the VIA phrase.'

It must be noted that the DDLC moved away from the DBTG's implication of 'as close as possible'. It is also worthy of note that the wording of the DBLTG is so close to that of the DDLC that it is probably copied.

In fact, the DDLC/DBLTG wording is rather ill chosen. To substantiate this, consider a single V structure, i.e. member with two owners:

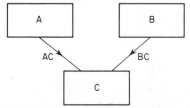

Record type C could well have a location mode of CALC or DIRECT, in which case the data base key is assigned without any consideration of its participation in the two set types as a member. If, however, the record type has a location mode VIA BC SET, then its membership in BC must mean something that its membership in AC does not. When a C record is stored, it will quite probably be connected into a set of AC *and* into a set of BC, *irrespective* of the location mode of C. Hence, if the mention of one set type and not the other in the location mode clause means anything at all, then it must imply an attempt to achieve physical contiguity of the participants (owner and members) in a set.

In practice this is what VIA SET means in most implementations, and this attempt to influence physical contiguity is the difference between a location mode of VIA SET and a location of SYSTEM (or DIRECT with null values).

4.7.1 Retrieval with Location Mode VIA SET

Again, in the DBTG report we observe the reference to 'selection on the basis of its LOCATION MODE clause' (again rectified by DDLC). As with location mode DIRECT, this is misleading. There is *no* special retrieval option for record types with a location mode VIA SET. Of course, a record type with this location mode is *ipso facto* a member in a set type and that fact does add extra retrieval possibilities over and above what will be possible if the record type were not a member in the same set.

4.8 Realms (Areas)

In the discussion of location mode CALC, we briefly introduced the realm concept, and now can go into more detail on this topic. In this book, we will use the DBLTG term *realm* rather than the DBTG and DDLC term *area* even though the latter is used in most implementors' specifications.

The reason that the DBLTG made this change is that the word *area* already has a use in COBOL, where it may be defined as a set of positions (normally contiguous) in high speed memory. COBOL also has the concept of a *saved area*. The CODASYL Programming Language Committee's philosophy on terminology is to avoid using the same word in situations where the semantics of any operation performed are clearly different. The DBLTG recognized some potential confusion with the word *area* and found another word for the concept.

A realm was defined by the DBTG (page 13) to be 'a named sub-division of the addressable storage space in the data base and may contain occurrences of records and sets or parts of sets of various types'.

The DDLC modified this definition and came up with the following:

'An area (i.e. realm) is a named collection of records which need not preserve owner/member relationship. An area may contain occurrences of one or more record types, and a record type may have occurrences in more than one area. A particular record is assigned to a single area and may not migrate between areas. An area may ...'

The DDLC was clearly trying to get away from the DBTG's reference to *addressable storage space*. At least in terms of available implementations, this is precisely what a realm is.

The whole realm concept has been something of a bone of contention from the beginning. The main fact which emerges is that the data administrator must map record types to realms as indicated in the DDLC's definition. Furthermore, he must assign each realm to a device type using the Device Media Control Language (see Section 2.6) and indeed he may be allowed to control in some detail the way records are distributed within the realm. The programmer needs to be aware only of how the record types are assigned to realms. The other details normally do not help him (except when using one rather specific DML FIND option as will be discussed).

If the data administrator does not like the realm concept for some reason or other, then he may assign the whole data base, that is all its record types, to one all embracing realm. Admittedly, the programmer must still 'ready' (i.e. open) this realm at the beginning of his program and 'finish' (i.e. close) it at the end.

The advantages of partitioning the data base into realms are numerous. One is to allow the assignment of the data base to different types of direct access device.

Another is to give a chance of better overall performance in a concurrent processing situation. The disadvantages of the way the DBTG designed their approach to the problem comes in the requirement for the programmer to include a READY statement in his program. The opponents claim (with reasonable justification) that this readying could be implicit in the use of the sub-schema.

4.8.1 Record Type to Realm Assignment

The process of assigning a record type to one or more realms is a fairly simple one. It is included in the part of the Schema DDL called the Record Entry, which is the part where all the properties of each record type (such as its location mode) are declared.

The DBTG syntax is as follows:

```
; WITHIN realm-name-1 [{realm-name-2} ...
           REALM-ID IS dbd-name-2]
```

We have changed the word AREA to REALM to be consistent with the narrative.

Most of the time a record type is assigned to one realm only and the syntax is very simple, as follows:

```
; WITHIN real-name-1.
```

If the data administrator knows that there will be tens of thousands of records of a given type and he does not want his realms to be too big, then he may assign the record type to two or more realms. It may be that there is a limit on the maximum size of a realm imposed by the implementor, but the problem is more likely to be one of the wanting to keep the realms to a manageable size.

There must be a basis or criterion for the partitioning of a record type into two or more realms. This means more work for the programmer who is writing the program to store new records of this type in the data base. What happens is that a data item, namely dbd-name-2 has to be initialized by the programmer to contain the name of one of the realms listed in the WITHIN clause. Hence, the decision to assign a record type to two or more realms is taken by the data administrator; the decision on which records of this type are stored in which realms is a completely procedural one left in the hands of the programmer who writes the updating program.

DDLC added two new capabilities to the WITHIN clause, neither of which has been widely implemented. Their syntax (modified) reads as follows:

$$
\text{WITHIN} \left\{ \begin{array}{l} \text{real-name-1 [\{realm-name-2\} ... \underline{REALM-ID} IS dbd-name-1]} \\ \qquad\quad \text{[USING \underline{PROCEDURE} db-procedure-1]]} \\ \underline{\text{REALM OF OWNER}} \end{array} \right\}
$$

The first of the additions can be related to the above paragraph discussing who decides what. If the data administrator decides that he wishes to control the detailed assignment of records to realms, then he may write a data base procedure to do this job. In this case, it is the data administrator's procedure which automatically initializes the item dbd-name and the programmer has no say in the matter. However, this capability depends on the availability of data base procedures which are not as yet widely available.

The other DDLC idea is to allow the data administrator to assign record types with a location mode of VIA SET (see Section 4.4) to the same realm as the owner of the set type named in the location mode clause. This makes a lot of sense if the location mode VIA SET is interpreted in terms of physical contiguity as was suggested in this book. In fact, in some implementations, the implementor has made this a rule anyway. It does not make much sense to choose a location mode of VIA SET and then assign the owner and members record types to different realms. The DBTG proposal did not include such a rule. The DDLC goes as far as to allow the option.

4.8.2 Temporary Realms

We cannot leave our discussion of the assignment of record types to realms without mentioning the temporary realm. It must be emphasized that this capability has not been implemented to a great extent, which reflects partly the inherent difficulties in doing so and possibily the implementor's belief in its value to the user.

A temporary realm is one which the programmer uses as a 'scratch' region during the course of execution of his program. He must ready it for use and when his READY statement is excuted, a *copy* of the realm is available for his use. This does not contain any records and after he has finished with the realm any records which he may have stored cease to exist.

There are these two important differences between a *permanent* realm and a *temporary* one. If two concurrently executing programs ready a permanent realm, they are then 'in contact with' the same physical data. If two concurrently executing programs ready a temporary realm, each gets its own copy of that realm, e.g. its own disc tracks. This is one of the reasons why the concept is hard to implement. Present day operating systems do not support this idea and it is often hard for the DBMS implementor to bring about changes to the host operating system.

Assuming that one has the temporary realm capability available, how can one use it? The host language, be it COBOL, FORTRAN or PL/1 will provide some kind of facility to the programmer to store records on direct or sequential access storage temporarily during the course of execution of a program. The only possible role for the temporary realm is then to store data records which are structured into set types. However, the data administrator is responsible for defining record types, set types and realms. If the programmer is to use temporary realms, then the data administrator must foresee this need and define the temporary realms and the assignments of record types to these realms.

The DBTG predicted one problem with the temporary realm and introduced a rule to prohibit the situation. They said (DDLC wording page 3.25 modified):

'Records in a temporary realm cannot participate either as owner or member records in sets which contain records that are not in temporary realms.'

(The whole rule would have been better written in the singular rather than plural form.) The effect of this rule is that if a temporary realm is to be used to contain data records structured into sets, then the owner and members must both be assigned to the realm. This implies further that such record types are necessary, special 'working' record types or else each record type concerned is assigned to at least one permanent realm and at least one temporary realm (using the REALM-ID option in the WITHIN clause). This latter alternative means that the program must be able to juggle records between temporary realm and permanent realm, a requirement that we hope is rarely necessary.

4.9 Summary

In this chapter we have discussed the general topic of assigning record type to storage. This has necessitated the introduction of the data base key concept and the realm concept, both of which are very fundamental to the DBTG ideas.

To give the complete overview, the relevant parts of the DDLC syntax for the Realm Entry and the Record Entry are repeated with two earlier samples.

{REALM NAME IS real-name-1 [; REALM IS TEMPORARY ...]} ...

{RECORD NAME IS record-name-1

$$; \underline{\text{LOCATION}} \text{ MODE IS} \left\{ \begin{array}{l} \underline{\text{DIRECT}} \left\{ \begin{array}{l} \text{dbd-name-1} \\ \text{db-id-1} \end{array} \right\} \\ \underline{\text{CALC}} \begin{array}{l} \text{[db-proc-1] USING db-id-2 [, db-id-3] ...} \\ \underline{\text{DUPLICATES}} \text{ ARE [\underline{NOT}] ALLOWED} \end{array} \\ \underline{\text{VIA}} \text{ set-name-1 SET} \\ \underline{\text{SYSTEM}} \end{array} \right\}$$

$$; \underline{\text{WITHIN}} \left\{ \begin{array}{l} \text{realm-name-1 [\{, realm-name-2\} ... REALM-ID IS dbd-name-2} \\ \text{[USING PROCEDURE db-proc-2]]} \\ \text{REALM OF \underline{OWNER}} \end{array} \right\} ...$$

This syntax deliberately omits several features not yet discussed and all the whole process of defining the intra-record structure. The following examples illustrate only the widely implemented features.

4.9.1 Worked Examples

Example 1

REALM NAME IS SUPPLIER-REALM.
RECORD NAME IS SUPPLIER-CONTROL;

LOCATION MODE IS CALC USING CALC-KEY
     DUPLICATES ARE NOT ALLOWED;
WITHIN SUPPLIER-REALM.
RECORD NAME IS SUPPLIER;
LOCATION MODE IS VIA SUPPLIERS SET;
WITHIN SUPPLIER REALM;
RECORD NAME IS PURCHASE-ORDER;
LOCATION MODE IS CALC USING PURCHASE-ORDER-ID,
                PURCHASE-ORDER-SEQ-NO
     DUPLICATES ARE NOT ALLOWED
WITHIN SUPPLIER-REALM.
RECORD NAME IS PURCHASE-ORDER-LINE;
LOCATION MODE IS VIA PURCHASE-ORDER-CONTENTS-SET;
WITHIN SUPPLIER-REALM.

This example illustrates the language which would be used for defining a realm and for record types within that realm. Two of the record types have a location mode of CALC and the other two have VIA SET. Hence, we see mention of two set types, the definition of which is yet to be discussed. Following the WITHIN clause for each record type would normally come a list of the items in the record type and their various parameters. This will be discussed in Chapter 9.

References

1. V. Y. Lum, P. S. T. Yuen and M. Dodd, 'Key-to-Address Transformation Techniques: A Fundamental Performance Study on Large Existing Formatted Files', *Communications of ACM*, April 1971, 228–239.
2. W. Buchholz, 'File Organization and Addressing', *IBM Systems Journal*, June 1963, 86–111.

Chapter 5

Mapping a Set Type to Storage

5.1 Recapitulation

In Chapter 3 we introduced the set type as an inter-record structuring technique and compared it with the more traditional intra-record structuring which came into vogue during the sixties as a means of representing a modest hierarchical structure on sequential storage media.

We explained the role of the owner record type and member record types and identified the three classes single member set types, multi-member set types, and system owned set types, and stressed that each set type must be named. We explained that, for each set type defined in the Schema DDL, there may be several sets (or set occurrences) in the data base, although some of these sets may be 'empty'. This means that the set comprises an occurrence of the owner, but no occurrence of any member record type.

The chapter concluded with some illustrations of how the set type could be used to build various data base structures. As one looks back at these figures, it is easy to think of the set type as a relationship between record types, but we must not lose sight of the fact that many relationships may be identified between any two record types, but very mundane considerations make the data administrator decide whether or not to include them in the data base structure. In blunt terms, he has to decide whether a set type is justified because of its utilitarian value as an access path to expedite the down to earth process of accessing records.

Remember in the discussion of location mode we asserted that 'there are always many ways of accessing a record' and emphasized that giving its record type a location mode of CALC added a way. We must now recognize that defining a set type in which a record type participates (especially as a member) adds yet another way. A record type can have only one location mode, but it can participate in several set types, and each participation adds yet another way (or access path to the record).

Before discussing the details of how a set type is mapped to storage, we must observe that there is absolutely no requirement at all that a single relationship set type be explicitly defined for a data base. It is quite acceptable for a data administrator to define a data base containing one record type, or even a hundred record types without a single set type. In this extreme case, none of the record types may have a location mode of VIA SET. Using a DBMS based on the CODASYL proposals without using set types would be a strange way of using it, but the fact remains—there is no requirement to define set types. As we will see during the sub-schema discussion, even if set types are defined in the Schema DDL, there is no need to use them in the sub-schema. There is also the matter of implicit relationships which will be discussed in Chapter 24 when relational theory is presented.

5.2 Mapping Consideration

When we discussed the mapping of record types to storage, we were concerned with the various alternatives for placing the actual records in one realm or the other and how the decision was made within the realm chosen. Although the discussion concerned *placement*, it was really a relative placement within a realm (or realms) rather than an utterly physical matter of which disc pack and which cylinder and track thereon.

Turning to mapping of set types, it must be clear that there is no conflict and only some interaction between the mapping to storage of set type and the mapping to storage of its participating owner and member record types. The records of the various types are placed where the location mode clause and the WITHIN clause indicate. In discussing the mapping of a set type, we are talking about *how* the set type is *represented* in storage.

This whole topic is so much emphasized in any short tutorial on the CODASYL proposals (including the author's own[1]) that the casual reader may well feel that this is what DBTG is all about. Hopefully, this book is clarifying that there is much more to a CODASYL-based DBMS than the set type—and its representations.

5.3 Set Mode

DBTG introduced the term *set mode* to identify the choice which the data administrator must make for each set type in the data base. DBTG identified two alternative set modes called *chain* and *pointer array*. If the former is chosen, then there are more lower level decisions to take—as will be discussed.

The DBTG clearly felt that the concept of set mode and the two alternatives chain and pointer array were a vital cornerstone in their thinking, as a considerable part of the presentation of concepts addressed these aspects. One of the most significant changes made by the DDLC in their report was to remove the whole idea of set mode as a data administrator option. The impact of this action will perhaps become clear after the details have been presented. The concept of chains, and to some extent pointer arrays, are so inherent in most implementations that no tutorial would be complete without a full treatment.

5.4 Chain Representation of a Set Type

The example in Figure 3.5 of a single member set type as repeated in Figure 5.1 can be used to illustrate the chain.

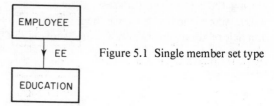

Figure 5.1 Single member set type

The reader will recall that in this book, rectangles represent record types, circles represent record occurrences.

An occurrence of this set type is illustrated graphically in Figure 5.2.

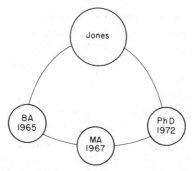

Figure 5.2 Occurrence of single member set type

The lines in Figure 5.2 (deliberately without arrows) merely indicate that the three EDUCATION records and the one EMPLOYEE record are all in the same set. The phrase used in this book is to say that the EDUCATION records are *connected* into the set. (This reflects the DBLTG's DML statement CONNECT which supersedes the DBTG's DML statement INSERT.) Just *how* the connection is made depends on the details of the set mode.

5.5 Chain Linked to Next

The simplest chain representation is a *chain linked to next*. This is depicted in Figure 5.3.

The implication here is that the owner record contains a pointer to the 'first' record in the set, namely the 'BSc 1959' record in Figure 5.3. The way this is implemented in practice is that the data base key value for the 'BSc 1959' record is

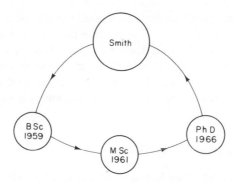

Figure 5.3 Chain linked to next

stored in the 'Smith' record. (Data base keys were discussed at length in Section 4.2.) Furthermore, the data base key of the 'MSc 1961' record is stored in the 'BSc 1959' record and so on.

In Figure 5.3, the last record, namely 'PhD 1966', contains a pointer to the owner record 'Smith', hence making the chain a 'closed' one (as compared with the open ended structures provided in some other systems).

The effect of this chain structure is to support a way of accessing the member records consecutively. Assuming that the location mode of owner record is CALC, then it is possible to make an access to it from outside the data base. From that point, it is possible to examine each of the connected member records in turn. In terms of the example, it would be possible to look at Smith's three education records in turn.

It must be emphasized that the EDUCATION record type could well have a location mode of CALC which means that education records could be accessed from outside the data base as well as from inside the set.

The details of the processing facilities will be presented later, but before moving on to the next type of chain, there are a few points to make on the chain linked to next.

5.5.1 Problems with Chain Linked to Next

Let us consider a typical real world situation where there may be 2,000 member records connected into a set. (There is nothing unreal about only having three, but the case to be made is so much clearer with 2,000.) It is a relatively frequent requirement to erase (or delete) a record from the data base completely. This means that the DBCS (note *not* the programmer) has the job of updating the pointers. The problem is that the DBCS has to access the record *preceding* the one being deleted to modify the pointer to point to the record after the one being deleted. It is this access to the preceding record which causes the problem. The only way to get to the record is to go all the way round the chain. If each of the 2,000 records in the chain is on a different disc track, then this means 2,000 distinct disc accesses—a very time consuming process.

The astute systems programmer accustomed to tailoring his own system might at this point suggest that it would be possible to retain the data base key of the record preceding the one to be deleted on the assumption that one would go round the chain to get to the record to be deleted. Unfortunately, this assumption is not valid here. While 'going round the chain' is certainly one way of getting to a record in order to delete it, there are other ways, and it is necessary to take this into account.

5.5.2 When to Use Chain Linked to Next

The advantage of the chain linked to next structure is that it uses less storage space than the other ways of representing a set type. If the sets are mostly small, but there are a lot of them (say 1,000 sets with a maximum size of 10 records), then one could get away with this option. Even then, if the deleting activity is heavy, one of the other alternatives might be more advisable. However, if the data administrator feels it is appropriate, he could designate the location mode of the member record types as VIA SET (using the set type under consideration). This should imply that the member records have a reasonable chance of being on the same page of the realm as each other and the chain linked to next might be given added justification. The data administrator needs to do his calculations in terms of page size, record size, pointer (i.e. data base key) size, set size and delete frequency to decide whether indeed this particular alternative is viable.

5.6 Chain Linked to Next and Prior

The problems discussed in Section 5.5.2 which can occur with chain linked to next can easily be obviated by choosing a different storage representation for the set type. This second alternative is called chain linked to next and prior. It is depicted in Figure 5.4.

There are now two pointers (that is, data base key values) stored in each record in the set. However, the problem mentioned for the chain linked to next has been solved. If a record is to be deleted from a large set, then the records on either side

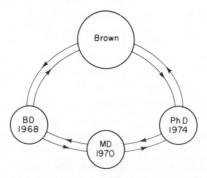

Figure 5.4 Chain linked to next and
prior

of it are easily accessible because the pointers in both directions are contained in the record to be deleted.

5.6.1 Effect of Single and Multi-member Set Types

So far, the discussion on chain linked to next and chain linked to next and prior has concerned itself with single member set types. It is important to note that both of these two set modes are quite independent of whether the set type is single member or multi-member. In fact, it is quite possible for the member records in an occurrence of a multi-member set type to be interspersed with respect to type. Hence, these chain representations are necessary properties of the set type rather than of the member record.

An occurrence of the multi-member set type from Figure 3.6 is shown in Figure 5.5.

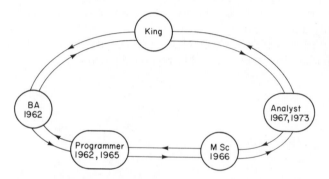

Figure 5.5 Occurrence of multi-member set type

It must be noted that the sequence of member records in any given set is quite independent of the set mode. It depends on a property of the set type called *set order* which will be discussed later. The intermixing of JOB-HISTORY and EDUCATION records in Figure 5.5 is quite possible.

5.6.2 Disadvantage of Chain Linked to Next and Prior

The chain linked to next and prior is a fairly useful set mode option and is probably more widely used than the chain linked to next. After all, deleting records is a fairly usual event in data processing.

There is a potential problem which arises equally with both chain linked to next and chain linked to next and prior. This arises if there is a requirement to access the owner of a given set from a member. The reader must now bear in mind that the programmer is not constrained to any one given way of processing through the data base. As a single example, suppose that the EDUCATION record type in Figure 5.1 has a location mode of CALC. It is then possible to access an EDUCATION record without any prior reference to an EMPLOYEE record.

However, having found the EDUCATION record, the next step is to gain access to its owner. This is always possible, but if the set mode option chain linked to next or chain linked to next and prior apply, then when the owner is accessed, the DBCS has to go all around the chain—again a potentially time consuming process.

5.7 Chains Linked to Owner

If the data administrator predicts that there will be frequent accesses to the owner from member records of a given type, then he may designate that the member in the set type has also a link to owner. It must now be observed that the link to owner is a property of a member—not of a set type. However, if the set type is a single member set type (especially if the DBMS only allows single member set types), then there is no difference.

The definition of a link to owner is also quite independent of whether there is a link to prior or not, although the arguments that justify a link to owner will often also justify a link to prior.

Several new set type representations are now possible. Single member set types with a link to owner are depicted in Figures 5.6 and 5.7.

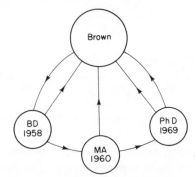

Figure 5.6 Single member set type as chain with link to next and to owner

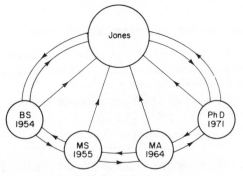

Figure 5.7 Single member set type as chain with link to next, prior and to owner

It always happens that two of the pointers are identical in the case of the first and last records of a set with links to prior and to owner. Even so, the pointers are stored in the records as if they were different. This makes it so much easier when new records are inserted into the set adjacent to the owner. Adjacent to the owner does *not* mean physically close. When we talk about positions in a set or chain, we are talking on a fairly abstract level. This topic will be discussed further when we come to set order.

Returning to the link to owner, in a multi-member set type it is quite possible for one member record type to have such a link, but not the other as shown in Figure 5.8.

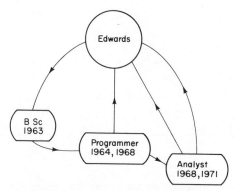

Figure 5.8 Multi-member set type as chain linked to next with one member linked to owner

If the multi-member set type has more than two members, then any member can be linked to the owner (even all of them). It is trivial to extend Figure 5.8 to include as well either a link to prior, or a link to owner for the EDUCATION record or both. Needless to say, the EDUCATION record could be linked to owner and not the JOB-HISTORY record.

In summary, the link to prior and each link to owner have to be assessed on their merits. It might be tempting to the data administrator to make a policy decision to include as many of these links as possible—'just in case'. This is not good data base design practice. If the data base is small enough, he may well get away with it. If the data base is large, but large because there are many small sets and many records are clustered by well chosen use of the VIA SET location mode, then the links to owner and prior may be a complete waste of storage space *and* possibly updating time.

5.8 Pointer Arrays

The whole concept of chains with the links to next and the choice of links to prior and owner has all been adopted by the DBTG from the tried and proven commercial product IDS developed by Bachman at General Electric in 1962.[2]

50

IDS (now IDS/1) did not in fact use the term set type (or set). The only set type in IDS/1 is the chain type.

DBTG identified the concept of chains as sets and decided to add a new way of representing sets in storage in addition to the chain. This new way is the pointer array.

To explain and justify the pointer array, it is best to start from a chain representation of either a single member or multi-member set type in which there is a link to prior and *all* members are linked to owner. For the multi-member set type of Figure 3.6, this would be as in Figure 5.9. Here it can easily be seen that *each* member record contains no less than *three* pointers.

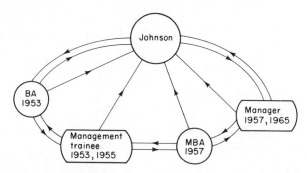

Figure 5.9 Multi-member set type as chain linked to next and
prior with both members linked to owner

In order to see what a pointer array looks like, each next pointer is moved into an array of such pointers; each prior pointer is 'thrown away' and each owner pointer is left where it is. The result is shown in Figure 5.10 which, for the sake of comparison, is the same set as in Figure 5.9.

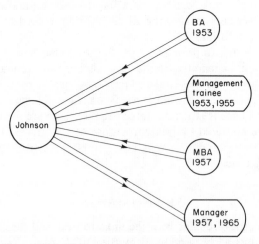

Figure 5.10 Multi-member set type represented as a
pointer array

The figure shows the arrows pointing away from the owner record and to each member record. This is not intended to leave the reader with the impression that the 'next' pointers from the chain structure are now all stored in the owner record. In fact, this is the last place they are likely to be stored. They may not be physically contiguous to the owner record. Just where the pointer array is stored and how is entirely a function of implementation.

The important aspect of the pointer array is that the execution time flexibility of the chain linked to prior with all members linked to owner is achieved at the expense of one pointer less per member record. In other words, the pointer array uses *two* pointers per member record compared with the chain's (Figure 5.8) *three* per member record.

In the case of the pointer array, the programmer can process in either direction through the set and from any member to the owner without the risk of excessive execution time.

5.8.1 Implementation of Pointer Arrays

The pointer array capability has not been widely implemented. Most implementors have decided that GE's (subsequently Honeywell's) experience with chains showed that there were no hidden snags and chose to economize on their implementation effort by leaving out pointer arrays or at least postponing this capability. Chains are possibly easier to implement than pointer arrays and certainly a 'chain only' implementation is more viable commercially than a 'pointer array only' implementation. A 'chain only' implementation allows a data administrator the extra control over the storage time versus processing time trade-offs, and this control is not really so difficult to exercise. However, it is predictable that pointer arrays will gain acceptance as time goes by.

5.9 DDLC Removal of Set Mode Option

As indicated earlier, the DBTG specifications included provision for the data administrator choosing between a chain and a pointer array for each set type in a data base. If chains were selected for a set type, then the option of a link to prior for that set type and a link to owner for each of its members would be available.

It is important to note that whatever set mode is chosen and whatever links are included in the case of a chain, the way the programmer writes his program is completely unaffected. Hence, the set mode is really something in the Schema DDL which the programmer does not *need* to know about; but it does help him to write better programs if he knows about it.

It was presumably the fact that the programmer does not need to know which caused the DDLC to remove the set mode option from the Schema DDL. In point of fact, they only removed two thirds of the evidence and decided (in that rather arbitrary way peculiar to committees intent on finding a compromise acceptable to all members) to leave behind the idea of a *prior processable* set and the idea of a link to owner. All references to chains and pointer arrays were taken out.

Another possible argument for the purge is that the DBTG's extensive discussions of chains and pointer arrays were 'too implementation oriented'. In view of the indisputable fact that the programmer 'does not need to know', one could also argue that the set mode concept belongs in the DMCL rather than the Schema DDL. However, the claim has never been made by the CODASYL committees that the Schema DDL contains *only* what the DML programmer needs to know.

No apology is offered here for including a full tutorial presentation of the ideas of chain and pointer array. They are felt to be completely intrinsic to an understanding of the CODASYL approach to data base management. If the concept were glossed over, the reader could understandably feel that something of considerable value were being hidden.

5.10 Set Mode Syntax

Using the Schema DDL, the definition of a data base is divided into a number of four so-called *entries*. In the sequence to be used, they are

schema entry
realm entry
record entry
set entry

In the previous chapter, we discussed various critical parts of the realm entry and the record entry. As with the record entry, the set entry is divided into two sub-entries. These are called the *set sub-entry* and the *member sub-entry*. It will soon be clear why the set sub-entry is part of the set entry.

The DBTG syntax for the relevant part of the set entry was (pages 126–7, adapted)

SET NAME IS set-name-1

; MODE IS $\begin{Bmatrix} \text{CHAIN [LINKED TO PRIOR]} \\ \text{POINTER-ARRAY} \end{Bmatrix}$

- - - - - -
- - - - - -

; OWNER IS $\begin{Bmatrix} \text{record-name-1} \\ \text{SYSTEM} \end{Bmatrix}$.

{MEMBER IS record-name-1 {} {}[LINKED TO OWNER]

- - - - - -
- - - - - -
- - - - - -

        } . . .

Parts of the set entry which have not yet been discussed in this text have been deliberately omitted.

This syntax can be compared with the DDLC's approach (pages 3.4.0 and 3.4.1, adapted)

<u>SET</u> NAME IS set-name-1

; <u>OWNER</u> IS $\begin{Bmatrix} \text{record-name-1} \\ \underline{\text{SYSTEM}} \end{Bmatrix}$

[; SET IS <u>PRIOR</u> PROCESSABLE]

- - - - - -
- - - - -

{<u>MEMBER</u> IS record-name-1 {} {} [LINKED TO <u>OWNER</u>]

- - - - - -
- - - - -
- - - - - -

      } . . .

The DDLC made a minor change by moving the owner clause up from the end of the set entry to the beginning which makes sense, and is consistent with the fact that the name of the member is declared at the start of the member sub-entry.

5.10.1 Examples of Set Declarations

Using the above DBTG syntax which will be more frequently encountered in practice, some of the various set representations illustrated earlier in this chapter would be defined as follows:

Example 1. (see Figures 5.1 and 5.3)

  SET NAME IS EE ; MODE IS CHAIN;

  OWNER IS EMPLOYEE.

  MEMBER IS EDUCATION.

Example 2. (see Figures 5.1 and 5.4)

  SET NAME IS EE ; MODE IS CHAIN LINKED TO PRIOR;
  OWNER IS EMPLOYEE.
  MEMBER IS EDUCATION.

Example 3. (see Figures 3.6 and 5.5)

  SET NAME IS EJE ; MODE IS CHAIN;

OWNER IS EMPLOYEE.
MEMBER IS EDUCATION.
MEMBER IS JOB-HISTORY.

Example 4. (see Figures 5.1 and 5.6)

SET NAME IS EE ; MODE IS CHAIN;
OWNER IS EMPLOYEE.
MEMBER IS EDUCATION LINKED TO OWNER.

Example 5. (see Figures 3.6 and 5.8)

SET NAME IS EJE ; MODE IS CHAIN;
OWNER IS EMPLOYEE.
MEMBER IS EDUCATION.
MEMBER IS JOB-HISTORY LINKED TO OWNER.

Example 6. (see Figures 3.6 and 5.9)

SET NAME IS EJE ; MODE IS CHAIN LINKED TO PRiOR;
OWNER IS EMPLOYEE.
MEMBER IS EDUCATION LINKED TO OWNER.
MEMBER IS JOB-HISTORY LINKED TO OWNER.

Example 7. (see Figures 3.6 and 5.10)

SET NAME IS EJE ; MODE IS POINTER ARRAY;
OWNER IF EMPLOYEE.
MEMBER IS EDUCATION.
MEMBER IS JOB-HISTORY.

Finally, it is instructive to note that if the DDLC's syntax were used, then there would be no difference between Example 6 and Example 7. Both would be written as

Example 8.

SET NAME IS EJE ; OWNER IS EMPLOYEE.
SET IS PRIOR PROCESSABLE.
MEMBER IS EDUCATION LINKED TO OWNER.
MEMBER IS JOB-HISTORY LINKED TO OWNER.

In Example 8, we have included the LINKED TO OWNER clause for each member record type. However, the DDLC syntax for the member clause indicates quite clearly that it is optional. We quote from DDLC page 3.71, Rule 4:

'The optional LINKED TO OWNER phrase causes the DBMS to select preferentially for the set type whose declaration contains this sub-entry, an implementation method which allows the owner record of the set containing an occurrence of this member record to be accessed directly from that member record. The . . .'

Since the DDLC's Schema DDL, as stated, calls for no awareness of the subtle differences between chains and pointer arrays, the implications of *omitting* the LINKED TO OWNER phrase are unclear. If the phrase is included, the implications of the potentially loaded expression 'to select preferentially' in the above rule are also unclear. However, it is clear that the DBMS could itself still have a choice, and an astute data administrator would surely like to know how it made it.

The idea of a pointer array *without* a link to owner is just about unacceptable. If the programmer is to be protected from needing to know how a set type is represented, then his attempt to find an owner record from a member would only be realizable in such circumstances by examining each owner record in turn to see which pointed to the member record the search starts from—not an enticing thought.

References

1. T. W. Olle, 'Tutorial on CODASYL Data Base Management Concepts', Proceedings of British Computer Society Symposium held October 1974 on *Implementations of the CODASYL DBMS Proposals*. Available from BCS at £2.50.
2. C. W. Bachman and C. B. Williams, 'A General Purpose Programming System for Random Access Memories', *Proc. FJCC*, **26** 411–422 (1964).

Chapter 6

Set Order and Search Keys

6.1 Recapitulation

The previous chapter discussed how a set type could be represented in storage. Most facets of this problem were discussed and the reader should now be fully cognizant with the ideas of chains and pointer arrays. He realizes that these are almost certainly independent of how the record types are mapped to storage. Indeed, if we forget the location mode VIA SET, then we could claim complete independence.

6.2 Set Order

We now come to the question of how the members in a set are sequenced relative to each other. In the previous chapter we mentioned in passing that one record in a set would be the 'first' and another would be the 'last'. What does 'first' mean? Is it time of arrival? In other words, does 'first' imply 'of longest standing' or 'oldest'? Does 'first' have something to do with the physical position in the realm or in the page? The safest answer to all these questions is 'no'. It is the aim of this chapter to explain the concepts of set order, first and last which in a sense could justifiably be thought of as a facet of the mapping of set to storage.

6.2.1 Reason for Set Order

When using magnetic tape files, it is natural because of the physical performance characteristics of the device type to try to sequence the records in the order in which they will be used. An access to any specific record in a tape file involves passing the whole file anyway and if the record is to be updated, then the whole file must be copied.

This neat concept of keeping records in some kind of usage oriented order seems to carry over naturally from the tape processing world to the direct access DBMS world. IDS/1 has always allowed for sorted chains and this capability carried over to DBTG without any question as to its utilitarian value. As any experienced data administrator knows to his cost, it is *not* always the best decision to have the set sorted as one would tend to if it were a tape file. Hence, there are other set order options as well which we will collectively refer to as chronological, although the CODASYL committees do not use this term or any other for that matter. If there is a way of talking about one class of set order, then logically there should be a way of talking about the other classes. We will use *sorted* and *chronological* in this book.

There are some important processing time trade-offs to be controlled in the choice between the two as we hope to clarify. Most of the time there is no storage space involved—but even that can come in as we shall see.

6.2.2 Data Administrator or Programmer Decision

If the data administrator decides that the set type is to be sorted, this means that whoever writes the programs to update the data base (and hence its records and sets) whenever these programs are run, the member records in the set are maintained in a very specific order, often sorted on some date, name or number. There is probably nothing the programmer can do to get a record into a set in a way he, the programmer, would prefer. In this case, we can regard the set order as a centrally controlled data administrator decision—central with respect to the several programmers who are writing programs to update the data base.

The various sorted set alternatives each represents a data administrator decision to control the set order centrally. A chronological set can go either way. The data administrator can choose an option which leaves the decision on set order to the programmers or he can take another option which means that the member records form either a stack (last in, first out) or a queue (first in, first out). DDLC introduced yet another alternative called IMMATERIAL, which implies 'nobody cares', although, as will be pointed out, this option seems to be of very marginal value in practice.

6.3 Sorted Sets

(It probably does not matter too much whether we talk about 'sorted sets' or 'sorted set types', although in all other aspects of the set type and set phenomenon, we have to be extremely careful.)

What happens is the following. In the Schema DDL, the data administrator may declare a set type as 'sorted'. This means that all sets of that type are maintained in a sorted order determined by a criterion which is common to the set type. Multi-member set types are so much more complicated than single member set types so we will consider the latter first.

6.3.1 Single Member Sorted Set Type

A single member set type may be sorted only if one item or more in the member record type is selected to serve as a sort key, where sort key has exactly the same meaning as in conventional data processing.

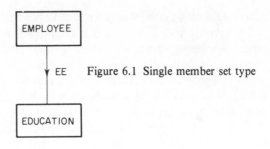

Figure 6.1 Single member set type

As an example we could return to our single member set type of chapters 4 and 5 as shown in Figure 6.1.

If this were designated as a sorted set type, then a typical item in the EDUCATION record to serve as a sort key might be the DATE-OF-QUALIFICATION item.

Why should the data administrator choose to designate a single member set type as sorted? In the above example which will clearly have only rather small sets, the reasons for and against sorting are fairly inconsequential. In a case where the sets are large, there are two situations which might justify it.

The first is that it might be a *frequent* requirement to generate a report containing data from the member records sorted in some sequence. Output sorting time is clearly saved if the records can be processed in that sequence. (Notice we did not say 'stored in that sequence'. This is another problem.) The other reason is if the programmer needs to do frequent searches through one or more sets of this type looking for records. If the sort key is the same as his search criterion, then the program can cause the search to terminate by testing values of the sort key item or items. In this case, we have a programmer taking advantage of knowledge of the sort key—a concept well understood in conventional data processing.

The reader must not get the impression that the sorted set type is free. Following the above discussion, one can always think of some basis for keeping sets of a given type in sorted order in case a programmer can take advantage of this sort order. However, at the time a new record is stored in the data base, it is usually connected into sets of at least one type and often more. How is this connection process effected? The DBCS has first to find the connection point. Whether the set type is represented by a chain or a pointer array, this could, in a large set, cause accesses to several hundred records. The risk can be minimized in an 'initial load' program which loads the data base from scratch, but the problem remains in updates performed subsequent to the initial load.

Before designating a set type as sorted, it is appropriate to look at the update versus retrieval time trade-off. It will often prove more advantageous to choose a chronological set type instead. However, it is usually possible to expend storage space to save processing time and the present situation is no exception. The way out is to designate the set type as indexed as well as sorted.

6.3.2 Indexed Set Types

Only sorted set types may be designated as indexed. The purpose of the index is to expedite the process of finding where a record is to be connected into a set. As far as can be ascertained from the specifications, there is no implication that such an index could assist at record retrieval time. It is fairly obvious that an index could equally well be used at both retrieval and update time.

The DBTG recognized that an index of this kind will necessarily require storage space. Furthermore, the data administrator might be anxious to assign the index to a faster kind of storage than the member record type or types which is indexed. Hence, there is an option for naming the index. This is the only index name in the whole Schema DDL and it is strange that the index to a sorted set should be singled out for special treatment. Why not pointer arrays and search keys?

If the index is not named, then where the index for each set of the sorted set type is stored is up to the DBCS. If it is named, then the idea is that in the DMCL the data administrator can assign it to a special realm.

6.3.3 Multi-member Sorted Set Types

In the case of a sorted set type with more than one member, there are a number of minor complicating factors. With single member sorted set types, there must be one or more items in the member record type which serve as a sort key. The four different options are discussed.

Sorted BY RECORD NAME

In a multi-member set type, the record name may or may not serve as a prime sort key. This rather obvious option was not provided for in DBTG, but DDLC, in a wholesale clean-up of the DBTG's confused thinking on set order, designated this option as SORTED BY RECORD NAME.

In this case, the data administrator *may* designate minor keys for any of the member record types. This process is best illustrated by reference to a previously used multi-member set type depicted in Figure 6.2.

If this set type is designated as SORTED BY RECORD NAME, then EDUCATION records will precede JOB-HISTORY records in each set because E sorts higher in any collating sequence than J. The reader should remember the

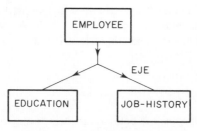

Figure 6.2 Multi-member set type

effect of this set order. Assume there are some records of both member types in a set and a programmer has found his way to the owner record EMPLOYEE. If he then asks for the NEXT in the set or the FIRST in the set, the record he will find will be an EDUCATION record. If instead he asks for the LAST in the set or the PRIOR, then the record he will find will be a JOB-HISTORY record.

The data administrator might decide that separating the EDUCATION records from the JOB-HISTORY records in this way is adequate. He might decide to go further and designate further sort keys for the JOB-HISTORY record type. (He could choose EDUCATION as well—or instead.) If he chooses as an ascending sort key in the JOB-HISTORY some obscure item such as JOB-START-DATE, then the EDUCATION records would be in some unpredictable order and the JOB-HISTORY records in ascending order of the date on which the employee started the job. This is illustrated in Figure 6.3. (No designation of pointers is given in this figure to emphasize that it is irrelevant to the present consideration of set order.)

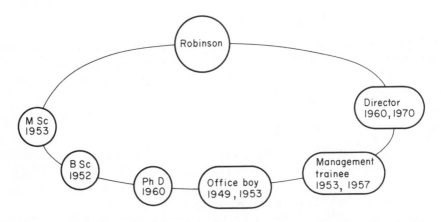

Figure 6.3 Multi-member set type sorted BY RECORD NAME

One question which might occur to the reader following this example is whether it is possible to get from the owner record to the first JOB-HISTORY record without passing through all the EDUCATION records first. In other words, is there anything the data administrator can do if he can predict this requirement to make it a more rapid process. The best answer is to make two separate set types. Within the multi-member set type, there is no easy way to achieve the goal otherwise.

Sorted BY DEFINED KEYS

In a multi-member set type, the data administrator may select an item or items which are the same in each member record type. 'Same' here implies that the value of the sort key items in one member record type can be sensibly compared with the value of the sort key items in the other member record types.

Using Figure 6.2 again as an example, one could choose DATE-OF-QUALIFICATION in the EDUCATION record type and JOB-START-DATE in the JOB-HISTORY record type. The set depicted in Figure 6.3 where the set type was sorted BY RECORD NAME would be sequenced as shown in Figure 6.4 if the two dates were the sort keys.

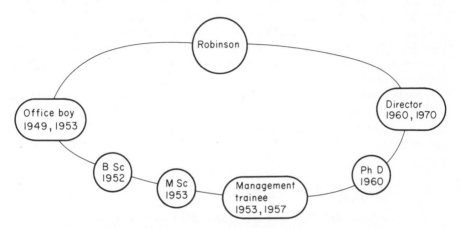

Figure 6.4 Multi-member set type sorted BY DEFINED KEYS

The DDLC specifications make no stipulations about the sort keys from the different record types, such as whether they have to be of the same length or not. Hopefully, such details will be taken care of by implementors providing this option. It is clear that the name of the sort keys will be different.

With the BY DEFINED KEYS option, there is a further option available to the data administrator and that is to take a position with respect to duplicate values of the sort keys. He has four alternatives available as follows.

1. He can prohibit them, which means that the attempt to store a record and connect it into the set can be unsuccessful if its sort key values collectively are identical to those in a record already connected.
2. He can decide that the records with duplicate sort key values are allowed, that he cares where they are connected relative to those records with the same sort key values already there, and specify that they be connected before or after them.
3. He can decide that the records with duplicate sort key values are allowed, but he does not care where they are connected relative to those records already connected.

In the last case, he may designate some kind of 'duplicate control' in the Member Sub-entry where he defines the sort keys.

Sorted BY DATA-BASE-KEY

This is one of the two sorted set type options originally provided for by the DBTG. (Both are felt to be of marginal value compared with the DDLC two new options already discussed.)

The effect of defining the set type as being SORTED BY DATA-BASE-KEY (DBTG preferred DATABASE-KEY) is to cause the member records to be sequenced in the set to which they are connected on the data base key (see Section 4.2). This is an option designed for the data administrator or programmer who are working on a very physical level. To use the option intelligently, *both* must understand how the data base key values are stored. Coupled with a location mode of VIA SET for the member record types, this set order option minimizes the number of physical disc accesses which are necessary when the programmer is processing the whole of a set by going through it one by one.

Whether the set type is multi-member or not could affect the process depending on how an implementation assigns data base key value to a record when it is stored. Conceivably, this could cause the records of different member types to be separated in each set (as in SORTED WITHIN RECORD NAME); possibly the records could be intermingled (as in SORTED BY DEFINED KEYS).

Sorted WITHIN RECORD-NAME

This is the other sorted set type option provided by the DBTG. It is deliberately discussed last, because an understanding of the preceding three should help the reader comprehend this somewhat strange marginal value option. (It is noted that it was not in IDS/1 or in the DBTG's October 1969 report.)

The idea is that each member record type may have its own sort keys. They are not minor to the record name in BY RECORD-NAME. They do not have to correspond so that their values may be compared as in the BY DEFINED KEYS OPTION. The result is that the records of different member types may turn out to be intermingled within a given set. There is a universal minor key which is used if no sort key is defined for one of the member record types and this is the data base key value. Hence, if the data administrator chooses this option but omits to specify application oriented sort keys for all member record types, then the effect is the same as SORTED BY DATA-BASE-KEY.

The relevant general rule governing this option is essentially the same rule in both DBTG and DDLC. The rule is quoted from the DDLC report in case it conveys something over and above the preceding discussion.

'The optional WITHIN RECORD-NAME phrase allows records to be sorted without regard to the order of other record types in the set. This does not mean that there is an implied major sort by record type. It means only that when a given type of record is considered independently of any other member record type, it is in sequence by its own sort control key. The sort control keys are specified by the KEY clause for each of the member record types. If the KEY clause is not used for any member record type, the data base keys of the occurrences of that record type are used as ascending key items.'

63

Readers more familiar with DBTG terminology should note that the clause they know of as ASCENDING/DESCENDING now has the neater name KEY clause.

The discussion of indexed set types in Section 6.3.2 was specific to the single member set type. However, the facility exists to define and name an index for any kind of sorted set type with any number of member record types. The index is a property of the set type and not of any specific member record type.

6.4 Chronological Set Types

As indicated earlier (Section 6.2.2), a chronological set may be defined such that the data administrator decrees exactly where new records are connected or alternatively he may leave the decision to the programmer. The former case is easier to explain so we will tackle it first.

6.4.1 Stacks and Queues

As with sorted set types, it is better to start by considering single member set types and then see what perturbations (if any) are introduced by allowing multi-member set types.

The two data administrator controlled options for a chronological set type have the effect that each new record is connected into the set 'adjacent' to the owner record. One is declared by using the syntax (DDLC) INSERTION IS FIRST and the other uses INSERTION IS LAST, where the words FIRST and LAST imply the equivalent of following the NEXT pointer round a chain. This does not mean that a chronological set type is tied in to the chain set mode, but using the chain concept is the best way of explaining what happens. To illustrate the concept of chronological set types, let us consider a completely different example of a set type as depicted in Figure 6.5.

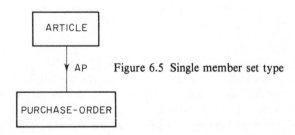

Figure 6.5 Single member set type

Assuming an on-line ordered entry system, as the day goes by clerical personnel may enter purchase orders (represented by occurrences of the PURCHASE-ORDER record type) into the data base. Each PURCHASE-ORDER record is automatically connected to the ARTICLE being ordered. If we assume that the set type AP has a chronological set order, then the situation at

64

five time intervals during the early part of the day is shown in Figure 6.6. The fact that a CHAIN LINKED TO NEXT is illustrated is arbitrary. Two items in the member record type are illustrated. These are CUSTOMER-NAME and QUANTITY-ORDERED. At time $t = 4$, it is clear that the set is sequenced quite differently from how it would be if it were sorted (at least on either or both of the items shown).

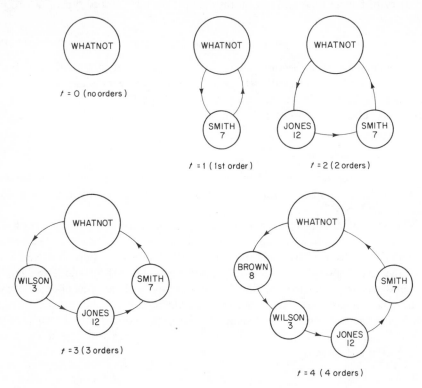

Figure 6.6 Occurrences of chronological set type at different times showing INSERTION IS FIRST

We regard the INSERTION IS FIRST as a stack (LIFO) because if the processing of the orders started at the ARTICLE record, then following the NEXT chain, the first order to be processed would be the last (that is, most recent) to be added. In practice, this would be rather unfair on the customers. However, the advantage of the stack is that the connection point for each new record is very quickly found and therefore the time taken to enter each new purchase order is minimized.

If the data administrator wanted to be fair to the customers at the expense of taking a little extra time to connect each PURCHASE-ORDER record, then he could define the set order as INSERTION IS LAST. The situation at time $t = 4$ in Figure 6.6 would then be as shown in Figure 6.7. The arrow between the last record in the set to be connected (but not in this case the most recent) and the owner is where the next record (in time) to be connected would go.

The reader will hopefully realize that the combination of CHAIN LINKED TO NEXT and INSERTION IS LAST, while quite legal, is not necessarily an optimum one.

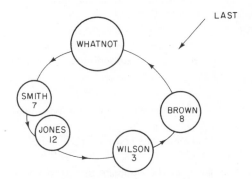

Figure 6.7 Occurrence of a chronological set type at one time showing INSERTION IS LAST

Again, physical contiguity plays a role. If the sets are all small but there are a lot of them, then the combination is appropriate, especially if the member has a location mode VIA SET. If the sets are large and the member record has some other location mode, then connecting a PURCHASE-ORDER record could be very time consuming, because the DBCS has to go all along the chain to the last record to find the connection point.

The INSERTION IS LAST option can be thought of as a queue (FIFO) and a more fair minded way of handling orders from customers.

We begin to see here how the various schema declarations of location mode, set mode and set order interact. There are many examples of such interaction and a skilled data administrator will learn that there are some combinations which are 'safe' and others which are to be avoided at all times.

We said that the two chronological options INSERTION IS FIRST and INSERTION IS LAST were such that the data administrator was dictating a set order in much the same way as in the sorted set types. However, it is not quite so dictatorial. In a batch processing environment, the programmer can surely achieve the order he wants by controlling the way the updating transactions are sequenced and fed in. In an on-line system, such as an order entry system, the programmer may need to know the set order criterion but he does nothing to influence the sequence in individual sets.

6.4.2 Insertion Next and Prior

If the data administrator wants a chronological set type and would like the member records sequenced in some very special way which none of the sorted set type options provides, then he must let the programmer build up each set procedurally.

The two other chronological set type options are referred to as INSERTION NEXT and INSERTION PRIOR. In order to explain these, we must jump ahead to a very basic execution time concept, namely the currency indicator. There are several of these the programmer should understand and they will be explained in full later. The important one here is called the Current of Set Type indicator.

At any point during the course of execution of a program, a Current of Set Type indicator contains a data base key value which identifies a record (owner or member) in a set of the set type corresponding to that indicator. One of these Current of Set Type indicators is maintained for each set type in the sub-schema the program is using.

At the time a new record is stored in the data base or connected into a set (which may be later) its position in the set is determined by the Current of Set Type indicator. If the declaration was INSERTION NEXT, then it is connected in the direction of the NEXT pointer. If the declaration was INSERTION PRIOR, then it is connected in the opposite direction which is the same as the PRIOR pointer if there is one. Again we are explaining Set Order in terms of chains and again we must not forget pointer arrays.

In the case of a pointer array, the array must be prised apart (figuratively speaking) to let in the data base key of the new record.

These two chronological set orders are illustrated in Figure 6.8 which is based on the same set type as that in Figure 6.5.

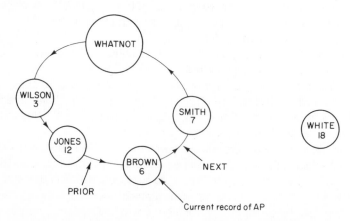

Figure 6.8 Occurrence of a chronological set type at one time showing INSERTION NEXT and INSERTION PRIOR

Figure 6.8 shows a chain linked to next only to define the direction of the next chain. (We have a habit of making them anticlockwise.) The Currency of AP indicator points to the PURCHASE-ORDER record from Brown for six 'whatnot' articles. If the set order was defined as INSERTION NEXT, then the order from WHITE for 18 whatnots is connected between the records for BROWN and

SMITH. If the set order was defined as INSERTION PRIOR, then WHITE's order goes between JONES and BROWN.

The combination of a set mode of chain linked only to next with a set order of INSERTION PRIOR is legal but as far as can be ascertained of remarkably little value. From the implementor's point of view, it may well be easier to allow than to prohibit.

In summary, the data administrator is delegating the set order decision to the programmer when he chooses INSERTION NEXT or INSERTION PRIOR, even though by his choice of NEXT or PRIOR he is dictating something about the whole affair. It is the logic in the program which determines how the current of set type indicator is adjusted and consequently the resulting set order in this case is very much up to the programmer.

6.4.3 Multi-member Chronological Set Types

The step from a single member to two or more members does not impact the chronological set types in the same way as it does the sorted set types. The chief impact in fact comes in processing the sets. The records in any set are likely to be randomly intermingled with respect to type in any of the chronological options, and the programmer will have the task of sorting them out. Fortunately, the statement which he uses to find his way around a set has an option which allows him to name the record type he wants. The search will then ignore records of other types. Even so, we would tend to discourage use of multi-member chronological set types.

6.5 Set Order Immaterial

While in the process of cleaning up the DBTG's thinking on set order, the DDLC chose to add an option which is neither sorted nor chronological. It is called IMMATERIAL and the implication is that the data administrator does not care about the set order and the programmer is not allowed to care. The exact wording of the DDLC's rule (page 3.77) is

'... that member records participating in an occurrence of this set type are to be maintained in the order most convenient to the DBMS.'

In view of the fact that the implementor is unlikely to conjure up any set order other than those already mentioned, this option could correspond to INSERTION FIRST for chains and INSERTION LAST for pointer arrays, although it may also be sensitive to a feature not yet discussed, namely set selection.

6.6 Permanent and Temporary Set Orders

Although this option is rarely provided, it is sufficiently relevant to merit presentation here. It is completely tied in with a DML statement which allows the programmer to change the sequence of the member records in a set during the course of execution of his program. The reader must be clear that it is *not* the basis for the set ordering which is changed. This would be very much a restructuring feature.

DBTG introduced this concept for chronological set types only. Their idea was that the programmer should be able to introduce order into a set occurrence on either a permanent or local basis. In the latter case, the actual member sequence in the data base would not be changed and the programmer would have a kind of 'local set' (not their terminology) to use during the course of execution of his program. Such a set order would not exist after the program terminates. Alternatively in certain circumstances, the programmer could in fact cause the record sequence in the data base to be changed. The certain circumstances were whether the data administrator definition would allow this or not.

To move to the DDLC's superior terminology for this discussion, each chronological set type must have its order declared as *permanent* or *temporary*. If permanent, no programmer may change it; if temporary, then he may. The option also applies if the set order is immaterial.

The reason the option is rarely found is that the DML statement ORDER is not generally implemented. Where this is the case, then all chronological set type orders are permanent.

6.7 Syntax for Set Order

We have presented the DDLC concepts for set order completely, and the DBTG's work is generally regarded as being weak in this area. Hence, we will restrict to the DDLC syntax. In the context of the Set Entry, it is as follows (from page 3.63):

SET NAME IS set-name-1;

OWNER IS $\left\{ \begin{array}{l} \text{record-name-1} \\ \text{SYSTEM} \end{array} \right\}$

[; SET IS PRIOR PROCESSABLE]

; ORDER IS $\left\{ \begin{array}{l} \text{PERMANENT} \\ \text{TEMPORARY} \end{array} \right\}$ INSERTION IS

$$\left\{ \begin{array}{l} \text{FIRST} \\ \text{LAST} \\ \text{NEXT} \\ \text{PRIOR} \\ \text{IMMATERIAL} \\ \text{SORTED INDEX NAME IS index-name-1} \left\{ \begin{array}{l} \text{BY DATA-BASE-KEY} \\ \text{BY RECORD NAME} \\ \text{WITHIN RECORD-NAME} \\ \text{BY DEFINED KEYS} \left\{ \begin{array}{l} \text{FIRST} \\ \text{LAST} \\ \text{NOT} \end{array} \right\} \text{ALLOWED} \\ \text{DUPLICATES ARE} \end{array} \right. \end{array} \right\}$$

If the set is a sorted set, then the data administrator has the option of defining sort keys in the Member Sub-entry. The appropriate DDLC syntax (page 3.64) is now as follows:

MEMBER IS record-name-1 {}{} [LINKED TO OWNER]

- - - - - -
- - - - - -

$$\left[; [RANGE]\ \underline{KEY\ IS} \begin{Bmatrix} \underline{ASCENDING} \\ \overline{DESCENDING} \end{Bmatrix} db\text{-}id\text{-}3 \right.$$

$$\left[, \begin{bmatrix} \underline{ASCENDING} \\ DESCENDING \end{bmatrix} db\text{-}id\text{-}4 \right] \cdots$$

$$\left[\underline{DUPLICATES}\ ARE \begin{bmatrix} FIRST \\ LAST \\ NOT \end{bmatrix} ALLOWED \right] \underline{NULL}\ IS\ [\underline{NOT}] \\ ALLOWED \right]$$

This is the clause which the DBTG called the ASCENDING/DESCENDING clause and DDLC has changed to refer to as the KEY clause.

The KEY clause *must* be used with the BY DEFINED KEYS option. It *may* be used with WITHIN RECORD-NAME and with BY RECORD-NAME. It is forbidden for all other set order options.

6.8 Examples of Set Order

It has not been feasible to discuss an example of every set order alternative in this chapter. Where possible, the examples of syntax use are referred back to earlier in the chapter.

Example 1. (see Figure 6.1)

SET TIME IS EE
OWNER IS EMPLOYEE
ORDER IS PERMANENT INSERTION IS SORTED BY DEFINED KEYS
MEMBER IS EDUCATION
KEY IS ASCENDING DATE-OF-QUALIFICATION

DUPLICATES LAST NULL NOT ALLOWED

Note that this example is a good illustration of potential problems with the two DUPLICATES clauses. Since there is only one member, the DUPLICATES control could be specified either in the Set Sub-entry or in the Member Sub-entry—or possibly both! However, if the data administrator specifies it at both places, then he must surely be consistent.

Example 2. (see Figures 6.2 and 6.3)

```
SET NAME IS EJE
OWNER IS EMPLOYEE
ORDER IS PERMANENT INSERTION IS SORTED BY RECORD-NAME
MEMBER IS EDUCATION
MEMBER IS JOB-HISTORY
KEY IS ASCENDING JOB-START-DATE
     DUPLICATES NOT ALLOWED    NULL NOT ALLOWED
```

This example follows the text of Section 6.3.3 by not having a sort key for the EDUCATION records. A decision not to allow an employee to start two jobs on the same date is implied in the above example.

Example 3. (see Figures 6.1 and 6.4)

```
SET NAME IS EJE
OWNER IS EMPLOYEE
ORDER IS PERMANENT INSERTION IS SORTED BY DEFINED KEYS

     DUPLICATES ARE LAST

MEMBER IS EDUCATION
KEY IS ASCENDING DATE-OF-QUALIFICATION
MEMBER IS JOB-HISTORY
KEY IS ASCENDING JOB-START-DATE
```

Comparing this with Example 1, we see that it is more concise to include the DUPLICATES control in the Set Sub-entry rather than in each Member Sub-entry. However, the Member Sub-entry DUPLICATES clause would allow us to prohibit null values. The Set Sub-entry DUPLICATES clause does not. Since nulls are generally allowed, we must assume that if there is no statement to prohibit them, then they are allowed.

Example 4. (see Figure 6.2 and Section 6.3.3)

```
SET NAME IS EJE
OWNER IS EMPLOYEE
ORDER IS PERMANENT INSERTION IS SORTED BY DATA-BASE-KEY
MEMBER IS EDUCATION
MEMBER IS JOB-HISTORY
```

Example 5. (see Figure 6.2 and Section 6.3.3)

```
SET NAME IS EJE
OWNER IS EMPLOYEE
ORDER IS PERMANENT INSERTION IS SORTED WITHIN RECORD-NAME
MEMBER IS EDUCATION
KEY IS ASCENDING DATE-OF-QUALIFICATION

    DUPLICATES ARE LAST   NULLS NOT ALLOWED

MEMBER IS JOB-HISTORY
KEY IS ASCENDING JOB-START-DATE

    DUPLICATES ARE LAST NULLS NOT ALLOWED
```

This example should be compared with Example 3. The reader should also note that if the two KEY clauses were omitted from Example 5, the effect would be the same as Example 4.

Example 6. (see Figures 6.5 and 6.6)

```
SET NAME IS AP
OWNER IS ARTICLE
ORDER IS PERMANENT INSERTION IS FIRST
MEMBER IS PURCHASE-ORDER
```

Example 7. (see Figures 6.5 and 6.7)

```
SET NAME IS AP
OWNER IS ARTICLE
ORDER IS PERMANENT INSERTION IS LAST
MEMBER IS PURCHASE-ORDER
```

Example 8. (see Figures 6.5 and 6.8)

```
SET NAME IS AP
OWNER IS ARTICLE
ORDER IS PERMANENT INSERTION IS NEXT
MEMBER IS PURCHASE-ORDER
```

Example 9. (see Figures 6.5 and 6.8)

```
SET NAME IS AP
OWNER IS ARTICLE
SET IS PRIOR PROCESSABLE
ORDER IS PERMANENT INSERTION IS PRIOR
MEMBER IS PURCHASE-ORDER
```

In this example, we have chosen to add a PRIOR PROCESSABLE clause to match up with the INSERTION IS PRIOR.

Example 10. (see Figure 6.2 and Section 6.5)

```
SET NAME IS EJE
OWNER IS EMPLOYEE
ORDER IS PERMANENT INSERTION IS IMMATERIAL
MEMBER IS EDUCATION
MEMBER IS JOB-HISTORY
```

In this example, we arbitrarily return to the multi-member set type on which the sorted set type examples were based.

6.9 Use of Set Orders

The potential data administrator might well be somewhat bewildered by this plethora of set order options and wonder which to choose and when. Among the nine options there are two or three 'work horses' and the rest will probably be used only very occasionally.

Before categorizing these, a comment is in order about the relatively new INSERTION IS IMMATERIAL, so far not known to be implemented although it should not pose problems to the implementor. If the latter interprets the DDLC's wording 'most convenient to the DBMS' in terms of the fastest execution of the connection into a set, with no regard to future retrieval from the set, then IMMATERIAL would be quite useful. If it becomes regarded as a 'don't care' option, then data administrators who care will not use it.

The real work horses, in estimated sequence of frequency of use, are

```
FIRST
BY RECORD-NAME
LAST
```

It must be noted that in a single member set type, BY DEFINED KEYS is the same as BY RECORD-NAME.

The others, in approximate estimated sequence of potential value, are

```
IMMATERIAL
BY DATA-BASE-KEY (see discussion in Section 6.3.3)
NEXT
BY DEFINED-KEYS (multi-member set type)
WITHIN RECORD-NAME
PRIOR
```

It must be emphasized that the above rankings are very intuitive and not based on empirical study. Relative usage may well vary from one implementation to another.

6.10 Search Keys

We have chosen to discuss search keys in the same chapter as Set Type Order partly with the aim of focusing attention on the relative role of the search key and the index. As discussed earlier (see Section 6.3.2), the data administrator may have the option of designating a sorted set type as indexed in order to expedite the process which takes place when a record is connected into a set occurrence. Conceptually there is one index built up and maintained for each set occurrence. Clearly, the index is maintained in the same sequence of the set members and the index key is necessarily identical to the sort keys. It must be emphasized that the role of the index is to expedite the storage process.

In case there is any confusion between the index and the pointer array, it must be recalled that the pointer array is intended to indicate participation in a set occurrence. The order of the members is indicated by the order of the pointers in the pointer array. There is nothing which ties the pointer array to the sorted set as a chronological (or 'immaterial') set type can equally well be represented as a pointer array. However, the point to be brought out is that the indexing facility is much easier to support in an implementation which also supports pointer arrays. The sort key values must be appended in some way to the entries in the pointer array. Nevertheless, although the DBTG specification does not prohibit the combination of indexed sorted sets with a set mode of chain, it is not felt to be of significant value.

Just as the index is designed to expedite the process of storing a record (specifically that part of the store which concerns connecting into a set) so the search key is intended to expedite the process of finding a record in a set. The search key is not tied to sort keys or for that matter to sorted sets in the same way as an index. As for an index, one must imagine as many search key indexes as there are sets. Again, the value of capability comes when the sets are large. A search key on a small set offers the user very little.

In order to explain the role of the search key completely, we must look ahead to the DML FIND statement which is the one used by the programmer when he wants to 'find' a record in the data base. There are numerous such 'finds' and one of these is designed to access a specific record in a set where the record contains certain programmer specified values for one or more items. If it happens that these items correspond to the search key, then the search key is used to expedite the search. (We will leave discussion of what happens when the items do not correspond until the appropriate chapter.)

The emphasis once again is on expending storage space ostensibly to expedite retrieval processing. Needless to say when the set is updated with new records or by deletion, then the search key index has also to be updated. Should the search key items and the sort key items in a sorted set happen to correspond, then in theory the search key could also be used to expedite updating. In this way it becomes clear that the sorted set index is a rather special form of the search key—even though the latter is intended for retrieval and the former for updating!

There are some unfortunate ramifications of this assertion which must be explored. The search key is a property of a member record type in a set type. As we shall see, the syntax does not allow the definition of a search key as a property of a set type even if search key items can be found in each of the member record types which correspond in a satisfactory way. If the set type is single member, then there is no problem; but in a multi-member set type it is possible to have one or more search keys for one member record type and none for the other member record types. In fact, the search key corresponds exactly to the index only in case that the set type is single member sorted but not 'by data-base-key'.

6.10.1 Syntax

The syntax used to define a search key is a part of the Member Sub-entry displayed in Section 6.7. Although DDLC modified DBTG's syntax very slightly, the change is outside the scope of material presented so far in this book. In context, it is as follows (from page 3.64 of DDLC)

MEMBER IS record-name-1 {} {} [LINKED TO OWNER]

$\left[\right.$; SEARCH KEY IS db-id-5 [, db-id-6] ...

USING $\left\{\begin{array}{l}\text{CALC} \\ \overline{\text{INDEX}} \text{ [NAME IS index-name-1]} \end{array}\right\}$

DUPLICATES ARE [NOT] ALLOWED $\left. \right] \cdots$

We see that a member record may have zero, one or more search keys and that each search key may be based on one or more items (which must of course have been defined as part of the record type being indexed).

The data administrator is seemingly allowed to choose how the search key will be represented. If he chooses the USING CALC option, then according to the DDLC's rules (page 3.84) '... the DBMS's standard key transformation algorithm is used in the selection of the sought record.'

Alternatively, if he chooses the USING INDEX option, then we are told

'... the DBMS's standard index mechanism is used in the selection of the sought record. The NAME phrase is provided to simplify references to specific indexes in the device media control language.'

(The word 'simplify' is ill-chosen here; without a NAME phrase, reference would be impossible.)

In point of fact, it is impossible to use the 'standard key transformation algorithm' or any other to randomize from a search key value *directly* to a record which has already been stored in the data base according to some other criterion (that is the location mode, possibly CALC, but certainly based on different items in the record type). CALC may be used in the search key, but some kind of table look-up (an index in other words) cannot be avoided.

One approach which falls between CALC and INDEX is to randomize the search key value to a data base key value which identifies some 'pseudo' record which contains in turn the data base key(s) of the record or records which contain the search key value sought. Another approach is, of course, a conventional table look-up which is more purely 'INDEX' than the first suggestion.

6.10.2 Example of Search Key

To end the chapter, two examples of search key definition follow.

Example 1. (see Figure 6.5)

```
SET NAME IS AP
OWNER IS ARTICLE
ORDER IS PERMANENT INSERTION IS FIRST
MEMBER IS PURCHASE-ORDER
SEARCH KEY IS SALES-OFFICE USING INDEX
        DUPLICATES ARE ALLOWED
```

The search key item SALES-OFFICE is necessarily defined in the PURCHASE-ORDER record type. It is interesting to note that an alternative way of collecting together all purchase-orders for a sales office is to use another set type as shown in Figure 6.9.

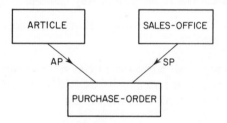

Figure 6.9 Alternative to using a search key

It is left as an exercise for the reader to assess the potential merits and demerits of each approach.

Example 2. (see Figure 6.9)

```
SET NAME IS AP PRIOR PROCESSABLE
OWNER IS ARTICLE
ORDER IS PERMANENT INSERTION IS SORTED
INDEXED BY DEFINED KEYS
MEMBER IS PURCHASE-ORDER
KEY IS ASCENDING ORDER-QUANTITY
        DUPLICATES FIRST NULL NOT ALLOWED
```

        SEARCH KEY IS ORDER-QUANTITY USING INDEX

            DUPLICATES ALLOWED

        SET NAME IS SP
        OWNER IS SALES-OFFICE
        ORDER IS PERMANENT INSERTION IS FIRST
        MEMBER IS PURCHASE-ORDER

This example illustrates a number of things. Firstly, a record type PURCHASE-ORDER is the member in a sorted set type AP and at the same time the member in a chronological set type SP. There is a search key on PURCHASE-ORDER within AP, but *not* within SP.

Most important, the example deliberately illustrates a minor DBTG inconsistency in treating indexes and search keys which the DDLC did not remove. In set type AP, ORDER-QUANTITY is both the sort key and the search key *and* the set type is indexed. Clearly, we want to allow duplicate values of ORDER-QUANTITY for any given ARTICLE. In the set order (and hence in the associated index) we are allowed to state where in the set records are connected relative to others with the same value. In the search key, we may only state whether or not we wish to allow duplicates. Who knows how the system will handle the problem?

6.10.3 Proposed Extensions to the Search Key Concept

The whole concept of indexed sorted sets should be removed and replaced by a rule for search keys reading:

'If the data items specified in one search clause correspond exactly to the sort key arguments in a set type sorted by RECORD-NAME, then the search key is used each time a new record is connected to a set of this type.'

Another extension to the search key concept which is generally accepted as being worthwhile is to allow the declaration as a search key as a global property of a record type. This should be additional to the existing intra set type capability. At present, if one needs a global secondary index on a record type, then it is necessary to define the record type as being a member in a system owned set type. This is a set type for which the whole system is the owner and since there is only one system, there is only one set occurrence. The result is that the data base incurs the overhead of the extra set type as well as the overhead of the search key.

Chapter 7

Storage Class and Removal Class

7.1 Background

Many people think of storage class and removal class collectively as set membership or membership type. The chief trouble here is not so much with the concepts as the manner in which the DBTG originally presented them. Their approach was perpetuated by the DDLC, but fortunately not by the DBLTG. How a concept is named and presented are both vital to how easy it is to comprehend that concept.

DBLTG recognized that we were not talking about one concept but two very separate and distinct concepts which really have little to do with each other—apart from the fact that they are defined in the same clause.

We will therefore introduce them separately and return to the fairly thoroughly ingrained thinking about set membership when we present the syntax. Storage class is much more significant than removal class, and it is appropriate that they be presented in that sequence.

7.2 Storage Class

A storage class must be declared for each member in a set type. The two storage classes are called *automatic* and *manual*. In a multi-member set type, it is quite permissible for one member to be automatic and the other manual. However, multi-member set types are really no more complicated with respect to storage class than are single member set types, so we can safely restrict our discussion to the latter.

To understand storage class, one must understand something about two DML statements, namely STORE and CONNECT. When a record is added to the data base for the first time, the programmer builds up the record in a special area in core and then causes a STORE to be executed on that record. This STORE statement is very simple syntactically but quite complex semantically. All kinds of Schema DDL declarations are taken into account during the course of execution of the STORE as we shall see when we come to discuss this statement in full.

However, one of the Schema declarations which is examined, for *each* set type in which the record type participates as a member, is the storage class.

The paths which are taken depending on the storage class are easy enough to describe. If the storage class is manual for a membership, then the new record is *not* connected into any set of the set type. If the storage class is automatic, then the new record is connected into one set of the set type. *Which* set of all those possible is chosen is a completely separate matter, depending on something called set selection which we shall consider in the very next chapter.

To reinforce understanding of storage class, an example will help and we choose a small part of an order entry system and depicted in Figure 7.1.

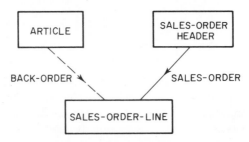

Figure 7.1 Record type automatic member in one
set type and manual member in another

Figure 7.1 is important graphically because it introduces for the first time in this book the way in which a set type manual member is depicted. Storage class is regarded as being sufficiently important to the immediate visual comprehension of a structure diagram that it merits its own graphic formalism and the dotted line is quite widely used for this.

To return to the example of Figure 7.1, each SALES-ORDER-LINE record must be connected to some SALES-ORDER-HEADER record. A SALES-ORDER-LINE would have very little meaning on its own; it probably contains data about which article is being ordered, quantity ordered, and some other miscellaneous data. If the article referred to is out of stock, then the normal procedure is to put in a 'back-order file'. (IDS/1 users would talk of a back-order chain, but here we must say a back-order set.)

When new stock arrives, then a program can be run to process those back-order sets for which stock is now available. However, the important fact about the BACK-ORDER set type is that at the time a SALES-ORDER-LINE record is stored in the data base, it is not known whether or not it must be connected to a BACK-ORDER set. Tests must be made, usually within the program which contains the STORE, and if the SALES-ORDER-LINE is to be connected to a BACK-ORDER set, then this may be done with a separate statement which DBLTG calls a CONNECT. DBTG called this statement INSERT and many earlier implementations use this somewhat unfortunate term. In the Schema DDL Set Order statement we said

ORDER IS PERMANENT INSERTION IS.....

Maybe one day this will become CONNECTION.

Storage class is a very powerful concept and hopefully the above example illustrates this. In the last analysis, the data administrator's choice of storage class is effectively dictating the semantics of the programmer's STORE statement. The question the data administrator should ask in choosing the storage class for a set type member is the following: 'Could a member occurrence meaningfully exist on its own without being specifically associated with an owner occurrence?'

If so, then the storage class for the member in that set type should be manual; otherwise it should be automatic.

7.2.1 Disconnected Records

Even if the storage class of a member is automatic, it is still possible to disconnect (or remove) it from a set after it has been connected there while a STORE was being executed. The DML statement which does this is called DISCONNECT. (DBTG used REMOVE which proved to be very difficult to explain; again, the reader will often encounter REMOVE in commercially available systems.)

Quite often when a member record is disconnected from one set, it is connected into another set two or three statements later. However, this is not necessarily the case and it is quite possible for a record to be 'left hanging loose' in the data base. This is also true for members of manual set types.

If a record is left hanging loose in this way, then the reader might well ask whether it can ever be found again. The idea of records being 'lost' in a data base without there being any way of finding them is indeed disturbing. If the location mode of the record type is CALC, then the problem could well be solved—as long as somebody knows the value of the CALC key item. What if the record type has some other location mode?

In the case of VIA SET alternative, we will usually find in practice that the implementor has made an extra rule that the storage class must be automatic. This means that when the record is first stored at least there has to be a set physically close to which the record can be placed. If this record is subsequently disconnected from one set and connected into another, then it is unlikely that the physical placement would be changed.

Some implementations have introduced an extra rule that if a record type is a manual member in a set type, then it must also be an automatic member in some other set type.

7.2.2 Double Connection

There is one very important rule (already mentioned in Section 3.4.1) regarding the matter of records being connected into sets. It is buried in the semantic rules for the MEMBER clause and in the DDLC JOD is stated as follows (from page 3.72):

'Each member record participates in at most one occurrence of each set type for which it is declared a member record type. That is, it may be associated with no more than one owner record for each set type for which it may be a member. A record may appear once in a given set.'

This rule affects what happens when a STORE and CONNECT is executed. As indicated in both, there is a process of set selection which takes place. The fact that it is rather different in each case is unfortunate but true. In the case of a STORE, the record is a brand new one and it cannot happen that the record is already connected into some other occurrence of the set type. However, with a CONNECT, the case is different. If the programmer makes a mistake, he may try to connect a record into a set when it is already connected into that set *or* into some other set of the same type. Since double connections are not allowed, the attempt to connect will not be successful. We shall discuss the implications of unsuccessful DML execution later.

7.3 Removal Class

Just as storage class is concerned with what happens when a record is stored, so removal class is concerned with what happens when a record is deleted from the data base. Removal class adds very little to the data administrator's structuring power. What it does offer the data administrator, according to the DDLC specification, is the ability to prohibit the situation where records 'hang loose' in the data base.

The two removal classes were called *mandatory* and *optional* by DBTG and DDLC. DBLTG decided in favour of *permanent* and *transient* respectively to convey these two classes. Clearly, the mandatory class implies that the connection once made is permanent and a record cannot be disconnected, although it can be deleted.

In addition, the choice of mandatory and optional affects the semantics of the ERASE (or DELETE) statement, but these semantics are so complex and in effect so completely dependent on the removal class that the only hint we can give is that it is all concerned with what happens to the members when the owner is deleted.

Removal class should probably be called 'disconnection class' to fit in with the name change of the REMOVE statement to DISCONNECT. If the data administrator wishes to allow flexibility, he would prefer the optional alternative every time. The mandatory alternative may have occasional merit.

7.4 Implementation Considerations

Removal class is the first capability we have encountered for which we can say that every implementation seems to be different, if not syntactically, then at least semantically. The implication on the STORE statements of choosing a storage class seems to have been treated in a fairly standard way, but some implementors let the storage class spill over into the semantics of the removal class, hence making the nice clean separation into storage class and removal class less meaningful. In other cases, the removal class could have a more restricted meaning than presented above.

7.5 Syntax for Storage Class and Removal Class

The definition of storage class and removal class both belong in the Member Sub-entry of the Set Entry (see Sections 6.7 and 6.10.1). The DDLC's Member. Sub-entry now appears as follows:

$$\underline{\text{MEMBER}} \text{ IS record-name-1} \begin{Bmatrix} \underline{\text{AUTOMATIC}} \\ \underline{\text{MANUAL}} \end{Bmatrix} \begin{Bmatrix} \underline{\text{MANDATORY}} \\ \underline{\text{OPTIONAL}} \end{Bmatrix} [\text{LINKED TO } \underline{\text{OWNER}}]$$

$$\left[\text{; } [\underline{\text{RANGE}}] \text{ KEY IS } \begin{Bmatrix} \underline{\text{ASCENDING}} \\ \underline{\text{DESCENDING}} \end{Bmatrix} \text{db-id-3} \left[\left[\text{, } \begin{matrix} \underline{\text{ASCENDING}} \\ \underline{\text{DESCENDING}} \end{matrix} \right] \text{db-id-4} \right] \ldots \right.$$

$$\left. \begin{matrix} ------ \\ ------ \end{matrix} \right]$$

7.6 Examples

To illustrate the definition of storage class and removal class we will take Figure 7.1.

```
SET NAME IS SALES-ORDER
OWNER IS SALES-ORDER-HEADER
ORDER IS PERMANENT INSERTION IS FIRST
MEMBER IS SALES-ORDER-LINE MANDATORY AUTOMATIC OWNER
SET NAME IS BACK-ORDER PRIOR
OWNER IS ARTICLE
ORDER IS PERMANENT INSERTION IS LAST
MEMBER IS SALES-ORDER-LINE OPTIONAL MANUAL LINKED TO
    OWNER
```

The reason why the BACK-ORDER set type should have a storage class of manual has been presented earlier in the chapter. However, we made the removal class in the SALES-ORDER set type mandatory because there is little likelihood that one would disconnect a line from the sales order to which it belongs. In the other set type, the member has a removal class of optional; once a back order has been met, it would be disconnected from the ARTICLE, but left in the data base.

Chapter 8

Set Selection Options

8.1 Recapitulation

So far we have considered two properties of a set type, namely set mode and set order, and three properties of a member record type in a set type, namely search keys, removal class and storage class. It would not be correct to call any of these purely structural properties, although the set type itself (as a property of two record types) is structural in the sense that it is defined to facilitate access to records of the member type. So indeed is the search key. Set mode is concerned with the representation in storage, and removal class and storage class are concerned with DML statement semantics. Where does the remaining property fit into the picture?

8.2 Set Selection Criterion

The set selection criterion is a property of a member record type in a set type. In terms of the above discussion, the set selection criterion is unequivocally concerned with DML statement semantics.

As we have hinted from time to time, there is a problem which occurs at execution time concerning which set of a given type a record is to be connected into or disconnected from or found in. In fact, the problem arises principally with four DML statements, namely

STORE
FIND
CONNECT
MODIFY

For some storage reason, there are two approaches to the problem. One is to use the CURRENT OF SET TYPE indicator. This was mentioned in Section 6.4.2 when we discussed set order and how the programmer could decide on the set order by the way he updated this currency indicator. The other approach to the problem of set selection is more complex—in fact it seems to be unnecessarily complex. It applies only in the case of the STORE and FIND statements. In the case of CONNECT and DISCONNECT, only one approach is possible, namely that based on currency indicators. Since this is also an option in the case of FIND and STORE, we will discuss it first and then go on to unravel the more obscure options.

8.3 Set Selection Based on Currency

To recapitulate, there is a current of set type indicator maintained automatically at execution time for each set type known to a program. As we shall see, the Sub-schema DDL allows the user to limit his view of the data base. If the data base schema defined 29 record types and 37 set types, one of its sub-schemas might limit this to 7 record types and 11 set types. A program using this sub-schema would be concerned with 11 current of set type indicators.

Each of these indicators contain null when the program starts to execute, but each time a FIND or STORE is executed, one or more of them may be updated. This means it would contain the data base key value of a record in the data base. This record is normally of a type which is an owner or member in some set types which means that the currency indicators for these set types are updated.

Supposing that the next thing to happen is that a record is to be stored, which is an automatic member in one set type (for the sake of simplicity). Since the storage class is automatic, the record will be connected to an occurrence of that set type. Which one? It is the setting of the currency indicator which determines which set. This indicator may point to the owner or one of the members. Whether or not the indicator is also used in deciding *where* in the set the new record is to be connected depends on the set order. Whether or not the indicator is used to determine *which* set the new record is to be connected to *may* depend on the set selection criterion; for the STORE it does, for the CONNECT it does not. Such are the ways of task groups and committees.

The DBTG's syntax for set selection based on currency was

SET OCCURENCE SELECTION IS THRU CURRENT OF SET

which DDLC elaborated to

SET SELECTION IS THRU set-name-1 OWNER IDENTIFIED BY CURRENT OF SET

(There is a fairly obvious string of typographical errors in the DDLC's presentation of set selection. Set-name-1 above is written as set-name-2 which gives the impression that the set selection is always by means of some set type *other* than the one named at the beginning of the Set Entry.)

8.4 Set Selection Based on Location Mode CALC

If in a given set type the owner record type has a location mode of CALC, then this fact can be used to select a set instead of the currency indicator. Referring back to the discussion on CALC record types (Section 4.5), we see that when the data administrator chooses this location mode, he must make a decision on whether the key is unique or not—in DBTG words whether or not duplicate values of this key are allowed.

If duplicate values of the key are not allowed, then the calc key acts as a unique identifier to the owner record and it may be used as a basis for set selection.

DBTG apparently had some delusions about the role of location mode DIRECT because their analogous capability was referred to as 'set selection through location mode of owner', and indeed they indicated that location mode DIRECT was similar in this regard to CALC. In fact it is not. DDLC recognized this and changed the whole syntax and semantics of this option.

The special feature of set selection based on CALC-KEY (as DDLC now calls it) is that at execution time the programmer must pass calc key values to the DBCS so that it can select an occurrence of the owner record and *ipso facto* a set occurrence. In the DBTG approach, these calc key values could be passed by using the record area in core for the owner record type. Each record type in the sub-schema has one corresponding record area in core (we will say more about this later). However, the data administrator could define other data items with the same characteristics to use as the parameter passing vehicle.

The DBTG syntax for this option (page 145) was

SET OCCURENCE SELECTION IS THRU LOCATION MODE OF OWNER

[USING db-id-5 (, db-id-6) . . .

{ALIAS FOR db-id-7 IS dbd-name-1} . . .]

It must be borne in mind that the syntax was supposed to cater also for the situation when the location mode of the owner was DIRECT.

DDLC's syntax is much clearer

SET SELECTION IS THRU set-name-1 OWNER IDENTIFIED BY

$$\text{CALC-KEY} \left[\text{EQUAL TO} \begin{Bmatrix} \text{db-id-1} \\ \text{dbd-name-1} \end{Bmatrix} \begin{bmatrix} , \text{db-id-3} \\ , \text{dbd-name-3} \end{bmatrix} \right]$$

The owner of set-name-1 must have a location mode of CALC. If the EQUAL TO option is omitted, then the actual CALC key items in the record area must be initialized before the set selection clause is invoked. If the EQUAL TO clause is used, then the items named may apparently be declared anywhere in the schema, that is to say in any record type. The value of each must be initialized before the set selection clause is invoked.

8.5 Set Selection Based on a Data Base Key Item

This particular option is rather like set selection based on a currency indicator, except that a user defined item is used instead of the system defined currency indicator. It is not clear when it offers an advantage over the currency indicator.

The system itself provides for *and* maintains the currency indicator anyway. If the data administrator decrees that a data item should be used, the programmer must move the contents of the currency indicator into the data base key item.

It was mentioned in Section 4.6.1 that it was possible to define data items in a record type which are of type DATA-BASE-KEY. This set selection option is another use for such items.

The DDLC syntax is

SET SELECTION IS THRU set-name-1 OWNER IDENTIFIED BY

$$\text{DATA-BASE-KEY} \left[\text{EQUAL TO} \left\{ \begin{array}{l} \text{db-id-1} \\ \text{dbd-name-1} \end{array} \right\} \right]$$

The DBTG syntax is as for location mode of owner. This set selection is conceptually quite independent of the owner record type's location mode. An owner record can be retrieved and hence a set selected if its data base key is known, whether the location mode is CALC, DIRECT, SYSTEM or VIA SET. However, DBTG had tied in retrieval of records using data base key with location mode DIRECT, whereas this kind of retrieval is possible quite independently of the location mode.

The three alternatives discussed so far are in the order presented the most frequently found in commercially available implementations. There is one other which may be encountered, however, and we will include it for completeness.

8.6 Hierarchical Set Selection

This matter will probably be best understood by readers with some knowledge of IMS since there seems to have been an attempt to perpetuate one of that system's quirks in the DBTG proposals.

To appreciate the problem (which has been carefully created so that a solution is necessary), we must recall that a set type is simply a building block to use when building up the complete data base structure.

Let us construct a hypothetical data base structure as depicted in Figure 8.1.

It is in this kind of situation that the hierarchical set selection comes into play. Yet again there has been a change between DBTG and DDLC, which has the effect of changing the problem the capability is intended to solve.

According to DBTG (page 147, rule 4), hierarchical set selection

'applies where the immediate owner record of the set occurrence cannot itself be uniquely selected except in terms of its membership in another set, ... This condition may occur to an arbitrary number of levels forming a continuous path from the specific owner of set-name-2 (Author's note: the set type for the members of which the set selection is being defined) to the specific owner of the set type of which the set selection clause is a part.'

In less formal words, considering Figure 8.1, the data administrator may wish to predefine a path from record type A down to record type D. The aim of this

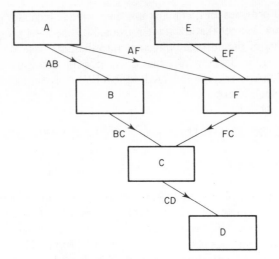

Figure 8.1 Hierarchy of set types

would be that when an occurrence of D was to be stored (or in some cases found) in the data base, the programmer could initialize a series of data items prior to execution of the STORE or FIND, thereby establishing a 'path occurrence' of the 'path type' identified by the data administrator. The idea is that the programmer has less to write. Without hierarchical set selection, the programmer must find his way 'down' the structure procedurally with a series of FIND statements.

Is the data administrator ever forced into a situation where he may have to use this hierarchical set selection? The answer to this is 'no', but the DBTG makes a special case out of the situation where record types B and C both have location mode of VIA SET. A being at the 'top' of the structure could not have such a location mode because it is not a member in any set type, but it is most likely to have a location mode of CALC.

The objective of the capability appears to be to avoid using set selection by means of currency indicators and hence also by setting data base key items. If we are defining the set selection criterion for D in set type CD, then we cannot use location mode of owner because C has a location mode of VIA SET. Hence, a C must be selected on the basis of its connection to a BC set. Again, B has a location mode of VIA SET, therefore a B must be selected on the basis of its connection to an AB set. Record type A has a location mode of CALC and therefore (assuming the calc key is unique) a unique A can be selected.

DBTG would like us to define this algorithm in the following way:

MEMBER IS D . . . .

SET OCCURRENCE SELECTION IS THRU BC
    USING LOCATION MODE OF OWNER AB
    USING A-CALC-KEY

where A-CALC-KEY is the calc key item in A.

In fact, the DBTG's statement quoted above about when hierarchical set selection applies, was rather misleading. Some understanding of the 'segment search argument' facility in IMS gives more insight into what the spirit of the capability was intended to be. The aim was to give the programmer a non-procedural way of finding or storing a record by path initialization. No machine time can possibly be saved, because the system has to find its way down the hierarchy anyway by accessing the records along the path.

8.7 Syntax

For completeness, the DBTG's syntax for the set selection clause follows. There are two formats, the first to cover the non-hierarchical situations and the second for the hierarchical case.

Format 1

SET OCCURRENCE <u>SELECTION</u> IS THRU

$$\begin{Bmatrix} \underline{CURRENT} \text{ OF SET} \\ \underline{LOCATION} \text{ MODE} \begin{bmatrix} \underline{USING} \text{ db-id-5 (, db-id-6)} \dots \\ \{\underline{ALIAS} \text{ FOR db-id-7 IS dbd-name-1}\} \dots \end{bmatrix} \\ \text{OF OWNER} \end{Bmatrix}$$

Format 2

SET OCCURENCE <u>SELECTION</u> IS THRU set-name-2 USING

$$\begin{Bmatrix} \underline{CURRENT} \text{ OF SET} \\ \underline{LOCATION} \text{ MODE} \\ \text{OF OWNER} \qquad [\underline{ALIAS} \text{ FOR db-id-8 IS dbd-name-2}] \dots \end{Bmatrix}$$

$$\left\{ \text{set-name-3} \begin{Bmatrix} \underline{USING} \text{ db-id-9 [, db-id-10]} \dots \\ \{\underline{ALIAS} \text{ FOR db-id-11 IS dbd-name-3}\} \dots \end{Bmatrix} \right\} \dots$$

The DDLC's syntax is equally complex but very different. It includes one special provision for multi-member set types. As indicated at the beginning of this chapter, set selection is a property of a member and not of the set type. Nevertheless, it is difficult to envisage when it might be advantageous to have two or more different set selection criteria in the same set type. The DDLC option allows the data administrator to say in the set selection for one member of a multi-member set type that it is the same as in one of the other members. In theory, this could save the data administrator writing out some lengthy hierarchical path twice. The DDLC also has two formats, but only one is within the scope of what has been discussed so far in this book, and the other is also adapted slightly.

SET SELECTION [FOR set-name-1] IS THRU set-name-2 OWNER
IDENTIFIED BY

$$\left\{ \begin{array}{l} \text{SYSTEM} \\ \text{CURRENT OF SET} \\ \text{DATA-BASE-KEY} \left[\text{EQUAL TO } \begin{Bmatrix} \text{db-id-1} \\ \text{dbd-name-1} \end{Bmatrix} \right] \\ \text{CALC-KEY} \left[\text{EQUAL TO } \begin{Bmatrix} \text{db-id-2} \\ \text{dbd-name-2} \end{Bmatrix} \begin{bmatrix} , \text{ db-id-3} \\ , \text{ dbd-name-3} \end{bmatrix} \cdots \right] \\ \text{MEMBER record-name-1 SELECTION} \end{array} \right\}$$

$$\left[\begin{array}{l} \text{THEN THRU set-name-3} \\ \left\{ \begin{array}{l} \text{WHERE OWNER IDENTIFIED BY db-id-4} \\ \left[\text{EQUAL TO } \begin{Bmatrix} \text{db-id-5} \\ \text{dbd-name-4} \end{Bmatrix} \right] \end{array} \right\} \cdots \end{array} \right] \cdots$$

One factor which could cause confusion is the difference between set-name-1 and set-name-2. The numeric suffixes are appended to facilitate an unambiguous reference to them in the syntax rules and general rules. However, when hierarchic set selection is ignored, then set-name-1 and set-name-2 necessarily refer to the same set type.

8.8 Use of Alternative Set Selection Criterion

The factor which complicates set selection in both DBTG and DDLC is the hierarchical path. In practice it is only implemented in one or two DBMS and the reader will not encounter it unless he is involved with those implementations.

Our advice here to data administrators is to avoid it where possible, and to use set selection via currency indicators as the lesser of a number of evils, unless the facility discussed in the next section is provided. The programmer who is concerned with set types has to understand and work with these indicators anyway and requiring him to program his set selection by means of them is not asking too much.

8.9 Important Set Selection Options

It may not be completely clear that this recent DDLC modification in fact remains a very important additional capability which not only facilitates a considerably simpler approach to the messy problem of set selection, but also address the whole problem of how the logical representation of a set type should be handled.

In the DBTG approach, and therefore in most of the commercially available implementations, a one to N relationship between two record types is defined *explicitly* by writing

SET NAME IS set-name-1

   OWNER IS record-name-1

   · · · · · · · · · ·

   MEMBER IS record-name-1

   · · · · · · · · · ·

In other words, the relationship exists because it is defined to exist and not because of any inherent implication that it exists. To avoid any confusion here, the only way of *implying* a relationship (in the generic sense) between two record types is to include common data items in the two record types. This is best illustrated by an example. Consider two record types

01 DEPT LOCATION MODE IS CALC USING DEPT-NO

                 DUPLICATES NOT ALLOWED

   02 DEPT-NO   PICTURE 999
   02 DEPT-NAME   PICTURE X(15)
   02 LOCN-CODE   PICTURE 99
   02 SIZE   PICTURE 999

01 EMPLOYEE LOCATION MODE IS CALC USING EMP-NO

                 DUPLICATES NOT ALLOWED

   02 EMP-NO   PICTURE X(4)
   02 EMP-NAME   PICTURE X(12)
   02 EMP-UNIT   PICTURE X(4)
   02 EMP-DEPT-NO PICTURE 999
   02 BIRTH   PICTURE 9(6)

The important line in these two schema record type declarations is the penultimate line in the EMPLOYEE record type, which defines an elementary data item EMP-DEPT-NO. Is this necessarily the same item as the item DEPT-NO in the DEPT record type? More precisely, do the two items take their values from the same permissible set of values? These questions address in effect the semantics of the data.

If one can assert that the values of these two items are in fact drawn from the same pool of values, then the act of including EMP-DEPT-NO in the EMPLOYEE record type is tantamount to making a declaration, that each department contains zero, one or more employees and that each employee belongs to zero or one department.

So far no set type relationship has been brought into the picture and it is interesting to explore the impact of *not* declaring the existence of the relationship which is implicit in the data items. One effect is that it will be more time consuming to perform any process which involves all the employees in a specific department. This reflects the access path implication of describing a set type relationship (see Section 3.5). Another effect to explore is whether it would be possible in any way to match the value of EMP-DEPT-NO with a value of DEPT-NO. Such a matching *could* normally take place at the time the EMPLOYEE record is stored in the data base *if* the storage class is automatic (see Section 7.1). However, there is nothing in any of the syntax discussed for the Schema DDL which provides a way of validating the value of an item in a member record type with the value of a 'matchable' item in the owner record type.

This discussion may appear to be somewhat out of place in a chapter on set selection, but in fact the set selection options are completely pertinent. If it were possible to use the value of EMP-DEPT-NO to select the set occurrence, and if, for a given EMPLOYEE record occurrence, the value of EMP-DEPT-NO is not equal to any value of DEPT-NO already in the data base, then no set would be selected. If the storage class is automatic, then the effect would be an unsuccessful execution of the STORE EMPLOYEE statement and a data base exception condition. Using this approach to set selection has the effect of specifying a validation to be performed on the item in the member record type whose values are used as the basis for set selection. This could be called an inter-record type validation.

The DBTG facility discussed earlier, specifically set selection based on location mode CALC (see Section 8.4) is not equivalent to the capability discussed in the preceding paragraph. Using this facility one could write (using DBTG syntax)

SET NAME IS D-E

   OWNER IS DEPT

   . . . .

   MEMBER IS EMPLOYEE

   . . . .

   SET OCCURENCE SELECTION IS THRU LOCATION MODE OF
                     OWNER USING DEPT-NO

It is not permitted to write EMP-DEPT-NO instead of DEPT-NO, because the rules state explicitly that 'all data-base-identifiers must refer to declared data items of the owner record of the set(s) referenced'.

However, with the revised DDLC syntax, it would be possible to write the set selection clause as

SET SELECTION FOR D-E IS THRU D-E OWNER IDENTIFIED
   BY CALC-KEY EQUAL TO EMP-DEPT-NO

This syntax is somewhat clumsy, but at least the desired effect can be achieved. It would be preferable if the member item on which the set selection is based were called the set item and the syntax of the whole set selection clause simplified to

$$\text{SET SELECTION IS VIA} \begin{cases} \text{SYSTEM} \\ \text{CURRENT OF SET} \\ \text{SET ITEM dbd-name-2 [, dbd-name-3] \dots} \end{cases}$$

Under the existing rules governing the interaction between set selection and storage class, any set selection option may also be declared for a set type in which the member has a manual storage class (see Section 7.1). The effect of declaring a manual storage class is that a member record is not connected into any set when it is stored in the data base, but it may be connected subsequently by means of a CONNECT statement (still to be discussed in detail, see Section 16.5). This statement does not invoke the set selection option and hence it would be possible to connect an EMPLOYEE record to a DEPT record when the department numbers are different. If the data administrator is interested in the validation effect of declaring a set type (as well as access to the member records), then the choice of automatic storage class is strongly advocated.

Chapter 9

Intra-Record Type Structures

9.1 Introduction

In Section 3.2, the concept of a record type was explained largely for the benefit of the reader more oriented to the concepts of scientific programming. However, this was more expository than discursive and it remains still to examine the precise nature of the Schema DDL's intra-record structure. In Section 3.3, the important difference between intra-record structure and inter-record structure was explained. So far this book has been concerned chiefly with inter-record structure, which constitutes one of the basic cornerstones of today's data base management systems. DBTG introduced a number of novel ideas into intra-record structure, and it is the purpose of this chapter to explain them.

9.2 History

Digging back into history to the DBTG's October 1969 report, it is noticeable that DBTG had already then drifted away from their initial charter of 'extending COBOL' to the extent that the word COBOL was not mentioned after the chairman's preface where it was stated

'It is our hope that the Data Description Language will form the basis of an industry standard and that individual host languages will interface with it.'

and furthermore

'The semantics and syntax of the Data Manipulation Language, on the other hand, are proposed as an extension of COBOL and as a prototype of the manipulation capabilities required in the host language. For other host languages, appropriate semantics and syntax could be developed.'

There were two problems at the time with this praiseworthy aim. The first was that in 1969, IBM were still trying hard to foist PL/1 on a somewhat reluctant market place, and the second was that the October 1969 Schema DDL intra-record structure was pure and unadulterated COBOL. IBM protested cleverly that the Schema DDL was too COBOL oriented and that therefore claims for a multiple host language DDL were invalid. The result was that, as some kind of glorious placebo, the DBTG replaced the Schema DDL's COBOL oriented intra-record structure by a PL/1 oriented intra-record structure, which is what appeared in the April 1971 report. Although the PL/1 push has abated between 1971 and 1973, the DDLC did not revert to COBOL. However, *all* the implementors of CODASYL based DBMS have reverted in one way or another. This does not mean that they do not wish to support PL/1; it means rather they do not wish to support the PL/1 intra-record structure (which is a different matter).

There are two approaches chosen by implementors to get back to COBOL intra-record structure. One is to use COBOL capability and COBOL language. The other is to use COBOL capability expressed in PL/1 language. This amounts to a sub-set of the DBTG or DDLC proposals.

9.3 Role of the Intra-record Structure

The intra-record structure is a major point of contact between the data base and the host language. As we have indicated in the preceding chapters, the inter-record structure capabilities are supported by corresponding facilities in the DML. Intra-record data manipulation is entirely the task of the host language.

Without doubt, the PL/1 intra-record structure is more powerful than that of COBOL. 'Powerful' here implies more item types, and more nested repeating group facilities.

Interestingly enough, events in this respect have turned a full circle since IBM introduced PL/1 in 1964. More recently, IBM Research has been extolling the virtues of something mysteriously called 'relations in third normal form'. Analysis of this seemingly abstract phenomenon reveals that this implies (in everyday data processing terminology) that intra-record structure is undesirable. One has a better view of the data base if each record type consists only of elementary items with no repeating groups. We concur.

When occurrences of a repeating group vary in size from one record occurrence to another, then the record length is variable—a feature which is certainly catered for in ANSI COBOL. As indicated in Section 3.3, the intra-record structure is a historical approach; the set type is a new one (relatively speaking). It would be difficult for any committee to kill the intra-record structure, but at least its use can be discouraged. Some implementations do not allow variable length records and hence there is no COBOL OCCURS DEPENDING clause or its equivalent. It is predictable that this feature will fall by the wayside as years go by. On this discouraging note, we will present, if only for the sake of completeness, the Schema DDL intra-record type structure.

9.4 Item Types

Each elementary item is normally defined by either a TYPE clause or a PICTURE clause but not by both. The TYPE clause is understood to be pure

PL/1 and reflects PL/1's ability to handle complex numbers, bit strings, character strings, and different kinds of real numeric items. The exact syntax of this clause from the DDLC (page 3.55) is

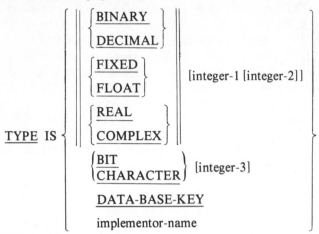

The first part of this piece of syntax refers to the numeric items. For illustration, the four REAL combinations are listed.

REAL BINARY FIXED
REAL BINARY FLOAT
REAL DECIMAL FIXED
REAL DECIMAL FLOAT

Just how many of these are provided in a given implementation depends on the number of possible hardware representations of numeric data items; integer-1 is the precision of the item. For fixed point items only, integer-2 is the scale.

Items of type BIT are bit strings (not possible in COBOL, integer-3 is the length of the string. Character strings or items of TYPE CHARACTER are familiar to COBOL oriented readers as DISPLAY items.

We have already had to introduce the idea of items of type DATA-BASE-KEY in Section 4.6.1, and here we see the idea in the context of the intra-record structure. It is important to remember that, although each record stored in the data base has a data base key value associated with it, there is *never* any need for a data administrator to define an item of type DATA-BASE-KEY in a record type in order to accommodate the data base key value of each record. The facility is provided for the physically oriented data administrator who is prepared to allow programmers also to work on a very physical level. Depending on how the restructuring facilities work, using items of type data base key could be a dangerous practice.

The DBTG was rather fond of leaving 'hooks' for the implementors to include capability which the DBTG thought might exist, but did not feel sufficiently strongly about to include in the specifications. DDLC removed all of these 'implementor hooks', except this one. If an implementor wishes to support a host language which is able to manipulate an item type other than those provided for in PL/1, and therefore in the Schema DDL, the suggestion is that he is not to be inhibited from allowing such items in the data base. Examples of such item types are dates, times, and longitudes and latitudes.

9.5 Repeating Groups (or Aggregate)

A repeating group is a named group of items which may have a variable number of occurrences in a record occurrence. In COBOL, there are two kinds of repeating groups. In the first, the number of repeats is fixed for all occurrences of the record. In the other, it may vary. There is no restriction in COBOL on how many of the former are allowed in a record type. The number of variable length repeating groups is restricted to three and these must be at the end of the record type.

PL/1, and therefore the Schema DDL, are less restricted on the matter of the nesting of repeating groups and where in the record they may be found. PL/1 uses the term 'aggregates' to talk about nested repeating groups, and hence this term is also found in the Schema DDL.

The Schema DDL syntax for defining repeating groups is simpler and more direct than that of COBOL. It is

$$\text{OCCURS} \left\{ \begin{array}{l} \text{integer-1} \\ \text{db-id-1} \end{array} \right\} \text{TIMES}$$

If an integer is used, it must be greater than zero and the size of the repeating group is fixed. There are the same number of occurrences of the group in each record occurrence. If db-id-1 is used, then this must be an elementary item in the record being defined, and it must also be of TYPE REAL FIXED which implies that it takes only integer values.

The OCCURS clause is used to define a data aggregate. A vector is a rather special case of a data aggregate in that there is only one component elementary item. If this item happens to be a numeric item type, then the FORTRAN idea of a one dimensional array is present.

9.6 Pictures

A picture clause may be used instead of a type clause to specify the characteristics of a data item. The concept of a picture clause is very familiar to any COBOL or PL/1 programmer. For the benefit of the FORTRAN programmer, we should explain that the picture clause is a way of specifying the form of an item value. If the data being processed is purely numeric, then the clause has no value, since its chief role is with non-computable data such as telephone numbers, dates, names, addresses, and such like.

Examples of pictures are

BIRTH-DATE   PICTURE IS   99X99X99

PHONE-NO   PICTURE IS   999X999X9(4)

96

In these, the 9 means that any decimal digit between 0 and 9 is valid. X means that the position may contain any character in the character set. The (4) in the second example illustrates a repetition factor and could equally well have been written as

PHONE-NO   PICTURE IS   999X999X9999

However, the repetition factor is more useful when a character type repeats many times as in the following example,

LAST-NAME   PICTURE IS   A(12)

which would mean that the permitted values of LAST-NAME may contain alphabetic characters and blanks only.

The DBTG's Schema DDL PICTURE clause along with the rest of the intra-record structure is based on PL/1. Implementations tend to restrict to COBOL and hence the PICTURE clause is also pure COBOL. With this in mind, it is proposed to avoid the details and refer the reader to any good COBOL primer.

9.7 Source Items

A *source item* is an item which is defined as part of two record types in a set type. In the owner record type, it is defined in the normal way just as any other item. In the member record type, the item is defined as a source item which means that there is an exact correspondence between the values of the item in each connected member and the value in the owner.

The DDLC's syntax for this capability (page 3.53) is as follows:

IS $\left\{ \begin{array}{l} \text{ACTUAL} \\ \text{VIRTUAL} \end{array} \right\}$ AND SOURCE IS db-id-1 OF OWNER OF set-name-1

If the source item is classed as 'actual', then the value of the item is stored in the member record at the time the member record is first connected into a set (which may be the time it is first stored). The implication is that during the course of execution of the STORE, the owner record must be accessed and the item value copied from the owner into the member. Hopefully (but not necessarily) the access to the owner record is not too time consuming. The COBOL JOD does not need to define syntax for such a capability, but it does need to refer to it. The terminology used (page IV–1–5) 'derived item', because the item value is derived at execution time of the DBCS. The JOB does not distinguish between source items as described here and result items to be described in Chapter 10.

If the source item is virtual, then the process of copying the value from the owner record into the member takes place at the time the record is retrieved and *not* at the time it is stored. In earlier chapters, we have referenced an important DML statement called FIND. The copying of the source item does not take place during the course of execution of the FIND, but during the course of execution of an associated DML statement GET. This will be discussed in more detail later.

The aims of the source item facility are to achieve consistency and further to allow control over a space time trade-off. If an item (elementary or group) in a record type is the same as one in another record type, and if it is justifiable to define a set type relationship between these two record types, then the item in the member record type could be a source item. The next question to ask is whether the values of the item correspond in any way to the algorithm for connecting members into a set. If so, then the case for making the item in the member record type a source item is strengthening.

To finalize it, it is necessary to consider processing time problems. If at all processing times, the *whole* owner record must be in core each time a connected member is being processed, then the case falls. There is no point in duplicating the item in owner and member irrespective of whether the space used is core only (virtual source item) or direct access space as well (actual source item).

If only the item under discussion is needed and not the rest of the owner record type, then it is quite probable that core space can be saved by making the item in the member a source item. If direct access space is at a premium and the sets are large, then the better approach would be a virtual source item, although it must be understood that this may involve an access to the owner record. To economize on processing time at the expense of direct access space, the member record types item can be made actual.

It is predictable that actual source items would be considerably more extensively used than virtual source items. The programmer does not need to know whether an item he is processing is 'normal' or source. If he does know, there is nothing much he can do about it except to avoid unnecessary retrievals of virtual source items.

9.8 Item Validation

'Garbage in, garbage out' has long been a criticism of computerized data files. As the technology advances to integrated data bases, it is long overdue that some effort be expanded by the specification committees and the implementors to provide the data administrator with tools to enable him to specify validation criteria that an item value must satisfy before being admitted to the data base.

The DBTG's efforts in this direction consisted of the CHECK clause which in an abbreviated form was as follows (see page 92):

$$\underline{\text{CHECK}} \;\; \text{IS} \left\Vert \begin{array}{l} \underline{\text{PICTURE}} \\ \underline{\text{RANGE}} \; \text{OF literal-8 THRU literal-9} \end{array} \right\Vert$$

DDLC modified this to read (page 3.30):

$$\underline{\text{CHECK}} \;\; \text{IS} \left\|\; \begin{array}{l} \underline{\text{PICTURE}} \\ \underline{\text{VALUE}} \; [\underline{\text{NOT}}] \;\; \text{literal-1} \;\; [\text{THRU} \;\; \text{literal-2}] \\ \qquad\quad [, \;\; \text{literal-3} \;\; [\text{THRU} \;\; \text{literal-4}] \ldots \end{array} \;\right\|$$

The meaning of the option CHECK IS PICTURE is not as obvious as it may appear at first sight. To appreciate it fully, the reader must be aware of a proposed sub-schema capability which is not yet implemented. This is the capability for an item in the sub-schema to be of a different type from the corresponding item in the schema. At execution time conversion takes place from one to the other. The conversion can be in one of two directions depending on whether the item value is being stored or retrieved. The effect of declaring CHECK IS PICTURE for a given item is to prevent such conversion taking place.

This is a strange capability. In effect, it could be interpreted as the person defining the schema exercising control over the permitted sub-schema declarations. If the former uses CHECK IS PICTURE, then there may be little point in using a different item type in the sub-schema, although the sub-schema item characteristics may be a sub-set of those defined for the same item in the schema. DBTG uses the phrase 'characteristics of a data item' to refer to the TYPE and PICTURE clauses discussed earlier in this chapter.

The use of RANGE, or as the DDLC prefers CHECK IS VALUE, is more clearly associated with validating item values. The DDLC's clause is a clear improvement over that of the DBTG, because the new one allows the data administrator to specify a set of values, or a number of discrete ranges or some mixture of both. Examples are

CHECK IS VALUE 3 THRU 10, 15, 20 THRU 30

and

CHECK IS VALUE NOT 5, 10, 15, 20.

9.9 Data Item Sub-entry

It is now time to refer back to Chapter 4 where we discussed record types in general and to Section 4.6 where the syntax of that chapter is summarized. No record type is complete without at least one item and the DBTG refers to the complete definition for a record type as being a Record Entry Skeleton. This consists of a Record Sub-entry (as defined in Section 4.6) and a Data Sub-entry which may appear several times.

In point of fact, the DBTG's syntax (page 90) allows for a record type without items, but this is either a mistake or else it implies that some esoteric usage may call for it.

The Data Sub-entry as discussed in this chapter would be as follows:

[level-number] dbd-name-1

$$\left[\; ;\; \underline{\text{PICTURE}}\;\; \underline{\text{IS}}\;\; ''\; \left\{ \begin{array}{l} \text{character-string-picture-specification} \\ \text{numeric-picture-specification} \end{array} \right\}\; '' \right]$$

$$\left[\; ;\; \underline{\text{TYPE}}\;\; \underline{\text{IS}}\; \left\{ \begin{array}{l} \left\| \left\{ \begin{array}{l} \underline{\text{BINARY}} \\ \underline{\text{DECIMAL}} \end{array} \right\} \right\| \; \left\| \left\{ \begin{array}{l} \underline{\text{FIXED}} \\ \underline{\text{FLOAT}} \end{array} \right\} \; \left\{ \begin{array}{l} \underline{\text{REAL}} \\ \underline{\text{COMPLEX}} \end{array} \right\} \right\| \quad [\text{integer-1, [, integer-2]}] \\[2em] \left\{ \begin{array}{l} \underline{\text{BIT}} \\ \underline{\text{CHARACTER}} \end{array} \right\} \; [\text{integer-3}] \\[1em] \underline{\text{DATA-BASE-KEY}} \\[0.5em] \text{implementor-type} \end{array} \right\} \right]$$

$$\left[\; ;\; \underline{\text{OCCURS}}\; \left\{ \begin{array}{l} \text{integer-4} \\ \text{db-id-1} \end{array} \right\}\; \text{TIMES} \right]$$

$$\left[\; ;\; \text{IS}\; \left\{ \begin{array}{l} \underline{\text{ACTUAL}} \\ \underline{\text{VIRTUAL}} \end{array} \right\}\; \underline{\text{AND}}\; \begin{array}{l} \underline{\text{SOURCE}}\; \text{IS db-id-4} \\ \text{OF } \underline{\text{OWNER}}\; \text{OF set-name-4} \end{array} \right]$$

$$\left[\; ;\; \text{CHECK}\;\; \text{IS}\; \left\| \begin{array}{l} \underline{\text{PICTURE}} \\ \underline{\text{VALUE}}\; [\underline{\text{NOT}}]\; \text{literal-1}\; [\underline{\text{THRU}}\; \text{literal-2}] \\ \qquad [\text{, literal-3}\; [\underline{\text{THRU}}\; \text{literal-4}]]\ldots \end{array} \right\| \right]$$

The level number is optional as in PL/1, but if used should be between 1 and 99 inclusive.

A Data Sub-entry must include one of the following six possible combination of clauses:

1. PICTURE
2. TYPE
3. SOURCE
4. OCCURS
5. OCCURS and PICTURE
6. OCCURS and TYPE

A data item (i.e. an elementary item) is defined by 1, 2 and 3 of the above. A vector is defined by 5 or 6. A repeating group would use 4, but the components of a repeating group may be further repeating groups. The phrase 'data aggregate' is the PL/1 term used to refer to either a vector or a repeating group (in other words, a Data Sub-entry containing an OCCURS clause).

9.10 Examples

The following examples are intended to illustrate various practical uses of the intra-record structure rather than the esoterica of PL/1 which will not be encountered in the commercially available systems.

Example 1

In Section 5.6.1, Example 1, it was shown how the set type of Figure 5.1 would be declared. If the data administrator preferred to use an intra-record structure rather than an inter-record structure, the Record Entry would be as follows:

```
RECORD NAME IS EMPLOYEE;
LOCATION MODE IS CALC USING EMPLOYEE-NO;
WITHIN REALM-1.
   02 EMPLOYEE-NO; PICTURE IS 9(8).
   02 EMP-NAME; PICTURE IS A(14).
   02 BIRTH-DATE; PICTURE IS 9(6).
   02 NO-OF-QUALIFICATIONS; TYPE IS DECIMAL FIXED.
   02 EDUCATION; OCCURS NO-OF-QUALIFICATIONS TIMES.
      03 QUALIFICATION; PICTURE IS X(5);
         CHECK IS VALUE B.SC., B.S., M.S.C., M.S., PH.D., B.A., M.A., B.D.
      03 QUAL-DATE; PICTURE IS 9(6);
         CHECK IS VALUE 200101 THRU 760101.
      03 COLLEGE; PICTURE IS X(14).
```

Example 2

The previous example is expressed as a set type (as it was in Section 5.1.6), but the item EMPLOYEE-NO is to be repeated in the EDUCATION record as well as in the EMPLOYEE record. The declaration would be as follows:

```
RECORD NAME IS EMPLOYEE;
LOCATION MODE IS CALC USING EMPLOYEE-NO;
WITHIN REALM-1.
   02 EMPLOYEE-NO; PICTURE IS 9(8).
   02 EMP-NAME; PICTURE IS A(14).
   02 BIRTH-DATE; PICTURE IS 9(6).
RECORD NAME IS EDUCATION;
LOCATION MODE IS VIA SET EE;
WITHIN REALM-1.
   02 EMPLOYEE-NO; IS ACTUAL AND SOURCE IS EMPLOYEE-NO
      OF OWNER OF EE.
   02 QUALIFICATION; PICTURE IS X(5).
   02 QUAL-DATE; PICTURE IS 9(6).
   02 COLLEGE; PICTURE IS X(14).
```

```
SET NAME IS EE; MODE IS POINTER ARRAY;
   OWNER IS EMPLOYEE;
   ORDER IS PERMANENT INSERTION IS LAST.
   MEMBER IS EDUCATION.
```

Chapter 10

Other Data Administrator Facilities

10.1 Introduction

We have now discussed the most widely available concepts in the Schema DDL. Just about every capability mentioned has been implemented in one system or another. However, this does not mean that we have covered every capability defined (or in some cases only conceived) by the DBTG and the DDLC. In this chapter, some of the more advanced ideas, most of which have never been implemented, are presented. Some of these ideas may indeed never come to be implemented.

10.2 Classification of Capabilities

At the beginning of Chapter 8, a small classification schema for Schema DDL facilities was introduced. It contained in total four categories:

1. Structural
2. Facilitate access
3. Mapping to storage
4. Control DML semantics only

The Schema DDL facilities presented so far can each be placed in one of these categories as follows:

1. Structural: Record type, item.
2. Facilitate access: Set type, search key, location mode (CALC).
3. Mapping to storage: Location mode (not CALC), Area, WITHIN clause, set mode, set order, source item.
4. Control DML semantics only: Removal class, storage class, set selection, CHECK clause.

This breakdown may probably not be well received by some members of the DBTG and DDLC who would affirm vigorously that the set type is a logical structuring property and that each set type is a representation of a real world relationship. There is no argument against this, but (as mentioned in Section 5.1) it is considerations of processing time efficiency which help the data administrator to decide whether or not a real world relationship needs to be defined as a set type using the Schema DDL.

There is another very personal way of looking at each Schema DDL statement which will be much more meaningful later when the DML is presented. This other classification is essentially unrelated to the preceding one and categorizes Schema DDL statements in the following terms of 'programmer involvement'.

1. Programmer needs to know.
2. Programmer does not need to know but can profit from knowing.
3. Programmer does not need to know and cannot profit from knowing.

Needless to say, most of the thirteen Schema DDL facilities here fall into the first category. Three, namely search key, set mode and set order, fall into the second category, whereas none of those discussed so far fall into the last category. This last category will have more meaning when the DMCL is discussed in Chapter 24. Also, as we go through the esoteric yet to be implemented facilities, we will identify some candidates for class 3.

10.3 Data Base Procedures

Many of the capabilities never implemented depend on the very powerful idea of data base procedures. A data base procedure is one defined by the data administrator in some language or other which is automatically invoked at execution time when some situation arises, the situation being defined in the schema.

In a sense, every data base procedure used is a case of DML execution time semantics being defined procedurally by the data administrator. Most COBOL programmers are familiar with the idea of USE declaratives. In PL/1, an analogous facility is supported by the ON statement. However, COBOL and PL/1 provide for a single level of human definition. The programmer himself defines procedures which he knows will be invoked while his program is executing at times which he himself prescribes.

The data base procedure is defined by somebody *other* than the programmer, but it affects execution of the programmer's program.

The reason this excellent capability has never been implemented is that it is both difficult and expensive. It certainly would involve modification to the host language compiler and possibly to the operating system.

Some of the possible uses of data base procedures are now discussed in turn.

10.4 ON Clause

An ON clause can be found in the DBTG report at each of the following levels:

realm
record type
item
set type

DDLC added an ON clause at the schema level, but, more important, clarified and expanded the ON clause capability on the other levels.

As a simple example of the ON clause, we can consider the one on the item level, which in DDLC's report appears (page 3.3.6) as

$$\underline{ON} \; [\underline{ERROR} \; DURING] \; \left[\left|\begin{array}{l} STORE \\ GET \\ MODIFY \end{array}\right|\right] \; \underline{CALL} \; db\text{-procedure-1}$$

Since we have already said something about STORE in a previous chapter, consider the example

ON STORE CALL LOGPROC

This means that immediately after the execution of the STORE statement (before the execution of the statement immediately following the STORE in the host language/DML program), control is transferred to the procedure LOGPROC, and LOGPROC does whatever it is supposed to do. After LOGPROC has been executed, control returns to the statement after the STORE.

There is no way the programmer can circumvent LOGPROC, except by not using the STORE statement—which could be difficult!

The ERROR DURING option is the DDLC's major contribution to the ON clause. If the example is modified to read

ON ERROR DURING STORE CALL LOGPROC

then the invocation of LOGPROC takes place only when an error occurs during the execution of STORE rather than at the end of the execution. (As we shall see, a comprehensive set of errors have been identified by the DBTG and DBLTG.)

ON clauses on realms, record types and set types are not significantly different from the above discussion for items. DDLC modified the DBTG's record type ON clause slightly for aesthetic reasons of their own. Basically, the clauses on each level realm, record type, item and set type are expressible on the DML statements which can be used at the various levels.

10.5 Procedurally Defined Mapping to Storage

The Schema DDL is a definitional or declarative language. In other words, it is non-procedural in that it states *what* shall happen but not how. As an example of this we have

WITHIN realm-1 [{, realm-2} . . . REALM-ID IS dbd-name-2]

from Section 4.8.1. This statement says that records of a given type are assigned to one or more realms. It does not say *how*. That decision is in the hands of the implementor and the programmer storing the records.

The DDLC's idea was that the data administrator may wish to express how the records are mapped to realms and for this purpose he must be able to define and invoke a data base procedure. The WITHIN clause syntax was therefore modified to read

WITHIN realm-1 [{, realm-2} ... [REALM-ID IS dbd-name-2

(USING PROCEDURE db-proc-2)]

so that an option to use a data base procedure is available.

Another use of a data base procedure has already been discussed (see Section 4.5.3), and it is in connection with the CALC location mode option.

The next mapping to storage is in connection with the definition of a search key, discussed in Section 6.10. The two non-procedural alternatives CALC and INDEX are supplemented by a procedural alternative as follows:

$$\underline{\text{SEARCH}} \quad \text{KEY} \quad \text{IS} \quad \text{db-id-1} \ [, \ \text{db-id-2}[\ ... \ \left[\ \text{USING} \left\{ \begin{array}{l} \underline{\text{CALC}} \\ \underline{\text{INDEX}} \\ \underline{\text{PROCEDURE}} \ \text{db-proc-1} \end{array} \right\} \right]$$

Having defined a procedural possibility for assigning records to realms, the DDLC could well have gone the whole way and included a procedural option for set order. This was not done, even though it would be easier for a data administrator to write a data base procedure to connect a record in a set in a specific way than it would to store a record procedurally in a given realm. This assertion assumes that the host language and DML could be used to write the data base procedures.

10.6 Item Level Data Base Procedures

Three data base procedures are on the item level, in one case supplementing a clause already described in the previous chapter and in two cases in clauses not yet mentioned.

10.6.1 CHECK Clause

The full syntax for the CHECK clause is

$$\underline{\text{CHECK}} \quad \text{IS} \quad \left\| \begin{array}{l} \underline{\text{PICTURE}} \\ \text{data-base-procedure-1} \\ \underline{\text{VALUE}} \ [\underline{\text{NOT}}] \ \text{literal-1} \ [\underline{\text{THRU}} \ \text{literal-2}] \\ \quad , \ \text{literal-3} \ [\underline{\text{THRU}} \ \text{literal-4}] \end{array} \right\|$$

and all except the data base procedure option were described in Section 9.8.

The data base procedure would allow the data administrator to define 'cross item validations', which validate combinations of item values within the record. This is not the only kind of validation possible using a data base procedure since the data administrator may include any kind of computational or data processing in the procedure he desires.

10.6.2 RESULT Items

In order to understand *result items*, it is important to have understood the *source items* (see Section 9.7) which are similar in some respects. However, a source item is *defined* as an item in a member record type, whereas a result item is *defined* as an item in an owner record type. In a result item, the value is computed from members and stored (at one time or another) in the owner. (Source items imply value copying from the owner to members.) The same difference of actual and virtual is provided for in the result items and this controls when the computation is made, and hence when the item value is stored in the owner record. The reader should recall that the COBOL JOD refers to actual and virtual derived items (page IV–2–5).

The complication which is introduced with the result items stems from the range of applicability of the computation specified in the data base procedure. The very nature of this feature seems to imply numeric computation of a sum or some other quantity across a set of values in member records, although the rules do not restrict us to this.

There are three different ranges of applicability for the computation as follows:

1. The record occurrence in which the value of result items is to be stored.
2. All records connected to the record occurrence in which the value of the result item is to be stored. The connected records may be connected because of different set type relationships.
3. All records connected to the record occurrence in which the value of the result item is to be stored. The connected records may be of different record types all of which are members in the same set type.

The DDLC's syntax for this feature is as follows:

$$\text{IS} \begin{Bmatrix} \text{ACTUAL} \\ \text{VIRTUAL} \end{Bmatrix} \underline{\text{RESULT}} \text{ OF data-base-procedure-1}$$

$$\left\| \begin{array}{l} \text{ON THIS } \underline{\text{RECORD}} \\ \text{ON ALL } \underline{\text{MEMBERS}} \text{ OF set-name-1 [set-name-2]}\ldots \\ \text{ON record-name-1 [, record-name-2]}\ldots \\ \qquad\qquad \underline{\text{OF}} \text{ set-name-3} \end{array} \right\| \quad \left\| \begin{array}{l} \text{[USING db-id-1} \\ \text{(, db-id-2)}\ldots] \end{array} \right\|$$

The reader will remember that the vertical parallel lines mean that the user is allowed to include any or all of the options listed in any sequence.

The result item facility is a fairly powerful one. A relatively simple example from a banking application of its use would be to store in a BRANCH record the sum total of the values of item BALANCE in the CUSTOMER records. If we write

TOT-BALANCE IS VIRTUAL RESULT OF COMPUTE-TOTAL USING BALANCE OF CUSTOMER

then the value of TOT-BALANCE is computed using the procedure COMPUTE-

TOTAL each time a BRANCH record is retrieved from the data base. ON phrases are not permitted with the VIRTUAL option.

If the data administrator prefers to maintain the total balance as an on-going calculation, then he might write

TOT-BALANCE IS ACTUAL RESULT OF ADJUST-TOTAL
  ON THIS RECORD ON CUSTOMER OR BR-CUST
  USING TOT-BALANCE OF BRANCH, BALANCE OF CUSTOMER

In this case, the same effect is achieved as before, but in a different way. The total balance would be adjusted using the procedure ADJUST-TOTAL each time a value of BALANCE is modified in a CUSTOMER record, or a CUSTOMER record is connected to or disconnected from a set in which a BRANCH record is the owner. The procedure ADJUST-TOTAL would be quite different from COMPUTE-TOTAL in the previous example. Notice also that we have deliberately used the result item itself as a parameter to the procedure. The COBOL style qualification is probably not necessary, but was added to the parameters after USING for additional clarity.

10.6.3 ENCODING/DECODING Clause

The role of this option is tied in with the concept of conversion between the schema image of an item value and its sub-schema image. To quote from the DBTG's function definition for this (page 102), its job is 'to specify the procedure to be executed whenever a data item requiring special conversion is retrieved or updated'.

The syntax for the option is as follows:

FOR $\left\{ \begin{array}{l} \underline{\text{ENCODING}} \\ \underline{\text{DECODING}} \end{array} \right\}$ [ALWAYS] $\underline{\text{CALL}}$ data-base-procedure-1

An ENCODING procedure is invoked when a STORE or MODIFY is executed; a DECODING procedure when a GET is executed.

The capability has never been implemented, chiefly because implementors have avoided execution time conversions of any kind as will be discussed when the sub-schema is presented. In addition, it relies on the yet to be provided data base procedure.

In practice, one could use these procedures to compact data item values on storage, and de-compact on retrieval. It is not clear whether this is in accordance with the spirit of the specifications which are aimed at overriding a so-called standard conversion which may be implied in any difference between the schema item characteristics and the sub-schema item characteristics (see Section 12.6.3). The optional word ALWAYS, if used, means that the conversion defined in the clause is always invoked. If and when ALWAYS is omitted, the ENCODING or DECODING conversion is used only when the characteristics differ.

Chapter 11
Schema DDL Syntax

11.1 Introduction

We have now covered in varying levels of detail all of the ideas put forward by the DBTG and DDLC. Widely implemented and therefore important concepts have been emphasized and discussed fully. Rarely or never implemented concepts have been given a more cursory treatment. The whole question of privacy has been left for a separate and special treatment in a later chapter.

The purpose of this chapter is to gather together the snippets of syntax presented in Chapters 2 to 9 and show a 'syntax skeleton'. One way of assessing quickly what capabilities a given implementation supports is to review its syntax skeleton. The reader will quickly see that the skeleton in this book does not come from the cupboard of any one committee or implementor. By and large it is closest to the DDLC, but it includes influences from the COBOL JOD (i.e. *realm* rather than *area*) and perpetuation from the DBTG of the set mode clause.

11.2 Main Vertebrae in a Syntax Skeleton

The syntax skeleton for a DDL consists of four entries as follows:

Schema Entry
Realm Entry
Record Entry
Set Entry

In a given data base schema, a Schema Entry, Realm Entry and Record Entry are required. A Set Entry is optional. The reader will remember that two of the entries have sub-entries. Hence, the 'global' syntax for the Schema DDL is as follows:

```
schema entry
{realm entry} ...
{record sub-entry {data sub-entry} ...} ...
[set sub-entry {member sub-entry} ...] ...
```

This rather useful overview is not to be found in the DBTG or DDLC reports, although the COBOL JOD provides something like it for the COBOL Sub-schema DDL in their report. Identifying the Set Entry as optional is somewhat academic, in the sense that most meaningful uses of the Schema DDL would include a Set Entry.

11.3 Schema Entry

The Schema Entry has not in fact been discussed so far in this text. COBOL oriented readers can equate it to the conceptual equivalent of the Identification Division. There is very little to the Schema Entry because it consists of one clause

SCHEMA NAME IS schema-name-1

This is perhaps an appropriate time to point out that a given installation may have many schemas which are 'known to the DBMS'. As one might expect, each schema must be given a name different from the others.

11.4 Realm Entry

The Realm Entry was touched on in Section 4.8.1. In terms of syntax, specifying the realms and whether each is permanent or temporary, the task to be done is trivial. For *each* realm, the data administrator writes

REALM NAME IS realm-name-1 [REALM IS TEMPORARY]

Again, each realm in a data base must have a name different from the others in the same data base. In a multi-data base situation, there is no provision for qualifying realm names with schema names, and the practitioner may find that the realm is equated to an operating system file. This means that each realm in an installation would have to have a distinctive name.

Although the syntax is here fairly simple, in practice the task of deciding how many realms to use and the size and characteristics of each are major tasks for the data administrator who may use the extra facilities of the DMCL (to be discussed in a later chapter) to extract the maximum performance from the overall system.

11.5 Record Entry

The discussion on the parts of the Record Entry has been somewhat separated in this book. The reader should refer back to Chapters 4 and 9 respectively for the important concepts of record assignment to storage and intra-record structure.

Collecting together the syntax for the Record Entry, it is as follows:

RECORD NAME IS record-name-1;

$$\text{LOCATION} \atop \text{MODE IS} \left\{ \begin{array}{l} \text{DIRECT} \left\{ \begin{array}{l} \text{dbd-name-1} \\ \text{db-id-1} \end{array} \right\} \\ \text{CALC [db-proc-1] USING db-id-2 [, db-id-3]} \dots \\ \qquad\qquad \text{DUPLICATES ARE [NOT] ALLOWED} \\ \text{VIA set-name-1 SET} \\ \text{SYSTEM} \end{array} \right\} ;$$

$$\text{WITHIN} \left\{ \begin{array}{l} \text{realm-name-1 [\{, real-name-2\}} \dots \text{REALM-ID IS dbd-name-2]} \\ \text{REALM OF OWNER} \end{array} \right\}$$

[level-number] dbd-name-3

$$\left[\text{; PICTURE IS} \quad \text{"} \left\{ \begin{array}{l} \text{character-string-picture specification} \\ \text{numeric-picture-specification} \end{array} \right\} \text{"} \right]$$

$$\left[\text{; TYPE IS} \left\{ \begin{array}{l} \left\| \left\{ \begin{array}{l} \text{BINARY} \\ \text{DECIMAL} \end{array} \right\} \atop \left\{ \begin{array}{l} \text{FIXED} \\ \text{FLOAT} \end{array} \right\} \right\| \text{[integer-1, [, integer-2]]} \\ \left\{ \begin{array}{l} \text{BIT} \\ \text{CHARACTER} \end{array} \right\} \text{[integer-3]} \\ \text{DATA-BASE-KEY} \\ \text{implementor-type} \end{array} \right\} \right]$$

$$\left[\text{; OCCURS} \left\{ \begin{array}{l} \text{integer-4} \\ \text{db-id-1} \end{array} \right\} \text{TIMES} \right]$$

$$\left[\text{; IS} \left\{ \begin{array}{l} \text{ACTUAL} \\ \text{VIRTUAL} \end{array} \right\} \text{AND SOURCE IS db-id-4 OF OWNER OF set-name-4} \right]$$

$$\text{CHECK IS} \left\| \begin{array}{l} \text{PICTURE} \\ \text{VALUE [NOT] literal-1 [THRU literal-2]} \\ \qquad\quad \text{[,} \qquad\qquad \text{literal-3 (THRU literal-4)]} \dots \end{array} \right\|$$

Here we have excluded the possibility of handling COMPLEX item types. In addition, several other options will not be found in commercially available implementations.

11.6 Set Entry

The capabilities associated with the set type have been discussed more extensively than many other facets of the Schema DDL. The reader should refer back to Chapters 5, 6, 7 and 8 for an exposition of the concepts underlying the following syntax. The set mode option has been preserved in the DBTG form—mostly for reasons of completeness.

SET NAME IS set-name-1;

OWNER IS $\left\{\begin{array}{l}\text{record-name-1}\\\text{SYSTEM}\end{array}\right\}$;

SET MODE IS $\left\{\begin{array}{l}\text{CHAIN [LINKED TO PRIOR]}\\\text{POINTER-ARRAY}\end{array}\right\}$;

ORDER IS PERMANENT INSERTION IS

$$\left\{\begin{array}{l}\text{FIRST}\\[4pt]\text{LAST}\\[4pt]\text{NEXT}\\[4pt]\text{PRIOR}\\[4pt]\text{IMMATERIAL}\\[4pt]\text{SORTED INDEXED [NAME IS index-name-1]}\\[4pt]\left\{\begin{array}{l}\text{BY DATA-BASE-KEY}\\\text{BY RECORD-NAME}\\\text{WITHIN RECORD-NAME}\\\text{BY DEFINED KEYS [DUPLICATES ARE }\left[\begin{array}{l}\text{FIRST}\\\text{LAST}\\\text{NOT}\end{array}\right]\text{ ALLOWED]}\end{array}\right\}\end{array}\right\}$$

EMBER IS record-name-1 $\left\{\begin{array}{l}\text{AUTOMATIC}\\\text{MANUAL}\end{array}\right\}\left\{\begin{array}{l}\text{MANDATORY}\\\text{OPTIONAL}\end{array}\right\}$ [LINKED TO OWNER]

$\left[\text{[RANGE] KEY IS }\left\{\begin{array}{l}\text{ASCENDING}\\\text{DESCENDING}\end{array}\right\}\text{ db-id-3}\left[\text{, }\left[\begin{array}{l}\text{ASCENDING}\\\text{DESCENDING}\end{array}\right]\text{ db-id-4}\right]\dots\right]$

$\left[\text{; SEARCH KEY IS db-id-5 [, db-id-6]}\dots\right.$

$\text{USING }\left\{\begin{array}{l}\text{CALC}\\\text{INDEX [NAME IS index-name-1]}\end{array}\right\}$

$\left.\text{DUPLICATES ARE [NOT] ALLOWED}\right]\dots$

; SET <u>SELECTION</u> IS <u>THRU</u> set-name-1 OWNER IDENTIFIED BY

$$\left\{ \begin{array}{l} \underline{\text{SYSTEM}} \\ \underline{\text{CURRENT OF SET}} \\ \underline{\text{DATA-BASE-KEY}} \left[\underline{\text{EQUAL TO}} \left\{ \begin{array}{l} \text{db-id-1} \\ \text{dbd-name-1} \end{array} \right\} \right] \\ \underline{\text{CALC-KEY}} \left[\underline{\text{EQUAL TO}} \left\{ \begin{array}{l} \text{db-id-2} \\ \text{dbd-name-2} \end{array} \right\} \left[\begin{array}{l} \text{,db-id-3} \\ \text{,dbd-name-3} \end{array} \right] \cdots \right] \\ \underline{\text{MEMBER}} \text{ record-name-1 SELECTION} \end{array} \right\}$$

[THEN <u>THRU</u> set-name-3

$$\left\{ \underline{\text{WHERE}} \text{ OWNER IDENTIFIED BY db-id-4} \left[\underline{\text{EQUAL TO}} \left\{ \begin{array}{l} \text{db-id-5} \\ \text{dbd-name-4} \end{array} \right\} \right] \right\} \cdots \right]$$

11.7 Summary

The above syntax skeleton is predicated more on what one is likely to find available than on what the user is recommended to use in practice. Which option should be used and under what circumstances is the whole topic of data base design and merits its own tutorial text.

Chapter 12
Sub-schema Concepts

12.1 Introduction

The concept of a sub-schema has necessarily crept into the preceding chapters so frequently that the reader will already have an insight into its role and what is achieved by using it. In a complete CODASYL-based DBMS, the Sub-schema DDL is a component which must be provided by the implementor and must be used by the data administrator.

In essence, the Sub-schema DDL is used to define a sub-structure of the data base schema. Since we now know that the Schema DDL is used to define realms, record types, items and set types, it is easier to explain that the Sub-schema DDL must be used to select *some* of these in order to identify the part of the data base which is to be processed by one or more application programs.

12.2 Relationship to Host Language

A Sub-schema DDL is identified by the CODASYL committees as 'belonging' in some sense to an associated procedural language such as COBOL. Hence, we should speak of the COBOL Sub-schema DDL or the FORTRAN Sub-schema DDL. However, there is a compiler for each procedural language and the translator which takes the Sub-schema DDL statements and translates them is not part of that compiler. The Sub-schema DDL Translator is a component of the DBMS in its own right and, in practice, must be used to translate a sub-schema before a program which uses the sub-schema is compiled.

The chief relationship between a Sub-schema DDL and its associated procedural language is that the procedural language's intra-record structure is reflected in the Sub-schema DDL. One could hence envisage a DBMS supporting both COBOL and PL/1 with a COBOL Sub-schema DDL and a PL/1 Sub-schema DDL. The only difference between these two would be the part of the Sub-schema DDL which defines the intra-record structure.

As indicated previously, currently available implementations do not attempt to support PL/1 and hence the Schema DDLs do not support its intra-record structure. However, given a DBMS which supports COBOL, in the sense of the COBOL intra-record structure in the Schema DDL and a Sub-schema DDL, then it would be a trivial step to provide a PL/1 interface which was restricted to the COBOL intra-record structure.

In this chapter on the sub-schema capabilities and in the chapters dealing with the DML, the treatment follows the CODASYL COBOL Journal of Development for 1976.[1] The specifications described therein for a COBOL Data Base Facility are the approved versions of the work of the Data Base Language Task Group. The DBLTG's work was published early in 1973. After the usual period of review and modifications, the DBLTG's proposals were approved by the CODASYL Programming Language Committee for inclusion in their 1976 Journal of Development.

Some of the widely used implementations of the CODASYL approach still adhere to the 1971 thinking and terminology of the DBTG and therefore it is proposed to follow the practice of presenting the COBOL Data Base Facility followed by the DBTG work where this is significantly or interestingly different. However, in both cases the presentation is strictly COBOL oriented.

12.3 Definition of a Sub-schema

In Section 2.4.1, we mentioned that the DBTG had been curiously ambivalent on the issue of who in fact should use the Sub-schema DDL in a given installation. DBTG said in their 1971 report that the data administrator *may* be responsible for defining the sub-schemas. Whether or not he *should* in a given installation seems to depend on the yet to be discussed question of privacy. If the data administrator wishes to control access to certain parts of the data base, then he should certainly be responsible for sub-schema definition. However, in an installation where privacy is not an issue, it should be possible for him to distribute copies of the schema declaration and let the application programmers write their own. In this case, there would be a need for the data administrator to catalogue the sub-schemas so defined in a library of sub-schemas. In this way he would be able to exercise some control.

There are arguments for tailoring each sub-schema to an application program. Although a sub-schema can be used by several application programs, it is quite likely in practice that the number of different programs using a given sub-schema will be quite low. One of the arguments in favour of the tailoring of sub-schemas is that of minimizing core usage. This is discussed in the next section.

12.4 Record Areas (User Working Area)

Any COBOL programmer knows that in his Data Division he must define a Working Storage Section. The purpose of this is to reserve areas in core into which data can be read from secondary storage files and from whence it can be written to such files. Since the image of a record type in core is invariably the same as it is on secondary storage, this means that the programmer has a certain amount of duplication in his Data Division.

If the programmer is processing data in a data base rather than in more conventional files, then he also needs working space in core for the data base records. The DBTG had the idea of relieving the programmer of defining such working space by making it completely implicit. Hence, the definition in the COBOL Sub-schema DDL of the sub-schema record types and items needed is tantamount to a definition of the working space reserved at execution time for each program using the sub-schema.

If a program uses a sub-schema which contains record types or items which the program does not process, then precious core space is being wasted.

DBTG coined the term *User Working Area* to refer collectively to the space reserved at execution time for the sub-schema record types. The DBTG report (page 20) gives the following very clear explanation of the User Working Area concept:

'Conceptually, the UWA is a loading and unloading zone where all data provided by the DBMS (i.e. DBCS) in response to a call for the data is delivered and where all data to be picked up by DBMS must be placed. Each program has to own UWA. The data in the UWA of a program is not disturbed except in response to the execution of a DML command or by the user program's host language procedures. There is no implication that the UWA locations are contiguous.'

The UWA is set up by the DBMS in accordance with the invoked sub-schema. Each data item included in the sub-schema will be assigned a location in the UWA and may be referenced by its name as declared in the sub-schema . . .'.

Either by intention or by oversight, this explanation was omitted from the DBLTG's proposal. There was clearly a deliberate move to remove the term *User Working Area* from the specifications. This was presumably motivated by the feeling that the existing COBOL term *record area* was adequate. There may also have been a feeling that the DBTG's idea of working space being implicitly defined in the sub-schema was too constraining on the implementor.

Using the term record area is a way of emphasizing the one to one relationship between sub-schema record types and the working space reserved, but the term *User Working Area* could well be perpetuated as it is occasionally needed to refer to the collection of all record areas during execution.

12.5 Renaming

One optional part of the Schema DDL is that which the DBTG called the Renaming Section and the DBLTG redesignated the Mapping Division. DBLTG introduced divisions to make the COBOL Sub-schema DDL seem familiar to COBOL oriented users. The Mapping Division contains one section called the Alias Section.

There are two goals which could be met with the Mapping Division. The first is that of defining names which are acceptable to the host language if and when the names in the Schema DDL are not. To the COBOL user, this will not be of much value. Schema DDL names are required to follow exactly the same rules as COBOL and it is unlikely that a user of the COBOL Sub-schema DDL would have to use the Alias Section because the schema names are invalid.

One problem he might encounter, however, is that of reserved words. Somewhat unfortunately the DBTG perpetuated the COBOL idea of reserved words in the Schema DDL. This means that the data administrator should be careful to avoid naming record types, items, set types by such names as

AREA, ERROR, INDEX, KEY, LOCATION, MEMBER, MODE, NAME, OWNER, RANGE, RECORD, RESULT, SELECTION, SOURCE, STORE, SYSTEM AND TIMES,

to mention a choice of the more tempting ones.

However, if one looks at the list of COBOL reserved words, the data administrator who assigns names in the Schema DDL such as

ALTERNATE, AUTHOR, BLANK, CODE, CONFIGURATION, CONTROL, COPY, COUNT, DATA, DATE, DAY, DEPTH, DETAIL, DISPLAY, DIVISION, ENVIRONMENT, GROUP, INSTALLATION, LABEL, LIMIT, LINE, MESSAGE, PAGE, POSITION, REPORT, SUPERVISOR, TABLE and TEXT,

will find that some use of the Alias Section is called for because these names cannot be used in a COBOL program.

12.6 Schema to Sub-schema Conversion

It has already been mentioned in Section 9.2 and again in Section 10.6.3 that the DBTG envisaged the idea of execution time conversion between the schema image of a record and the sub-schema image. For purposes of discussion, we can regard these as the image of a record type as stored in the data base and the image of the same record type as processed by the application program. CODASYL parlance usually talks of the schema record and the sub-schema record. In the commercially available implementations, it is usually possible to omit schema items in the sub-schema record, but conversion from a schema item type to a sub-schema item type has yet to be provided.

The CODASYL reports are all very weak on terminology to discuss the concepts of conversion, so we will introduce and define three levels on which the conversion problem exists. These are

1. Record level
2. Group or aggregate level
3. Item level (i.e. elementary item)

12.6.1 Record Level Conversion

Of the three levels, this is the kind which one can meet in practice. If it is possible in the Sub-schema DDL to omit items from the corresponding schema record type, then there is a need at execution time to convert the one image to the other. Numerous problems rear their heads.

Can one omit just any item from the sub-schema record? There are several roles which an item can play in the schema, and these include the following:

calc key
sort key (ascending/descending)
search key
realm-identifier

There is immediately a tremendous difference between retrieval and updating. If a program using the sub-schema record type is not going to update occurrences of this record, then the case for being allowed to omit items playing the above roles is stronger.

Supposing that it is desirable to omit the search key item. Does this matter if the programs retrieving occurrences of the record type do not in fact make use of the search key? Similar arguments apply to the other three roles listed above.

Whoever specifies a sub-schema should think very carefully before leaving out an item which has a role to play for the record type in the data base. With retrieval programs, some omission may be tenable, but with programs updating the record type, it will certainly be necessary to include items which have a role to play.

Another problem comes with updating sub-schema records which are only a part of the schema record. There are, of course, different kinds of update, but what happens when a program stores a new record of a type in which certain of the items are unknown to the program? The official answer is that the value of these items is set to null (i.e. no value). If values are to be provided for these items at a later time, then this must be done by other programs which use a different sub-schema selecting the items.

12.6.2 Group or Aggregate Level Conversion

If the schema record type contains repeating groups (possibly nested) of the kind discussed in Section 9.5 and the sub-schema record type also contains repeating groups but different ones, then there could be a need for an execution time mapping between the two intra-record structures. DBTG overlooked this problem. DBLTG recognized it and gave it a fairly complete treatment in the JOD (see page IV–2–3) under the heading of 'mapping of table elements'. In COBOL, an intra-record repeating group structure is called a table and each item in the structure is referred to as an element in the table.

The sub-schema aggregate may be larger or smaller than the schema aggregate. If it is larger, then it should accommodate instances of the schema structure. If it is smaller, then truncation may be necessary. DBLTG has laid down rules for this. There is a good chance they will never be implemented, and if they are, there is a further likelihood that they will not be used. Even if PL/1 as a language is supported in a DBMS, it would not appear advisable to support its complex intra-record structure. However, the aggregate level conversion problem is not only a function of whether PL/1 record structure is supported or not. With the COBOL intra-record structure, it is possible for the sub-schema record type structure to differ from the schema record type structure on an aggregate level. In this case the DBLTG's rules are useful. However, every indication points to a planned decrease in the use of intra-record structures as the more flexible inter-record structures gain in acceptance.

For these reasons, aggregate level mapping is regarded as of passing interest, but not meriting a more complete discussion.

12.6.3 Item Level Conversion

The problem of item level conversion was recognized by the DBTG at the time the COBOL intra-record structure was replaced by the PL/1 intra-record structure. As many as possible of the mapping rules were specified in the General Rules for the TYPE clause (pages 120 to 122, rules 9 to 19). It may seem a little strange to find these mapping rules in the definition of the Schema DDL, and DDLC did not touch them in any way.

The topic of item level conversion is much more important than aggregate level conversion. The scientific fraternity is developing an interest in data base management systems and recognizes that these are relevant for handling all kinds of scientific data. COBOL in its present form is very limited in the way it handles numeric data, and this is one of PL/1's strong points. The question which arises is whether one would ever want to use the COBOL language to process PL/1 like numeric data in a data base.

There are three kinds of item level conversion envisaged by the DBTG. These are

1. DBTG defined (pages 120 to 122)
2. Implementor defined
3. Data administrator defined.

The data administrator may be involved in two ways. First, he may use a CHECK IS PICTURE for the item, which, as pointed out in Section 9.8, is tantamount to imposing a syntax rule on the Sub-schema DDL. If the data administrator uses this option in the schema, then the sub-schema item must have the same characteristics as the corresponding schema item. This means no conversion is possible or necessary.

Secondly, he may use his ENCODING/DECODING option (see Section 10.6.3) which will automatically override a conversion in the other two classes. He can do this for the conversions in both directions. In fact, it seems that if he encodes the item value on update, he must say how it is to be decoded on retrieval.

The chief difference between DBTG defined conversion and implementor defined conversion is that in some cases it was not possible for the DBTG to define the conversion because of differences in hardware representation. Consequently, the DBTG had to delegate the rules to the implementor.

SOURCE \ TARGET	BIT	USAGE IS DISPLAY	USAGE IS COMPUTATIONAL
TYPE IS BIT [integer]	TARGET LONGER— RIGHT ZERO FILL TARGET SHORTER— TRUNCATE ON RIGHT IF ZEROS ELSE ERROR	BIT 1 → CHARACTER 1 BIT 0 → CHARACTER 0	CONVERT UNSIGNED BINARY INTEGER TO BASE, SCALE, MODE, PRECISION OF TARGET. POSSIBLE ERROR
TYPE IS CHARACTER [integer]	CHARACTER 1 → BIT 1 CHARACTER 0 → BIT 0 OTHER CHARACTERS— ERROR NO CONVERSION	TARGET LONGER— RIGHT BLANK FILL TARGET SHORTER— TRUNCATE ON RIGHT IF BLANKS ELSE ERROR	IMPLEMENTOR DEFINED
TYPE IS CODED ARITHMETIC integer-1 [integer-2]	ABSOLUTE ARITHMETIC VALUE CONVERTED TO FIXED POINT BINARY. ZERO BITS ADDED OR REMOVED ON LEFT. POSSIBLE ERROR.	IMPLEMENTOR DEFINED	SPECIAL RULES

Figure 12.1 Table of item level conversions

For convenience, the DBTG's rules have been summarized in the table in Figure 12.1.

Referring back to the fact that an item may play a role in a record type such as calc key, sort key, etc., the data administrator should consider this when thinking about the possibility of allowing item level conversion. In fact, allowing conversion from schema to sub-schema does not raise as many problems as omitting the item from a sub-schema record type. Nevertheless, it is probably better avoided.

12.6.4 Summary of Schema to Sub-schema Conversion

We have discussed the three levels of schema to sub-schema conversion. In commercially available systems, record level conversion could be encountered today, aggregate level will hopefully never be encountered, and one can expect to meet item level conversion in the course of the next few years.

12.7 Modification of Set Selection

In Chapter 8, we discussed the thorny problem of set selection. It is possible for the person defining the sub-schema to modify the algorithm chosen in the schema. Why should one wish to do this? The problem arises with the kind of set selection which we referred to in Chapter 8 as hierarchical set selection.

The reader may remember that hierarchical set selection involves defining a path to the set type member in question from some 'higher' point in the structure at which a unique selection of an owner record is possible. In a sub-schema, one or two nodes (i.e. record types) along the path may not be included. If the programs which will use the sub-schema are going to store new member records or find existing member records using the set selection criterion, then a new path must be defined.

The problem of set selection is conceptually difficult. The DBTG and DDLC seem to have gone out of their way to develop an approach which is unnecessarily obscure and obfuscatory. DBLTG tried to reduce the problem to manageable terms, but their definition was only on the Sub-schema DDL level which is very much the tail of the DDLC's dog. We have then three divergent approaches to set selection in three different CODASYL reports. Fortunately in practice, there is only one known implementation of hierarchical set selection and that is based on the DBTG's original thinking. Most implementations avoid hierarchical set selection and provide the non-hierarchical options. In this case, there is no need to change the Schema DDL declared set selection criterion in the Sub-schema DDL.

12.8 COBOL Sub-schema DDL Syntax

The DBTG partitioned the COBOL Sub-schema DDL as follows:

SUB-SCHEMA IDENTIFICATION DIVISION
SUB-SCHEMA DATA DIVISION

RENAMING SECTION
AREA SECTION
RECORD SECTION
SET SECTION

The COBOL JOD Sub-schema DDL has more divisions and less sections and the language is partitioned as follows:

TITLE DIVISION
MAPPING DIVISION
[ALIAS SECTION]
STRUCTURE DIVISION
[REALM SECTION]
[SET SECTION]
[RECORD SECTION]

The reader should observe the deliberate resequencing of the record and set declarations by the DBLTG. From both the implementor's and user's point of view this was ill-advised. The person using the Sub-schema DDL considers which record types he wishes to include before he considers which of the set type relationships he will need to relate the record types he has selected.

In other respects, the DBLTG tried hard to make the COBOL Sub-schema DDL look more like COBOL and we will follow their ideas in this chapter.

12.9 Global Syntax

The general format of the COBOL Sub-schema DDL is as follows:

TITLE DIVISION sub-schema-description-entry
[ALIAS SECTION (alias-description-entry)...]
STRUCTURE DIVISION
[REALM SECTION [realm-description-entry]...]
[SET SECTION (set-description-entry)...]
[RECORD SECTION [record-description-entry]...]

In the following sections, we will follow the precedent of the earlier chapters in omitting all references to privacy locks. In addition, the DBLTG's 'record-description-entry' is almost pure and unadulterated CODASYL COBOL, and we will not present the details of the COBOL intra-record structure. Only the more important clauses are presented.

12.10 Title Division

The syntax for giving a name to a sub-schema is (page IV–4–4)

TITLE DIVISION
SS sub-schema-name WITHIN schema-name

The important fact to note here is that a sub-schema can be associated with one schema and no more. As previously indicated, several schemas may exist concurrently and be 'known' to a DBMS. There may also be several sub-schemas of a given schema.

Since we are now talking about a new part of the COBOL language, any names, such as sub-schema, which are defined using the Sub-schema DDL must follow the COBOL rules for names.

12.11 Mapping Division—Alias Section

This section is optional. If and when used, the COBOL JOD syntax is (page IV–4—5):

ALIAS SECTION

$$\underline{AD} = \text{pseudo-text} = \begin{bmatrix} \text{REALM-NAME} \\ \text{SET-NAME} \\ \text{RECORD-NAME} \end{bmatrix} \underline{\text{BECOMES}} \begin{Bmatrix} \text{real-name} \\ \text{set-name} \\ \text{record-name identifier} \end{Bmatrix}$$

The pseudo-text must reference a name defined in the associated schema. The names after the BECOMES are the names to be used in programs referencing the data included in the sub-schema. The new names should also be used in the REALM, RECORD and SET Divisions. The new names do not replace the schema names and should be thought of as synonyms for the schema names.

The reference in the syntax to 'identifier' is the more COBOL way of referencing 'data-base-data-name' and 'data-base-identifier' of the Schema DDL.

12.12 Structure Division

The Structure Division is used to specify the content and structure of a part of the data base that is included in the sub-schema being defined. It consists of those sections Realm, Set and Record. It seems possible for a use of the Mapping Division to contain a Realm Section and a Record Section only, but this is not clear from the COBOL JOD.

12.12.1 Realm Section

In the Realm Section, the user may elect to include all Schema realms in one statement or he may name the specific realms he requires. The syntax is (page IV–4–7)

REALM SECTION

$$\underline{RD} \begin{Bmatrix} \underline{ALL} \\ \text{realm-name} \end{Bmatrix}$$

This section of the Mapping Division may have the associated entry repeated many times. Furthermore, this section must be included. In other words, a sub-schema must include at least one realm. If a realm is not included in a sub-schema, then a programmer using that sub-schema cannot reference the data in the realm—either explicitly or implicitly. 'Implicit reference' could imply that the realm contains a record type along the path of a hierarchical set selection. Alternatively, it could contain a search key index. Even more subtly, the realm might contain some of the occurrences of a member record type and another realm (included in the sub-schema) might contain others. When processing along a set occurrence, a record in the available realm might point to a record in a realm not available. There would be no way of going further along that set occurrence.

12.12.2 Record Section

We will consider the Record Section before the Set Section even though this is contrary to the sequence proposed by the DBLTG.

The syntax is less trivial than in the other sections. Therefore, it is appropriate to present it before any discussion. Combining two parts from the COBOL JOD (pages IV–4–10 and IV–4–12) we get

RECORD SECTION

    01   record-name [WITHIN {realm-name-1}...]
                    (REAL-ID IS identifier-1)]

$\left\{\text{level-number} \quad \text{data-name-1} \quad (\underline{\text{PICTURE}} \text{ IS character-string)}\right.$

$\left[[\underline{\text{USAGE}} \text{ IS}] \left\{ \begin{array}{l} \underline{\text{COMPUTATIONAL}} \text{ [-n]} \\ \underline{\text{DB-KEY}} \\ \underline{\text{DISPLAY}} \text{ [-n]} \\ \underline{\text{INDEX}} \text{ [-n]} \end{array} \right\} \right]$

$\left[\text{; } \underline{\text{OCCURS}} \text{ integer-1 TIMES} \right.$

$\left. \text{; } \underline{\text{OCCURS}} \text{ integer-20 TO integer-3 TIMES } \underline{\text{DEPENDING}} \text{ ON data-name-6} \right] \right\}...$

There are two additions to CODASYL COBOL here. The first is the WITHIN clause and its associated REALM-ID. The second is the possibility of having a USAGE DB-KEY.

The effect of the WITHIN clause is explained differently in the JOD specification from in the DBTG. We will present the JOD as it seems clearer.

If a record type is assigned to two or more realms in the schema, then it is possible that a sub-schema will want to select some but not all of the realms and hence some records of the type named, but not all. The user must be consistent in the REALM SECTION and the WITHIN clause and the REALM-ID clause seems rather redundant, in that the selection could surely be implied in the REALM SECTION.

The ability to assign an item a usage of DB-KEY reflects the corresponding Schema DDL capability (see Section 9.4), although the COBOL JOD has chosen an abbreviated form. As mentioned earlier, the practice of storing data base key values in the data base is one to be discouraged even though the user will find the capability to do so implemented. It should be possible to store data base key values in the programmer's working storage space in core during the course of execution of a program, but if one would have to define an item of this type in a data base schema record type, and then define it again in a sub-schema record type, it would be a very round about way of achieving a simple objective. Fortunately, the COBOL JOD now allows the definition of data base key items in the ordinary Data Division Record Description.

12.12.3 Set Section

Without the facility discussed in Section 12.7 for redefining the schema's set selection criterion, the Set Section syntax becomes as simple as that of the Realm Section. The COBOL JOD specification (page IV–4–19) read as follows

$$\underline{SD} \begin{Bmatrix} \underline{ALL} \\ \text{set-name-1} \end{Bmatrix}$$

However, if the user wishes to revise the set selection, he must name the individual set type and may not use the ALL option.

For completeness, the COBOL JOD non-hierarchical set selection modification option is

$\underline{SD}$ set-name-1 [; SET $\underline{SELECTION}$ FOR record-name IS

$$\underline{VIA} \text{ set-name-1 OWNER} \begin{Bmatrix} \text{SYSTEM} \\ \underline{\text{CURRENT}} \\ \text{identifier-1} \\ \underline{\text{VALUE}} \text{ OF identifier-2 IS identifier-3} \\ \text{[identifier-4 IS identifier-5]} \dots \end{Bmatrix} \dots$$

The following table defines the correspondence between the Schema DDL option in Chapter 8 and the above Sub-schema DDL option.

Schema DDL	Sub-schema DDL
SYSTEM	SYSTEM
CURRENT	CURRENT
DATA-BASE-KEY	identifier-1
CALC-KEY	VALUE OF
MEMBER	no corresponding facility

It will be clear that the DDLC's Schema DDL prefers to make the meaning of the third and fourth options explicit in the syntax, while the DBLTG has followed the unfortunate practice of burying the meaning in the semantics.

12.13 COBOL Sub-schema DDL Translation

A sub-schema has to be translated into object form using a DBMS component called the Sub-schema Translator. At the time this translator is used, the object schema of the schema identified in the Title Division must be available to the translator.

Chapter 13

Data Manipulation Language Concepts

13.1 Introduction

An understanding of the concepts of the DML is absolutely vital to a thorough grasp of the CODASYL approach to data base management. All too many tutorial expositions explain the concepts of set type, chains and possibly location mode and sub-schema. They then stop and leave the reader or listener with an uneasy feeling that he is looking at the tip of an iceberg.

The DML has been the subject of criticism on the basis that it is 'unnecessarily complex'. In some cases, this must be construed as a confession by the individual or group making the assertion, that he or they simply do not understand it. Indeed, the definitive prose of the DBTG and DBLTG is hard to understand. Most formal language definitions suffer from this problem. While a casual reader can usually grasp the idea of a set type and a chain, some of the more subtle ideas of manipulating such a structure are rather more elusive. It is the aim of this and the ensuing chapters to try to rectify the problem of a comprehensive expository approach and hopefully to explain in careful detail how the DML works.

13.2 Host Language Interface

As was clarified earlier in this text, the DBTG rightly chose a host language approach to data base management. This means that the application programmer is required to process the data in the data base using an enhanced version of the language he has always used—usually COBOL, but occasionally PL/1 or FORTRAN. The enhancements to the standard programming language are mostly statements to allow the programmer to move around the inter-record structure. The previously existing programming language statements are used to perform intra-record processing.

The new statements should be to all intents and purposes indistinguishable from the previously existing ones. In fact, it is predictable that within the course of a decade, the identification of some of the programming language statements as 'DML statements' will cease to be made. For the present, however, we regard the statements which have been added specifically to facilitate processing of data base records, as DML statements. In the case of COBOL, the new statements are mostly in the Procedure Division. In one or two cases, existing COBOL statements have been extended.

The COBOL application programmer believes he is writing in an enhanced version of COBOL. In theory, his source program should be compiled by a suitably modified and enhanced COBOL compiler. In practice, most implementors have chosen not to modify the COBOL compiler, but to provide a DML/COBOL Preprocessor (as mentioned in Section 2.5.1). This means that the programmer's source program is not handled by the COBOL compiler, but is translated by a pre-processor into a revised source form. The revised source form is recognizable by the standard COBOL compiler, because each DML statement in the Procedure Division has been translated by the pre-processor into a CALL statement with a number of parameters appropriate to the statement and its options found in the first program. Hence, the parameters in the CALL statement list are processed at execution time by the DBCS (execution time module).

The capabilities of the DML are not really dependent on whether a preprocessor approach is used or the COBOL compiler is modified. Pre-processors may differ from each other in practice in terms of how much work they do. On the simplest level, a pre-processor may merely recognize a DML statement and translate it into a CALL statement with parameters. A more sophisticated preprocessor may be involved with execution time semantics.

13.3 Binding to a Sub-schema

Each application program which is going to process data records in a data base must be bound to a sub-schema. In terms of the programming step required, this means that the programmer must include the name of a sub-schema in his program. The sub-schema must be one which has previously been translated.

The DBTG syntax for identifying a sub-schema is provided by an INVOKE clause in a new Schema Section of the existing Data Division. The programmer must then write

DATA DIVISION
SCHEMA SECTION
INVOKE SUB-SCHEMA sub-schema-name OF SCHEMA schema-name.

Only one INVOKE clause is allowed in each COBOL application program.

DBLTG modified this syntax to make it more COBOL-like and the result was a new clause for the Data Division as follows:

DB sub-schema-name WITHIN schema-name.

This clause has exactly the same effect as the DBTG's, although the syntax is rather different.

The reader should recall at this juncture one of the effects of the sub-schema facility, namely to reserve a working space in core for each record type named in the sub-schema. This was discussed in some detail in Section 12.4 and it is not proposed to duplicate the discussion here. However, an understanding of the role of the record area during the course of execution of a program is vital to an understanding of the DML.

13.4 Application Programs and their Run-units

The DBTG recognized that application systems built around a data base would tend more and more towards 'on-line' systems. Since there are many kinds of on-line systems, it must quickly be clarified that in a commercial environment, the most viable kind of on-line system is one in which pre-programmed transaction programs are invoked by non-programmers, whom we like to refer to as 'parametric users'. Such a system is sometimes called a transaction oriented system or a transaction driven system. Other kinds of on-line systems include program preparation system (often still called time sharing) and interactive query systems.

Examples of application based on a transaction oriented system include order entry, balance checking (in a bank), and theoretically airline reservation systems. The important point which we are leading up to here is that in such a system a given transaction program may be invoked two or more times simultaneously from different terminals. Each executing instance of the transaction program is then referred to as a *run-unit*.

It now becomes important to distinguish properties of an application program from properties of a run-unit, although once the term run-unit has been introduced and understood, the task of making the distinction becomes much easier.

In fact, we must now return to the discussion of record area. There is a record area in core for each record type in the sub-schema and for each run-unit using the sub-schema. An illustration of this situation is depicted in Figure 13.1.

There exist three sub-schemas of SCHEMA-1. Two application programs use SUB-SCHEMA-1 (namely AP1 and AP2), one application program uses SUB-SCHEMA-2 (namely AP3) and two use SUB-SCHEMA-3.

Furthermore, at a given point in time, a total of five run-units are executing, as follows:

1 of AP1, namely RU11
3 of AP3, namely RU31, RU32 and RU33
1 of AP5, namely RU51

It will be noted that at the point in time under consideration, *no* run-units of AP2 or of AP4 are executing.

Referring to the specific case of RU31, RU32 and RU33, *each* of these three run-units has its own record areas for each record type included in SUB-SCHEMA-2. In view of the fact that these run-units have nothing to do with each other apart from the fact that they are run-units of the same application program, this seems a very reasonable approach.

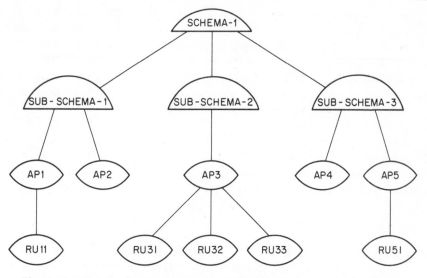

Figure 13.1 Relation between run-unit, application program and sub-schema

13.5 Data Base Registers

When the programmer communicates with the DBCS, he does so using fairly conventional parameter passing techniques. Either the parameter is implied in the DML statement syntax or else the DML statement references data items in core whose value is to be taken as the parameter value.

However, often the DBCS needs to communicate with the programmer and this is done using what the DBLTG called data base special registers. There are several of these, but the most important is called DB-STATUS. This register is set each time a DML statement is executed for a run-unit. It is now necessary to distinguish between successful execution of a DML statement and unsuccessful execution.

In the case of a successful execution of the DML statement, DB-STATUS is set to zero. In the case of an unsuccessful execution, it is set to a specific value depending on why the execution was unsuccessful. We must now examine why the DBLTG called the register DB-STATUS which is much preferred to the DBTG's ERROR-STATUS.

If the DML statement is unsuccessful, this could conceivably be for a number of reasons. Not all of these reasons constitute errors, although to be fair most of them do. The DBLTG used the phrase *data base exception condition* because it does not have the unfortunate connotation of error. DBTG called all conditions error conditions and therefore this will be found in a number of implementations.

There is also a difference between how the DBTG's and DBLTG's exception conditions are represented. DBTG used four digits and the DBLTG used seven digits. In each case, the first two of the digits represent a code for the DML statement, but the two codes are otherwise totally different.

We do not propose to give a full list of data base exception conditions in one place as this has little or no tutorial value. The conditions which can occur during the course of execution of each DML statement will be discussed in the section for each DML statement. However, a few general remarks are appropriate.

If and when a data base exception condition occurs, the programmer should plan to take appropriate action. He may feel that all occurences of a given condition anywhere in his program should be treated in the same way and in this case he may use a Declarative Procedure. (For the benefit of non-COBOL programmers, this is a procedure which is declared to be executed when a certain event happens during the course of execution of the program—in this case a data base exception condition, although COBOL allows for certain others.) Alternatively, if the programmer wishes to treat each occurrence of a condition in a specific way, he must build in a test of the form

IF DATABASE-STATUS EQ . . . .

after each DML statement in which the condition may occur. Hopefully for the sake of the programmer, the former technique is more generally applicable than the latter.

The action to be taken when a data base exception condition occurs may involve some programmer diagnosis of what has happened. To facilitate this, the DBCS sets a value in certain other data base special registers, three of which are identified as follows:

DB-REALM-NAME
DB-SET-NAME
DB-RECORD-NAME

There is one of each of these for each run-unit. Each register is capable of containing a COBOL name which is 30 characters.

The idea is that if a data base exception condition occurs, then the register is set to contain the name of the realm, set type or record type associated with the exception condition. Usually, the situation is fairly clearly defined and there is no ambiguity about which record type etc. should be named in the register. However, the meaning depends on the meaning of the condition which has occurred.

The DBTG identified two other special registers, namely ERROR-TYPE and ERROR-COUNT. The former is concerned with problems of concurrent processing. The latter is intended as a count of the number of 'errors' occurring during the course of execution of a DML. (The other register would refer to the *first* error detected.)

DBLTG sensibly dropped the idea of ERROR-COUNT and renamed ERROR-TYPE as DB-CONFLICT—a rather better indication of its role in the scheme of things.

13.6 Currency Indicators

One of the most vital concepts in the DML is that of the currency indicators. Introduction of one of the currency indicators was unavoidable when chronological set types were presented in Section 6.4.2 and again when set selection was considered in Section 8.3. Hence, the reader should already have some inkling about these indicators, but now is the appropriate place to present a full treatment.

Each currency indicator is a system maintained quantity which normally points to a record in the data base. This means that the normal contents of a currency indicator is a data base key value, although the content can also be a null value (as at the commencement of the run-unit).

The number and type of currency indicators maintained by a run-unit depends entirely on the sub-schema used by the program to which the run-unit belongs (if one can talk of a run-unit 'belonging' to a program). They are identified as follows:

CURRENT OF RUN-UNIT	1 only
CURRENT OF SET-NAME	1 per set type in sub-schema
CURRENT OF REALM-NAME	1 per record type in sub-schema
CURRENT OF REALM	1 per realm in sub-schema

Hence, if a sub-schema includes 4 set types, 6 record types and 3 realms, each run-unit of a program using the sub-schema will automatically maintain $1+4+6+3=14$ currency indicators.

It is important to note that the significance of the four classes of indicator varies considerably. The first two classes, namely CURRENT OF RUN-UNIT and CURRENT OF SET-NAME, are infinitely more important than the other two classes. To place matters in perspective, as a rough estimate, 80% of application programs could be written quite efficiently without using the CURRENT OF RECORD-NAME and CURRENT OF REALM-NAME indicators.

Two statements affect the setting and updating of the currency indicators. These are the FIND and the STORE. Many statements, including these two, may reference one or more indicators during the course of their execution.

The CURRENT OF RUN-UNIT indicator is rather special in that it is often the way in which the DBCS knows which record in the data base to act on. For example, one of the DML statements options appears as

ERASE record-name

There may be 10,000 occurrences of the record type named 'record-name' and the system needs to know which of these to delete from the data base. It is the CURRENT OF RUN-UNIT indicator which determines this and the programmer therefore has to include a FIND in his program prior to the ERASE in order to establish the presence of the record to be erased.

The CURRENT OF SET-NAME indicator is often used in DML statements to select a set of the type named in the statement. As an example of this, consider the statement

CONNECT record-name TO set-name

In fact, here the CURRENT OF RUN-UNIT is used to identify the record to be connected and the appropriate CURRENT OF SET-NAME indicator is used to determine the occurrence of 'set-name' into which the record is to be connected.

The programmer must remember that all indicators are null at the beginning of the run-unit. Hence, he must take care in the first DML statement of the program to avoid using one which tests or uses a currency indicator in any way.

A final point on currency indicators must be mentioned. It is possible for the program to use an option in the FIND and STORE statements which has the effect of preventing the updating of some or all of the currency indicators. This option is not available for the CURRENT OF RUN-UNIT, but it is with all other indicators. DBTG referred to the capability as 'suppressing currency updates'. DBLTG modified this to 'retaining currency'. The effect of the option is the same in both cases.

While the idea of the programmer controlling the updating of the currency indicators in this way is logically powerful, it is one which should be used with utmost care. Playing around with currency indicators is not a practice to be recommended for the neophyte programmer.

13.7 DML Philosophy

Before giving a brief discussion of each DML statement, it is useful to gain some perspective on the approach chosen by the DBTG for manipulating data records. The approach follows that pioneered in the early sixties in IDS and happens to be the same as that in other commercially available systems such as IMS and TOTAL.

We have emphasized that there is a record area in core available for each record type in the sub-schema used by the run-unit. Many of the DML statements which act on the record level transfer data between this record area and the data base. The important thing to note is that when a record level DML statement is executed, *one* record and one record only is directly affected. Possibly other records may be indirectly affected in that they are accessed incidentally during the course of execution of the DML statement.

The DBTG's DML approach has been characterized as a 'single record at a time logic'. In that this approach is tried and proven in the market place, and that any other is at best speculative, the DBTG cannot be criticized for selecting this approach. Possibly, in the course of time it will be supplemented, and maybe even ultimately replaced, by a more powerful multiple record logic. For the time being, the DBTG's approach is the one against which others are to be measured.

13.8 DML Statements

The DBTG and DBLTG chose to present the DML statements to their readers in alphabetic order. This is useful if one wishes to reference the report to check what a rule is. The tutorial value of this sequence is zero.

It is useful to categorize each DML statement in terms of the level on which it operates. Before launching into a full scale tutorial exposition of each statement, we will then give a one paragraph discussion of the function and role of each statement in order to give the reader a global appreciation for the statements as a whole.

Many of the DBTG's statement names were carefully changed by the DBLTG for a variety of reasons—some good, some bad, sometimes obscure, sometimes obvious. In Figure 13.2 we give both names. We will comment on the changes when discussing the individual statements.

Level	COBOL JOD	DBTG
Realm (area)	READY FINISH	OPEN CLOSE
Set	ORDER	ORDER
Record only	FIND, STORE ERASE STORE	FIND DELETE STORE
Record and item	GET MODIFY	GET MODIFY
Linkage	CONNECT DISCONNECT	INSERT REMOVE
Currency Indicators	ACCEPT	MOVE
Conditional	IF	IF
Declarative	USE	USE
Concurrency	KEEPT FREE REMONITOR	KEEP FREE (not provided)

Figure 13.2 Relation between COBOL JOD and DBTG DML statements

13.8.1 READY Statement

A READY statement must be the first DML statement in a program which will access the data in the data base. It is necessary for the programmer to communicate to the DBCS which realm or realms he is planning to process, how he is going to process each (retrieval or update) and finally what attitude he has to other run-units which also plan to process the same realms. READY is a very important statement because it is the one concerned with concurrent processing. Conceptually, a READY realm is rather like an 'OPEN file' in conventional processing.

13.8.2 FINISH Statement

A FINISH statement is the opposite of a READY and would normally be the last DML statement to be executed in a program. It is conceptually similar to a CLOSE file.

13.8.3 FIND Statement

FIND is surely the most important of the DML statements. It is used to establish the presence of a record in the data base. If it is successful, the data in the record cannot be processed by the host language statements (such as MOVE) until a GET has also been executed. There are several kinds of FIND options, and the programmer needs to be aware of DDL declarations such as set types and location mode in order to use these intelligently.

13.8.4 STORE Statement

The programmer may build up a new record in the record area and then cause it to be stored in the data base using a STORE statement. He must have previously executed a READY FOR UPDATE on the realm in which the record is to be stored. Depending on the location mode and set selection, he may have some parameters to initialize prior to the STORE. Although this statement is syntactically quite simple, its semantics are fairly complex.

13.8.5 GET Statement

The GET statement complements the FIND in that it is used after a FIND to move the found record from the DBCS's own system buffer into the run-unit's record area corresponding to the record type. It is possible to move some or all of the items in the record type into the record area.

13.8.6 ERASE Statement

ERASE is used to 'wipe out' a data base record. Before an ERASE can be executed successfully on a record, its presence in the data base must be established using a FIND. ERASE has a number of options which allow several records to be erased in one statement execution. These options depend on the 'removal class' discussed in Section 7.2.

13.8.7 MODIFY Statement

The MODIFY statement is used to replace a record in the data base with a different image of the same record in the record area in core. 'Same record' in this context means that it has the same data base key value. Normally, the sequence of statements preceding a MODIFY would be FIND, GET, and then MOVE. The

MOVE statements (as many as necessary) change item values in core. The MODIFY makes the changes in the data base. MODIFY can work on the item level.

13.8.8 CONNECT and DISCONNECT Statements

If a record type has a storage class of automatic in a set type (see Section 7.1), then it is connected into a set of that type when initially stored in the data base using a STORE. However, it can be disconnected using a DISCONNECT, and it can be connected into a set using a CONNECT. With a CONNECT, the matter of set selection arises.

13.8.9 ORDER Statement

This statement is not widely implemented, but it could be useful when available. It is involved with the DDL Set Order declaration (see Section 6.2), and allows the programmer to sequence an occurrence of a chronological set type either temporarily for the duration of his run-unit or possibly permanently such that the order in the data base is changed—but *not* the basis for ordering as used when records are later connected into the set.

13.8.10 ACCEPT Statement

The ACCEPT statement may be used to copy currency indicators into user defined data items. Such items must have been defined as having an item type of DB-KEY. ACCEPT can also be used to copy a realm name into a user defined alphanumeric elementary item defined to hold such a name.

13.8.11 IF Statement

The existing COBOL IF statement is extended to allow the programmer to make several tests on the most recently found record to see whether it is connected to a set of a specified type in any way. Another option allows a test to be made on whether a set of a named set type is 'empty' or not.

13.8.12 USE Statement

The existing COBOL USE statement has been extended to allow a USE FOR DB-EXCEPTION. This facility is vital for performing diagnosis in relation to the various data base exception conditions which may arise during the course of execution of any of the DML statements.

13.8.13 KEEP, FREE and REMONITOR Statements

These three statements are concerned with the problems of integrity in a concurrent processing environment where two or more run-units are processing data records in the same realm. The DBLTG approach is complex and will be treated in full in the chapter on concurrent processing.

13.9 Conclusions

The COBOL DML consists of up to thirteen new Procedure Division statements and modifications to the existing IF, USE and ACCEPT statements. The sequence in which the statements were presented in the preceding sections is what is felt to be the tutorial sequence. This is roughly the sequence which the ensuing in-depth discussion will use.

Chapter 14

READY and FINISH

14.1 Introduction

As we start to look at the DML statements in detail, it is important to remember that the whole philosophy is predicated on the fact that the application programs which the programmer prepares have to be written with the consideration that they will execute concurrently with other programs. To be exact, it is the run-units which execute concurrently, and the chief problem is that the run-units may at some time during the course of execution be in contention for the same data record. If both wish only to retrieve the data, the contention is not too serious. If both wish to change it in some way (including deletion), then major problems can arise.

It would be nice if the DBMS designer could spare the programmer from considerations of concurrent processing and indeed this is well within the state of the art. However, as with many other factors from which it is possible to spare the programmer, this too has its price in terms of the machine efficiency with which the program will execute.

DBTG selected an approach which in some ways delegated the problem of concurrent processing to the data administrator, but only in the sense that it suggested tools to stop the programmer from getting involved in the problems.

The DBTG's approach requires us to focus attention initially on the READY statement, which is rather like an 'OPEN file' in that it communicates an intention to process the data in some part of the data base.

14.2 READY Statement Syntax

It will be easier to discuss the concepts of concurrent processing if the syntax and more important semantic rules of the READY statement are first presented. The DBLTG form of this statement is (page III–12–40)

$$\underline{READY} \; \begin{bmatrix} \begin{bmatrix} \text{set-name-1} \\ \text{realm-name-1} \end{bmatrix} \cdots \begin{bmatrix} ; \underline{USAGE\text{-}MODE} \; \text{IS} \; \begin{bmatrix} \underline{EXCLUSIVE} \\ \underline{PROTECTED} \end{bmatrix} \begin{Bmatrix} \underline{RETRIEVAL} \\ \underline{UPDATE} \end{Bmatrix} \end{bmatrix} \end{bmatrix}$$

This is slightly different from the DBTG's offering (page 247) which was as follows:

$$\underline{OPEN} \; \begin{Bmatrix} \underline{ALL} \; \text{FOR} \; \underline{SET} \; \text{set-name-1} \; [, \; \text{set-name-2}] \ldots \\ \underline{AREA} \; \text{area-name-1} \; [, \; \text{area-name-2}] \ldots \end{Bmatrix}$$

$$\begin{bmatrix} ; \; \underline{USAGE\text{-}MODE} \; \text{IS} \; \begin{bmatrix} \underline{EXCLUSIVE} \\ \underline{PROTECTED} \end{bmatrix} \begin{Bmatrix} \underline{RETRIEVAL} \\ \underline{UPDATE} \end{Bmatrix} \end{bmatrix}$$

Examination of the available implementations indicates a tendency to omit the facility to refer to set types in the first part of the statement, but to extend the USAGE-MODE clause in various ways. One way is to add an 'initial load' mode for use when records are being stored in the realm for the first time. Another tendency is to make explicit the usage mode implied by omitting both EXCLUSIVE and PROTECTED and to call it NON-PROTECTED.

14.2.1 Usage Modes

In the optional USAGE-MODE clause, the programmer is declaring two things. When he chooses between UPDATE and RETRIEVAL, he is stating how he himself intends to process the records in the realm. If he chooses RETRIEVAL, then he is restricted to using FIND, GET and IF statements. If he chooses UPDATE, he may in addition include STORE, MODIFY, ERASE, CONNECT, DISCONNECT and ORDER.

It is interesting to note that if he omits the USAGE-MODE clause altogether, the default is RETRIEVAL. This is an about face from IDS/1 which had the opposite default.

The more important part of the USAGE-MODE clause is where he chooses between EXCLUSIVE, PROTECTED and the 'third option', which we shall here for reference call 'unrestricted', although this term has not been used by the CODASYL committees. As we shall see, the unrestricted usage mode is the most important and we do need a word or phrase to identify it.

The reader should here note that there are a total of six different usage modes arrived at by combining each of RETRIEVAL and UPDATE with each of EXCLUSIVE, PROTECTED and UNRESTRICTED (capitalized for consistency).

The all important usage mode clause would then read

$$\underline{USAGE\text{-}MODE} \; \text{IS} \; \begin{Bmatrix} \text{EXCLUSIVE} \\ \text{PROTECTED} \\ \text{UNRESTRICTED} \end{Bmatrix} \begin{Bmatrix} \text{RETRIEVAL} \\ \text{UPDATE} \end{Bmatrix}$$

For ease of reference, we will identify the first option as the *concurrency mode* and the second as the *processing mode*. Together these two combine to make a usage mode. The only term used by the CODASYL committees is 'usage mode' which on its own is an inadequate basis for a clear exposition.

14.2.2 Exclusive Processing

When the programmer includes a READY FOR EXCLUSIVE in his program, he is saying that he is prepared to wait for any concurrently executing run-unit to finish with the realm. Furthermore, once his run-unit gets control of the realm, no other run-unit is allowed a 'look-in' until his run-unit has finished. Hence, 'exclusive' is a good word to describe this concurrency mode.

If the programmer furthermore wishes to update the records in the realm, then he is ensuring that there will be no interference from other run-units. They will all have to wait even if they only wish to retrieve one single record from the realm. The result is an inevitable slowing down of the whole application system. This may or may not be acceptable. There is no risk of the updating run-unit changing some of the records which a retrieving run-unit is processing to generate reports.

A usage mode of exclusive update makes reasonable sense and could be used on various occasions although not with great frequency. One example is when records are being loaded into the realm initially.

On the other hand, a usage mode of exclusive retrieval is one which must be classed as completely anti-social. If each programmer were to make a practice of using this option, the overall performance of an on-line application system would be slow indeed. Fortunately, the DBTG indicated a way in which the data administrator could prevent programmers from using such an option. This capability will be discussed in the chapter on privacy.

14.2.3 Protected Processing

The protected concurrency mode has been given slightly different interpretation by the DBTG and DBLTG. In the DBTG report (page 248, rule 7) it states:

'Use of the PROTECTED phrase prevents concurrent update and allows concurrent retrieval within the same area.'

The COBOL JOD is trying to be simpler, but more explicit when it declares (page III–12–41, rule 11):

'The PROTECTED phrase prevents any other run-unit from updating the affected realms.'

The COBOL JOD gives a definition of PROTECTED USAGE MODE which reads (page III–2–27):

'The state of a realm in which its records cannot be modified by another run-unit.'

All of these three quotations are open to interpretation. The most useful interpretation is that when a run-unit readies a realm for PROTECTED UPDATE, then there may be no other concurrently executing updating run-unit irrespective of the concurrency mode of the other run-unit. There may be other retrieving run-units, but clearly from the point of view of the *other* run-units, these would not have a concurrently mode of EXCLUSIVE RETRIEVAL.

When a run-unit readies a realm for PROTECTED RETRIEVAL, then this implies that there may be no concurrent updating run-unit, but there may be concurrent retrieving run-units.

Hence, the essence of the protected concurrency mode looking at the overall situation is that there may be no more than one updating run-unit and at the same time there may be retrieving run-units.

14.2.4 Unrestricted Processing

When a programmer readies a realm for unrestricted processing, one might initially feel that he is adopting a 'don't care' attitude to what goes on in concurrently executing run-units. In practice, use of the unrestricted concurrency mode means that the overall execution of the mix of run-units should be improved and also that the programmer has to take steps to protect the integrity of the data base. These steps involve the use of the KEEP statement presented in Chapter 17.

UNRESTRICTED RETRIEVAL means that the program is going to retrieve from the realm and others can do what they like. UNRESTRICTED UPDATE means that the program is going to *update* the realm and others can do what they like.

14.2.5 Overall View of Usage Modes

Now that each concurrency mode has been presented in turn, it is possible to look at the overall view of the situation. One way of doing this is to look at what will be called a conflict matrix or conflict table.

The situation is defined for a realm in terms of all the possible usage modes which may first take effect and all possible usage modes which may be attempted by another run-unit for that realm. Since we have six usage modes, this results in a 6 by 6 matrix in which each element is either Y for yes or N for no. This indicates the success of the *second* attempt to ready the realm. The 'first' attempt (in absolute time) from some run-unit or other is always successful irrespective of the usage mode.

The table opposite is taken from the DBTG report (page 250). The COBOL JOD regrettably omits this useful piece of definition which also has considerable tutorial value.

While the implication of a Y is fairly clear, more must be said about an attempt to ready a realm which is unsuccessful because an earlier attempt from a concurrent run-unit causes a conflict.

DBTG is very clear on this point (page 250, rule 14 modified):

FIRST READY	CONCURRENT	EXCLUSIVE		PROTECTED		UNRESTRICTED	
	READY	RETRIEVAL	UPDATE	RETRIEVAL	UPDATE	RETRIEVAL	UPDATE
EXCLUSIVE	RETRIEVAL	N	N	N	N	N	N
	UPDATE	N	N	N	N	N	N
PROTECTED	RETRIEVAL	N	N	Y	N	Y	N
	UPDATE	N	N	N	N	Y	N
UNRESTRICTED	RETRIEVAL	N	N	Y	N	Y	Y
	UPDATE	N	N	N	N	Y	Y

'Any attempt to execute a READY statement which would result in usage-mode conflict for a realm will result in the run-unit attempting to execute the READY statement going into a wait-state.'

The implication is that the failure to execute the READY is only temporary. Just what happens to a run-unit in 'wait-state' is entirely up to the implementor. Possibly, the run-units waiting for a realm are queued in some way and when the realm is released (that is to say 'finished') by the run-unit in control of it, then the run-units in the queue should be processed on a first come first served basis.

However, one cannot forget the possibility of priority schemes which may come into play at this juncture. This topic is rather outside the scope of the present book.

Another way of looking at the overall picture of concurrency modes is to list some permissible combinations of usage mode which may be in effect at a given point in time. In the following table, the first in the list is the first kind of usage mode to gain control. The remaining modes in the list are prefixed by N x if an arbitrary number of such usage modes is acceptable.

1. EXCLUSIVE RETRIEVAL.
2. EXCLUSIVE UPDATE.
3. PROTECTED RETRIEVAL—N x PROTECTED RETRIEVAL,
       N x UNRESTRICTED RETRIEVAL.
4. PROTECTED UPDATE—N x UNRESTRICTED RETRIEVAL.
5. UNRESTRICTED RETRIEVAL—N x PROTECTED RETRIEVAL,
       N x UNRESTRICTED RETRIEVAL,
       N x UNRESTRICTED UPDATE.
6. UNRESTRICTED UPDATE—N x UNRESTRICTED RETRIEVAL,
       N x UNRESTRICTED UPDATE.

Examination will show that this 'co-existence table' is compatible with the conflict table presented earlier.

14.2.6 Readying Several Realms

So far we have looked at the matter of readying a realm from the point of view of 'one READY, one realm'. Looking back at the syntax, we are reminded that a single READY can act on several realms, and this complicates the possible course of events. Fortunately, the semantic rule is fairly simple. If a READY addresses several realms, then success must be achieved for all of them. If there is one conflict, then the READY is not executed for any of the realms and the run-unit is placed in the queue as discussed earlier.

As indicated, the option which includes set types in the READY statement has not been implemented. However, the meaning is fairly obvious. If the programmer writes

READY EJE

where EJE is the name of a set type (see Figure 3.6), and if the three record types

EMPLOYEE, JOB-HISTORY and EDUCATION are each in a different realm, then an attempt is made to ready all three realms.

It should be noted that all realms which are addressed explicitly or implicitly in a READY statement should be in the sub-schema used by the application program. Furthermore, the fact that a realm is readied successfully does not mean that the records in the realm can be processed by ensuing DML statements. This fact depends on whether or not the record type is included in the sub-schema being used.

If a record type is assigned to two or more realms, then it is possible that not all of these realms are included in the sub-schema. A READY executed on a set type which has the record type as a member would not affect all the realms to which the record type is assigned, but only those in the sub-schema.

14.2.7 Possibility of Deadlock

If a run-unit needs to ready two or more realms with a concurrency mode other than unrestricted and a concurrently executing run-unit is trying to do the same thing to two of the same realms, there is a chance of a deadlock occurring. This situation is sometimes described by the more graphic term *deadly embrace*.

The situation is best illustrated by the following example of two run-units trying to ready two realms, X and Y, for exclusive retrieval.

Time T	*Run-unit A*	*Run-unit B*
1	READY X USAGE-MODE EXCLUSIVE	
2		READY Y USAGE-MODE EXCLUSIVE
3	READY Y USAGE-MODE EXCLUSIVE	
4		READY X USAGE-MODE EXCLUSIVE

The problem is that if the two readies at lines 1 and 2 are both successful, then run-unit A's attempt to ready Y at T=3 will be unsuccessful, and run-unit A will be placed in the queue. Control will come eventually to run-unit B at time T=4, and the attempt to ready realm X will also be unsuccessful because run-unit X already has control over the realm. Hence, the two run-units are deadlocked. Neither can proceed until the other has finished with a realm it is waiting for.

There are a number of solutions to this problem. The more obvious one relies on programmer discipline. Instead of writing two READY statements, he writes only one

READY X, Y USAGE-MODE EXCLUSIVE

More generally speaking, he writes the minimum possible number of READY statements, bearing in mind that there can be only one usage mode in a READY.

Also, he should avoid readying and finishing realms unnecessarily during the course of his program.

Another solution which is available in one implementation is to have a special system program monitoring each run-unit for activity. When this program detects that a run-unit is stagnant for more than an acceptable period of time, it can break the deadlock.

14.2.8 Possible Data Base Exception Conditions

Since this is the first DML statement to be considered fully in this book, it is an appropriate time to state the policy which will be adopted when presenting exception conditions.

An attempt will be made to consider conditions identified by DBTG and DBLTG and to give the text which these groups specified to identifying the conditions. Where this is felt to be inadequate, an alternative will be suggested. Privacy conditions are considered only in the special chapter on privacy matters.

The COBOL JOD identifies four non-privacy DBECs which could occur during the course of execution of a READY. They are

1. An unavailable realm has been requested by the DBCS.
2. Realm in ready mode.
3. Usage mode conflict in a concurrent run-unit.
4. DBCS space is exhausted.

It is not clear how the first of these could occur during the course of execution of a READY. The DBEC is more oriented towards other DML statements which may invoke a hierarchical set selection criterion (see Section 8.6).

The second DBEC in the list would be better described as

Realm already readied for this run-unit

which seems to be the intent of the condition. If this condition arises, the most likely reason is that there is an error in the program which has caused a transfer of control back to the start of the program. The sensible action when this DBEC is detected is to abort the run-unit.

The third DBEC is probably the most frequently occurring. The action to be taken where this is detected is up to the programmer.

The fourth DBEC is only applicable in the case of a READY FOR UPDATE (irrespective of the concurrency mode). However, the DBLTG felt that this DBEC could occur with *all* DML statements. Surely, the critical point for this situation is when it is *first* detected, which would normally be during the course of an updating DML statement such as STORE, MODIFY or CONNECT. The value of this DBEC with any other DML statement is open to question.

14.3 FINISH Statement

Compared with the READY statement, a FINISH realm (also known as CLOSE area) is extremely simple. The syntax (page III–12–31) is

$$\underline{\text{FINISH}} \quad \left\{ \begin{array}{l} \text{[set-name-1]} \dots \\ \text{[realm-name-1]} \dots \end{array} \right\}$$

The same rationale applies to use of set names as in the case of the READY. The effect of executing a FINISH is that subsequently executed update and retrieval DML statements may not reference records in the realm.

A problem could arise with currency indicators which point to records in a realm being finished. Since there is a currency indicator for the realm being finished, some rule for what happens is necessary. DBTG recognized this problem and specified that the value of any affected currency indicator should be set to null. However, if the programmer finishes the realms he uses at the end of his program, then any problems caused by null currency indicators are avoided.

The only DBEC which can occur when a FINISH is executed is that the realm has not in fact been readied. As in the case of an attempt to ready a realm already readied, this would normally imply that there is an error in the program and the most appropriate action to take is to abort the run-unit.

It should be noted that when a run-unit is aborted because of some other DBEC in some other DML statement, then any of the realms which are readied are normally finished automatically as part of the abort process.

14.4 Syntax Errors in READY and FINISH

Data base exception conditions are conditions which arise during the course of execution of a program. Syntax errors can normally be detected during the use of the compiler or pre-processor.

The chief syntax rules which must be checked during the compilation process concern whether the realms or set types addressed are in fact in the sub-schema. If the compiler or pre-processor does not detect such errors, then logically this places an extra load on the DBCS.

Chapter 15

FIND and GET Statements

15.1 Introduction to FIND Statement

The FIND statement is the cornerstone of the DML. It is necessary to find a record in order to perform any other function on it. The only exception to this is the STORE which will be treated later.

There are many different FIND formats. Both DBTG and COBOL JOD (page III–12–12) present the FIND in seven different formats, although JOD resequenced the DBTG's seven and modified the syntax. In both cases, the sequence of the breakdown seems to be somewhat arbitrary and it is felt that a more tutorial exposition can be achieved by ignoring both. Instead we shall give a breakdown into three main categories and then discuss each category in turn.

We will reference the DBTG and JOD format numbers where necessary as DBTG 4 for Format 4 of the DBTG report and JOD 7 for Format 7 of the COBOL Journal of Development.

15.2 General Format of a FIND

In both DBTG and JOD, the FIND statement has the following general format.

FIND record-selection-expression [   ]

The square brackets contain the optional expression to suppress updating of the currency indicators (in DBTG terms) or to retain currency (in JOD terms). We will return to discuss this option at the end of the chapter.

DBTG created the term record-selection-expression to refer to the remainder of the FIND statement after the FIND. It is perhaps somewhat unfortunately grandiose and might lead one to think in terms of Boolean selection facilities and the like. This is not the case. As pointed out in Section 13.7, the DML adopted a 'single record at a time' logic. Each time a FIND is executed, either *one* record is found, or *no* record is found. With some options, several records may be accessed during the course of execution of the FIND, but there is no way such records can be made available to the application program after execution of that FIND. Many observers regard it as a major weakness in the CODASYL approach that no multi-record FIND is provided.

15.3 Categories of FIND

The following categories of FIND are felt to be useful in promulgating an understanding of how the FIND works.

1. Out of the blue
2. Relative
3. Repeated

It must be emphasized that since the data base is in direct access storage, *all* accesses to data base-records are 'direct' and hence the word has no value in terms of identifying any specific class.

In each category of FIND, there are factors of which the programmer must be aware in order to use the FIND. Sometimes these factors are Schema DDL declarations, sometimes they are currency indicators. The programmer must *always* bear in mind which record types and set types are in the sub-schema he is using in a given program.

As each FIND is discussed, we shall list the factors which the programmer needs to remember. The only certain effect of successfully executing a FIND is to update the current of run-unit indicator. The other possible effects are to update the other indicators, although the programmer may choose to suppress these updates.

15.4 Out of the Blue FIND

An out of the blue FIND is one which is made from outside the data base without reference to any record previously found. Such a FIND does not reference currency indicators and hence the first FIND to be executed in a run-unit should be one in this class.

Two of the formats, DBTG 3 and DBTG 5, JOD 4 and JOD 2 respectively allow a FIND in this class. One of them is for CALC record types only and is far more useful and predictably more used than the other.

15.4.1 Finding a Calc Record

The DBTG 5 syntax for this class of FIND is

FIND record-name-1 RECORD

JOD 2 is a modified form of this.

FIND ANY record-name-1

As mentioned, record-name-1 must have a location mode of CALC. The reader should refer back to Section 4.5 for the discussion of CALC location mode.

The programmer has to know that the location mode is CALC. He also has to know which of the items in the record type comprise the calc key. Furthermore, immediately prior to the FIND, he must move values for the calc key into the items in the record area. Here we see the record area being used to pass parameter values from the program to the DBCS.

If the FIND is successful, the current of run-unit indicator is updated. The record found is *not* copied into the record area. (That calls for a GET to be executed.)

The reader who has brushed up his knowledge of CALC location mode will remember that the data administrator had to choose in the Schema DDL between allowing duplicate values of the calc key and prohibiting them. If he prohibited them, and there is a record in the data base with the calc key value which the programmer is seeking, then all is well. However, if the data administrator allowed duplicate calc key values and there are indeed several records in the data base with the calc key value sought, which of them does the 'out of the blue FIND' pick out?

The answer to this is arbitrary but quite sensible. In fact, the record found will be the one with the lowest *data base key* value. The programmer needs to know that there *may* be duplicates and he has a way of finding them. We regard the FIND used to find records which are duplicates of one just found as a *relative* FIND and will discuss it later.

There is a third possibility and that is that there is no record in the data base whose calc key values correspond to those in the record area. (Whether duplicates are allowed or not is irrelevant here.) This situation is a good example of a data base exception condition which is certainly not a programmer error and is a good example of why the DBLTG moved away from the phrase 'error condition' in favour of the certainly more long winded 'data base exception condition'.

We may be dealing with a customer record type in an on-line environment. A query arises. 'Do we have a customer called PHIPPS?' The parametric user types in the identification of a transaction program designed to handle queries of this kind is followed by the parameter value PHIPPS. The FIND in the program is executed, a data base exception condition is established, the program tests the DBEC and transmits the correct answer 'no customer called PHIPPS'.

This particular FIND option is one of three or four 'work horses' among several less valuable FIND options.

We will end discussion of this option by listing again the factors the programmer must remember when using the option:

1. Location mode of record type
2. Calc key of record type
3. Whether duplicates allowed or not

We will summarize possible DBECS for the FIND at the end of this chapter.

15.4.2 FIND within a Set

This option appears with justification to be one of the most complex FIND options available. It is quite powerful and properly used can be very valuable.

The DBTG 6 and JOD 7 syntax are only slightly different. In both cases, there is an associated option of the same format which relies on the current of set name indicator. We class this as a relative FIND and discuss it later. The relevant portion of the DBTG 6 is

<u>FIND</u> record-name-1 <u>VIA</u> set-name-1

[<u>USING</u> db-id-1 [, db-id-2] ...]

while the corresponding portion for JOD 7 is

<u>FIND</u> record-name-1 <u>WITHIN</u> set-name-1 [<u>USING</u> db-id-1 [, db-id-2 ...]

It is this FIND option which causes the set selection criterion discussed in Chapter 8 to be invoked. If the set selection is based on the current of set name indicator, then this is here regarded as a relative FIND.

The chief set selection option of interest here is that which is based on the owner record type of the set type having a location mode of CALC (see Section 8.4). In this case, duplicate values of the calc key are not allowed and the programmer has to initialize the calc key prior to the FIND.

Next comes the basic problem of finding a record in the selected set. There are four alternatives.

1. USING clause not used
2. db-id-1, db-id-2 correspond to a search key
3. db-id-1, db-id-2 correspond to range key
4. Other

In the first case, the first record in the selected set is the one found.

The second case is the most interesting one because a search key (see Section 6.10) is used to expedite the FIND. Assuming the set selection is based on the CALC location mode of the owner, then the FIND takes place in two stages. In the first stage, an owner record is selected which effectively selects a set of the record set type. Then using the intra set type search key, a member record connected to the set is found whose values correspond to those in the record area. As with finding records based on location mode CALC (Section 15.4.1), duplicate values of the search key might have been allowed. However, in this case, it is not so clearly defined which of the duplicates is the one to be selected. The DBLTG rule states that 'the record identified is the first one meeting the above requirement', the requirement being a match of the values in the record with those in the record area.

The third case implies a sequential search through the connected members in the set. The fact that the search is based on a sort key (or range key, see Section 6.7) means that the system is able to cut short the search after it has passed the values being sought. In this sense only does use of the sort key expedite the search.

In the last case, the search may have to go through all connected records in a set—a potentially time consuming process if the set is large.

15.4.3 Finding FIRST and LAST in Realm

Although the options are strictly speaking in the 'out of the blue' class of FIND, it is unlikely that a programmer would use them because he wishes to find one specific record in the data base. He would however use such a FIND to initiate a planned search through a realm.

The relevant portion of the JOD 4 syntax is

$$\underline{\text{FIND}} \begin{Bmatrix} \underline{\text{FIRST}} \\ \underline{\text{LAST}} \\ \text{integer-1} \\ \text{identifier-1} \end{Bmatrix} \text{[record-name-3]} \quad \underline{\text{WITHIN}} \quad \text{realm-name-1}$$

whereas the DBTG 3 syntax is rather more powerful and explicit

$$\underline{\text{FIND}} \begin{Bmatrix} \underline{\text{FIRST}} \\ \underline{\text{LAST}} \\ \text{integer-1} \\ \text{identifier-1} \end{Bmatrix} \text{[record-name]} \quad \underline{\text{RECORD}} \quad \text{OF} \quad \text{realm-name-2} \quad \underline{\text{REALM}}$$

When the programmer omits reference to a specific record type, he is effectively saying that he does not care which record type is retrieved, as long as it satisfies the rest of the record-selection expression.

The format allows the programmer to find the record possibly of a named type in the realm with either the lowest (FIRST) or highest (LAST) data base key value. If identifier-1 is specified in the FIND, then it must be defined in the application program or else in a record type in the sub-schema and must contain a positive or negative integer. From here on the rules are the same as for the case when an integer is specified explicitly in the format.

The specification of an integer (directly or indirectly) refers to an ordinal count upwards from the record with the lowest data base key value or downwards from the record with the highest. These are still 'out of the blue' FINDs because the programmer does not need to precede a FIND integer with a FIND FIRST or FIND LAST and no currency indicators are referenced.

The FIND FIRST may be of occasional use when a programmer wishes to access *all* records, possibly of the same type, in a given realm. FIND FIRST would then be used to initialize the currency indicator. Going through all the records in a realm does not call for an understanding of how the records are stored relative to each other within the realm.

The other three options using LAST or an integer are felt to be of somewhat marginal value. To make intelligent use of a statement such as

FIND 13 record-name

the programmer would need to understand exactly how the records of the named type are stored in the realm and in effect how the data base keys are assigned. Implementors seem to share this view and the capability to include an integer will not often be encountered in practice.

15.5 Relative FIND

Most of the FIND options can be regarded as in this class of relative FINDs. It means that an out of the blue FIND has been used (not necessarily the immediately preceding FIND) to initiate the search, and the result of executing the relative FIND under consideration is to go from the record just found to another record possibly using an access path. Needless to say, the FIND executed immediately preceding the FIND under consideration would often also be a relative FIND. Hence, the overall view emerges of initializing a search using an out of the blue FIND which is then followed by a series of relative FIND executions—possibly programmed in a loop with a test after the FIND statement.

The following six different relative FIND statement options are:

1. Using set type relationship
2. DUPLICATE value of calc key
3. OWNER from a connected record using set type relationship
4. Within a set possibly using the search key
5. NEXT DUPLICATE value of a search key or sort key
6. NEXT or PRIOR in realm

15.5.1 FIND Using Set Type Relationship

It is this option which capitalizes on the set type relationship declared in the Schema DDL. DBTG and JOD both treat it as *syntactically* the same format as the out of the blue option discussed in Section 15.4.2. It corresponds to DBTG 3 and JOD 4. Leaving out the reference to a realm, the DBTG's format reads

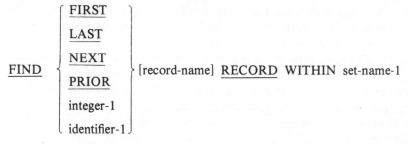

The first problem to look at is that of set selection. The programmer names a

set type in his FIND statement. When the statement is executed, it must refer to one specific set of that type. The discussion of set selection in Chapter 8 is strangely irrelevant here. The semantics of this FIND option dictate that set selection is based only on the current of set name indicator. This means that the programmer must ensure that the indicator is set as he wishes prior to the execution of the FIND. It must be remembered that a current of set name indicator may point either to an owner in a set or to a *connected* member.

Having discussed the all important problem of set selection, it is time to see what the individual options mean. FIRST and LAST represent only semi-relative options. We had no hesitation in classing the 'FIND FIRST and LAST in realm' options as 'out of the blue' because no reference to a currency indicator was called for. When a set type is named, a currency indicator is used to perform the set selection.

The 'first' record in a set is the one logically adjacent to the owner record, which is NEXT (rather than PRIOR) to the owner.

If the programmer plans a sequential search through all the records in a set, he has two options. He could make an out of the blue access to the owner and then execute a series of FIND NEXT statements. Alternatively, he could ensure that the current of set name indicator is correct, then do a FIND FIRST followed by a series of FIND NEXTs.

Before leaving FIND FIRST, let us consider one hypothetical problem. Supposing a set has 500 member records connected to it. For some reason, the current of set indicator points to one in the middle—number 250. When the FIND FIRST is executed, the DBCS has the job of getting from the 250th member to the first. There are three possible routes it might follow.

1. If there is a link to owner use it to find the owner, then find the first number.
2. If there is a link to prior, follow it to the first member.
3. Follow the link to next round to the first member.
4. With a pointer array, go straight there.

Systems will vary on how much 'intelligence' is built in. An intelligent system will be able to select the most direct path to the object record depending on the set mode and on the link available. The programmer could profitably be aware of how the system executes a FIND FIRST, in that he might avoid the option in certain circumstances.

FIND LAST is just about as marginally useful in the case of the set type as it is in a realm. It is left as an exercise for the reader to list the various paths to the last record from an arbitrary point in the middle of a long set.

FIND NEXT is one of the real work horses among the multitude of FIND options. The record to be found is the member logically adjacent to the one referenced in the current of set name, using the link in the next direction. If the currency indicator points to the last record in the set, then a data base exception condition arises. The same applies if the currency indicator points to the owner of an empty set.

FIND NEXT will always be executed with reasonable speed. Unless the implementation is very inefficient, it should never cost more than one physical access to the data base. This is not true of FIND PRIOR, which is fairly safe with a pointer array or with a chain having a link to prior. However, in the case of a chain which only has a link to next, the programmer could risk that the DBCS has to go all the way round a chain in the 'next' direction until it comes to the record preceding the one pointed to in the current of set name indicator.

The facility to include an integer (implicit or explicit) in this option is also of very marginal value and not regularly implemented. However, the option to name a specific record type is very valuable for processing multi-member set types with a chronological set order, since the different member record types are likely to be intermingled.

Considering the multi-member set type in Figure 3.6, the programmer could write

FIND NEXT EDUCATION RECORD WITHIN EJE

if he wishes to ignore the other member record type—JOB-HISTORY. On the other hand, if he wishes to process both record types, then he may write

FIND NEXT RECORD WITHIN EJE

It is important to note that the programmer must have his own way of testing which type of record is found as a result of execution of this particular FIND option when the programmer does not know a priori which record type it will be. The syntax of the GET statement also allows the programmer to omit the record name. This would mean, in the case of the example, that either the record area for EDUCATION or else the record area for JOB-HISTORY is changed. Hence, the programmer must build in a test of the value of items in these record area.

15.5.2 FIND DUPLICATE

In Section 15.4.1, we pointed out that an out of the blue FIND to a CALC record for which duplicate values of the calc key were allowed would result in the record with the lowest data base key value being found. In order to give access to the other records with the same calc key value, the programmer must use the same format as that for the FIND of the first duplicate.

In DBTG 5 this is achieved by writing

FIND NEXT DUPLICATE WITHIN record-name-1 RECORD

whereas JOD 2 is more simple,

FIND DUPLICATE record-name-1

It does not make sense to use this option unless the most recently executed FIND is either the out of the blue option or the same option.

The system looks in the designated record area at the calc key values and then accesses the data base to find the record of the same type with the same calc key values and the next highest data base key value to the one just found. Although it does not say so in any of the specifications, there is a fairly clear implication that duplicate CALC records should be linked together in some way so that there is a fairly easy access from one duplicate record to the next. This is, of course, a problem which the implementor should recognize and solve. If he fails to do both of these, then the programmer using this option can look forward to some fairly time consuming executions of programs.

One important rule must be emphasized in connection with this option, and that is that the FIND is actually relative to the current of run-unit and *not* relative to the record in the record area referenced in the syntax. If the programmer is processing two record types with a location mode of CALC, he must be very careful about intermixing the order of execution of these FINDs on the two record types.

15.5.3 FIND OWNER

This is surely the simplest of the seven FIND options proposed in both DBTG 4 and JOD 6; it merits a whole format of its own. The format reads

FIND OWNER RECORD OF set-name-1 SET

which DBLTG 6 abbreviated to

FIND OWNER WITHIN set-name-1

As with the option discussed in Section 15.5.1, the first problem is that of set selection. The solution is the same, namely to use the current of set name indicator. No reference is made to the set selection (see Chapter 8) which has been declared in the Schema DDL.

The reader should now refer back to Sections 5.4 and 5.5 where the chain linked to owner and pointer array were discussed. The programmer may use the FIND OWNER format whether *or not* there is a direct access path from the record identified in the current of set name indicator to the owner record. However, the speed with which the statement is executed certainly depends on the availability of an access path.

DBTG included a number of options which must be classed as FIND OWNER. DBTG 2 reads

FIND [OWNER IN set-name-3 OF] CURRENT OF { record-name-1 RECORD / set-name-1 SET / realm-name-1 REALM / RUN-UNIT }

In fact, the 'OWNER IN set-name-3 OF' phrase is optional and if excluded, it corresponds to several of the options in the third class defined. However, when the phrase is included as above, it provides four further options. These are somewhat complex semantically and DBLTG clearly felt that they were not of significant value because they dropped them completely. It should be noted that if set-name-3 and set-name-1 in the above DBTG 2 format are the same set type, then the option is the same as the one discussed earlier in this section.

15.5.4 FIND WITHIN SET

This option is closely associated to the out of the blue option discussed in Section 15.4.2. In fact, it is a different option of the same format (DBTG 6 and JOD 7) which reads

FIND record-name-1 VIA [CURRENT OF] set-name-1 [USING db-id-1

[, db-id-2] . . .]

and

FIND record-name-1 WITHIN set-name-1 [CURRENT] [USING db-id-1

[, db-id-2] . . .]

It should be noted that if set selection for record-name-1 in set-name-1 is based on the currency indicator, then the phrase CURRENT OF or CURRENT may be omitted and the effect is the same. However, if the set selection is based on a factor other than the currency indicator and the CURRENT phrase is included, then the latter overrides the set selection included in the schema.

When the set selection is based on the currency indicator, we here regard the FIND as being a relative one—in that it is relative to the record whose data base key value is stored in the current of set name indicator.

The role of the option USING phrase is identical to that described in Section 15.4.2. However, it is interesting to speculate on the ways in which the complete statement might be executed.

Supposing the currency indicator points again to the 250th record in a sorted set with 500 member records connected and the data base identifiers correspond to the sort key in the set type but not to any search key. The programmer initializes the values of the items to be named in the FIND format. These values, in fact, correspond to those of records 300, 301 and 302 in the set, but the programmer does not know that and neither does the system.

An intelligent system would compare the values sought with those in the record identified in the currency indicator. In this case, the values sought are higher (in terms of the sorting sequence) than those in the current record of the set. The system can then initiate its search key proceeding in the NEXT direction until it comes to record number 300 at which point it can stop.

A less intelligent system might want to start every search from the owner record, but it might involve a sequential pass through the remainder of the set to find the owner record.

In summary, we have a situation where this option is invaluable if the items used in the format correspond to a search key. In fact, this is the FIND option which makes the search key worthwhile. Its use when the item does not correspond to a search key is only slightly more than marginal.

The user of this option must think about the following factors:

1. Setting the current of set name indicator to select the required set.
2. Whether items used in format are search key, sort key or neither.
3. Whether more than one record with the same values may be connected to the set.

Regarding the third factor, the reader should remember that control over duplicates is exercised in three ways which are applicable here. The search key and the sort key are fairly obvious, but it is also possible for the data administrator to prohibit duplicate valued records in a chronological set type which does not have a search key.

The point about duplicates is that, if they may occur, then the programmer must be aware of the fact and have a way of accessing them. This leads us to the next relative FIND option.

15.5.5 FIND DUPLICATE in Set

Both DBTG and JOD provide a special format to allow the programmer to search for duplicate records in a set. This format in the JOD report *precedes* the one just discussed for some incomprehensible reason. Such presentation makes understanding rather harder, but we shall try to rectify the problem here.

The two formats used to find duplicate records in a set are DBTG 7 and JOD 3. The former reads

FIND NEXT DUPLICATE WITHIN set-name-1 using USING db-id-1 [, db-id-2] . . .

whereas JOD 3 appears as

FIND DUPLICATE WITHIN set-name-1 USING db-id-1 [, db-id-2] . . .

In both cases, the USING phrase is no longer optional as it was in the option discussed in Sections 15.4.2 and 15.5.4.

The meaning of this option relative to the previous one should be fairly obvious in the case that the items in the format identify a search key or a sort key. In each case, finding of the next duplicate value will be a fairly rapid process. In the permitted case that the items do not correspond to a search key or to the sort key, then what might happen is rather more open. JOD states:

'The DBCS begins its search for the identified record at the current record of the set type, and proceeds to search in the order defined by the set ordering criteria of that set type.'

It should be noted that this sentence, as it appears in the JOD, is independent of the kind of role played by the item named in the format. This would not make sense if the item is a search key, although it is appropriate for the other two cases.

Apart from the problem mentioned in the preceding paragraph, there is another problem which calls for some discussion. If the user goes to the trouble and expense to specify and maintain a search key index, he should be entitled to maximum advantage from it. The FIND option allows the programmer to use a search key to access a record in a selected set without accessing others in the set. Furthermore, he should then be able to access any duplicate valued records of a record just found in this way. The question arises as to what happens if an attempt to find a duplicate is unsuccessful because there is no further duplicate. The answer is a data base exception condition. However, the user may wish to go on to process the records with the next highest value to that recently found. In other words, he may want to go through the records in a set in ascending sequence of the search key item values. This may well be possible if the search key is implemented using an ISAM like index. The existing specifications make no provision for this kind of processing.

One might wish to do this kind of processing based on the location mode of CALC, but it is not allowed for there because CALC has historically become synonymous with randomizing to the exclusion of indexing. Overlooking the requirement for processing using a search key by index seems to be associated with the fact that it is not possible with a randomizing technique.

15.5.6 FIND NEXT or PRIOR in Realm

The last FIND option in the relative category is the one for very physical level processing. It is associated with the out of the blue option presented in Section 15.4.3 and is in fact a different option of the same format. The DBTG 3 syntax for the option is

$$\underline{\text{FIND}} \ \left\{ {\text{NEXT} \atop \text{PRIOR}} \right\} \ [\text{record-name-2}] \ \underline{\text{RECORD}} \ \text{OF} \ \text{realm-name-1} \ \underline{\text{REALM}}$$

whereas the JOD 4 syntax is

$$\underline{\text{FIND}} \ \left\{ {\text{NEXT} \atop \text{PRIOR}} \right\} \ [\text{record-name-2}] \ \underline{\text{WITHIN}} \ \text{realm-name-1}$$

In the case that the record-name is stated explicitly in the FIND, the record found is the one of the type named with the next highest (NEXT) or next lowest (PRIOR) data base key value to the record identified in the current of realm indicator. There is no implication that the record found must be of the same type as the one identified in the currency indicator used, although it seems that this would be what the user wants more often than not.

There are two ways a programmer might use this option. The first is as a quick and effective way of searching through all the records of a given type in a given realm. This may be necessary if the set type relationships in which the record type participates as a member are of no value for the search criterion. The programmer does not need to know any details of *how* the record type is stored in the realm, merely which record types are stored therein.

The other way is for the really 'physically involved' programmer who has an intimate knowledge and understanding of the details of the record to realm mapping as specified in the DMCL rather than in the Schema DDL. Processing the records in a realm in this way could then be done on a more selective basis.

15.6 Repeated FIND

A repeated FIND is a FIND on a record which has been found at a previous time, normally and most meaningfully in the same run-unit.

This means that the data base key value of the record has been stored in some system or programmer register. The systems registers provided for the storage of data base key values are clearly the currency indicators, although it is the system itself which must store the value in the register. There is no explicit facility provided for the programmer to set a currency indicator to a specific value, but there is a way he can achieve this.

The data administrator is allowed to define items in data base record types with an item type of data base key (see Section 9.4). The ability to define items of this type in data base records has been construed understandably as a facility to store data base key values in the data base—a practice which is to be severely criticized. In the JOD, a facility has now also been explicitly provided to define data items in the COBOL working storage section with a type of data base key.

Given either kind of user defined items with a type base key, one of the formats of the ACCEPT is provided to allow the programmer to move the content of any currency indicator into such an item.

The repeated FIND statements fall naturally into sub-classes, one based on system registers and the other on user registers. The former is essentially based on currency indicators and will henceforth be identified in these terms.

15.6.1 FIND Based on Currency Indicators

If any currency indicator contains the data key of a record in the data base, then it should be clear to the reader that that record must have been found by some previously executed FIND in the same run-unit.

The reader might ask why it should be necessary to perform a second FIND on a record which has already been found in the run-unit. The problem is that normally only one record occurrence of each type is retained in core in the record area. If the programmer predicts a frequent and significant requirement to have in core access to two or more records of the same type during the course of execution of his program, he can of course reserve working space in core and move the records into this space when first found. More often than not, the trade-off between core space and processing time is such that the programmer would prefer to retain in core the address of the record and retrieve it as and when necessary.

The DBTG 2 syntax appropriate to this option is as follows:

$$\underline{\text{FIND}} \;\; \underline{\text{CURRENT}} \;\; \text{OF} \left\{ \begin{array}{l} \text{record-name-1} \;\; \underline{\text{RECORD}} \\ \text{set-name-1} \;\; \underline{\text{SET}} \\ \text{realm-name-1} \;\; \underline{\text{REALM}} \\ \underline{\text{RUN-UNIT}} \end{array} \right\}$$

which JOD 5 modified to read

$$\underline{\text{FIND}} \;\; \underline{\text{CURRENT}} \;\; [\text{record-name}] \left[\underline{\text{WITHIN}} \left\{ \begin{array}{l} \text{set-name-1} \\ \text{realm-name-1} \end{array} \right\} \right]$$

Omitting WITHIN option is equivalent to finding the current of run-unit or else the current of record-name, so both these DBTG alternatives are catered for.

The purpose of a FIND of this class is to re-set the current of run-unit indicator to some value it had earlier in the run-unit before other more recent FIND statements caused it to change. Any successful execution of a FIND or a STORE statement will update the current of run-unit indicator; it will update the other indicators unless the programmer takes explicit action to prevent this.

In processing a network structure containing several set types, it is possible that the logic of the program may make an exploratory probe along some path in the network and then decide to return to an earlier point to pursue a different path. In this case, it is useful to be able to re-set the current of run-unit indicator to an earlier value.

The practice of suppressing the updating of other currency indicators is one which only the experienced DML programmer should attempt. In cases where such suppression does take place, the otherwise useless option

FIND CURRENT OF RUN-UNIT

is valuable to bring previously suppressed indicators up to date.

The most useful of these options is surely that based on the current of set name indicator. Those based on the current of realm and on current of record-name will not be used very much.

15.6.2 FIND Based on Data Base Key

Finally, we come to the option which both DBTG and JOD define is the first format. DBTG 1 is

$\underline{\text{FIND}}$ [record-name-1] $\underline{\text{USING}}$ identifier-1

JOD 1 is modified in order to improve readability. It is

$\underline{\text{FIND}}$ [record-name-1]; $\underline{\text{DB-KEY}}$ IS identifier-1

At one time there seems to have been some kind of understanding that this format was exclusively reserved for record types with a location mode of DIRECT. Indeed, on page 40 of the DBTG report one can read

'DIRECT. Retrieval is based on the unique identifiers assigned by the DBMS to each record occurrence in the data base. For this method to be used, the unique identifiers of the record to be selected must be made available by the run-unit to the DBMS and this must have been saved previously by the run-unit. . . . This is possible . . .'

If these sentences had been divorced completely from the location mode DIRECT, they would provide a good explanation of what is possible with Format 1 for record types with *any* of the three location modes.

If the programmer omits the reference to a record-name, he is implying that he either does not know or does not care what the record type is. As indicated in Section 15.5.1, he should in such circumstances program in a test to determine the record type. As an added word of discouragement to the practice of omitting the record-name from this and other formats when the practice is possible, it should be mentioned that the program becomes harder to read and understand.

The capability to remember a record which has been found at one point in the execution of a program and to find it again later is quite useful in practice and will probably rate as the third or fourth most useful FIND options. It is certainly quick to execute and the programmer need have no fear of problems caused by hidden semantics.

15.7 Data Base Exception Condition

Some of the DBECs which can occur during the execution of a FIND are quite independent of format or of options. These are the following (based on the JOD):

1. Realm not in ready mode for this run-unit.
2. Access to an erased record is specified.
3. Record type or set type not defined in the sub-schema.
   (In this case of a DBEC, it can sometimes be treated as a syntax error and sometimes as a DBEC.)
   The remaining DBECs in the JOD are option sensitive.
4. End of set or realm reached.
5. Unavailable realm requested by the DBCS.
6. No set satisfies set selection criterion.
7. No record satisfies record selection expression.
8. Current of realm, record type or set type indicator is null.
9. Current of run-unit is null.
10. Current of run-unit is not correct record type.

In the following table, each of the 11 sub-classes of FIND as presented in this chapter is tabulated with the above seven DBECs to indicate which DBEC is likely to occur with which FIND.

Section No.	Description	4	5	6	7	8	9	10
15.4	Out of the blue							
15.4.1	Calc record				Y			
15.4.2	In a set using set selection	Y	Y	Y				
15.4.3	FIRST and LAST in realm				Y			
15.5	Relative							
15.5.1	Using set type relationship	Y			Y	Y		Y
15.5.2	DUPLICATE calc				Y			
15.5.3	OWNER					Y	Y	
15.5.4	In a set using current of set				Y	Y		
15.5.5	DUPLICATE IN set	Y			Y	Y		
15.5.6	NEXT or PRIOR in realm	Y				Y		Y
15.6	Repeated							
15.6.1	Based on currency indicator					Y	Y	
15.6.2	Based on data base key				Y			Y

The above table deliberately omits DBEC 7 in cases for which it seems clear that some other more definitive DBEC will occur earlier during the execution of the FIND. The table is not taken from any CODASYL report or from the documentation on a specific implementation, but it is included here for the purpose of clarification.

15.8 Introduction to GET Statement

The GET statement complements the FIND and is invariably used immediately after it. Some implementations provide a non-standard combined statement as a supplement to the two separate.

15.8.1 GET Statement

The job of the GET statement can be defined quite simply. It causes the record identifier in the current of run-unit indicator to be transferred into the record area appropriate for its type. What may happen when a GET is executed depends on the capabilities provided and used.

The syntax of the GET statement is defined by the DBTG in two formats.

Format 1

GET [record-name]

Format 2

GET record-name; db-id-1 [, db-id-2] . . .

The JOD's one format is essentially the same, but it appears as

GET identifier-1 [, identifier-2] ...

where it allows for the fact that an identifier can be either an item name or a record name.

There are two basic options in both cases. The first acts on the whole sub-schema record type. The second acts only on the items, groups, and aggregates named in the GET statement. The former will be considered first.

15.8.2 Simple GET

When a GET (as opposed to a GET record-name) is executed, the DBCS looks first at the current of run-unit indicator to determine which record the GET applies to. In the case of all commercially available implementations, the record will be in core, but *not* in the record area. In fact, it will normally be in the system buffer which cannot be addressed by the application program.

We must now refer to the matter of schema to sub-schema record level conversion discussed in Section 12.6.1. If the schema record type contains say 31 items and the corresponding sub-schema record type contains only 23 items, then the record area for this record type has space only for the 23 items and, during the course of execution of the GET, the 8 items which are invisible to the application program must be stripped away.

Furthermore, any aggregate level or item level conversion must also be performed (see Sections 12.6.2 and 12.6.3). For most commercially available systems, that is just about the full story. However, if one takes into account some of the more esoteric features discussed in Chapters 9 and 10, then the execution of a GET statement could become a very time consuming process.

Examples of such features are

1. Virtual source item (see Section 9.7)
2. Virtual result item (see Section 10.6.2)
3. Decoding clause (see Section 10.6.3)

not to mention the more obvious ON clause which can be defined for any DML statement type and invoked each time statement of that type is executed.

The reader may remember that a VIRTUAL SOURCE item value is not stored in the record as it is stored in the data base, but it is 'materialized' from the owner record during the course of execution of a GET statement on a record of this type. Looking behind the scenes, this means that the DBCS has to access the owner record. Hopefully, the set type named in the schema declaration of the virtual item does have a link to owner, although there is no rule to say that it should have.

The effect is that, if the sub-schema record type contains virtual source items (or for that matter, virtual result items), execution of the GET will be more time consuming than a straight forward in-core MOVE.

When the simple GET is on its own (not GET record-name), it implies that the programmer does not know (or possibly does not care) which type of record the record identified in the current of run-unit indicator belongs to. The GET will be executed and the contents of one record area changed. It is then up to the programmer to find out which. This approach is consistent with the FIND RECORD options presented in Sections 15.4.3, 15.5.1 and 15.5.6 where the result of a successfully executed FIND can set the current of run-unit indicator to a record of some unknown type—although clearly one of those in the sub-schema.

15.8.3 GET Record-name

If the program in fact makes use of these FIND options, then one way the programmer can ascertain which type of record has been found is to use a series of GET record-name statements. This assumes that there is not a large number of record types that a given record could possibly belong to. The point is that when a record-name is included in the GET statement, the record type of the current of run-unit must be of that record type, otherwise a data base exception condition arises. Hence, the programmer can write GET record-name statements in his program, each followed by a test to see if the exception condition occurred.

15.8.4 GET Items

When the programmer references specific items in the record type, then only the values of those items, groups and aggregates are moved into the record area. The reader might wonder what happens to the values of other items in the record area which are not referenced in the GET. DBTG said that they are set to null. JOD states that they are unchanged. Both approaches could be encountered in practice.

15.8.5 Data Base Exception Conditions

There is a further difference between DBTG and JOD in terms of the kind of data base exception conditions which can occur, and in this case the DBTG's ideas seem more reasonable. However, we shall continue the practice of listing the possible conditions in a way which is independent of each specific report.

The inclusion of a virtual item among the items processed by the GET adds somewhat to the list of possible conditions, so this situation is considered separately. The following conditions are independent of virtual items.

1. Currency indicator is null.
2. Access to an erased record involved (this means the record will have been deleted by some concurrently executing run-unit *after* the FIND in the subject run-unit sets its current of run-unit indicator).
3. Current record of run-unit does not correspond to record type in GET statement (this condition is the one discussed in Section 15.8.3).
4. Conversion of item value not possible (possibly standard conversion, possibly a DECODING procedure).

If virtual items are referenced in the GET statement, the following conditions can occur.

5. Record containing source item (i.e. owner record) is in realm which has not been readied.
6. Current of run-unit not connected to any set of type named in virtual source declaration.

15.9 Relation Between FIND and GET

The fact that the FIND and the GET are separate statements frequently causes concern to those who are used to systems such as ISAM where the content of a record is available for processing as soon as the record has been retrieved from the file. DBTG's deliberate separation of the two follows the practice of IDS. The agrument in favour of the separation is that it is quite frequently useful to be able to execute a FIND simply by establishing the presence of a record in the data base without following the FIND with a GET. If the DBMS, in fact, supports some of the potentially time consuming things that might happen during the course of execution of the GET, then the case for the separation is strengthened.

However, quite a few implementations have provided the option of a combined FIND and GET, called either FETCH or OBTAIN. This option is supplementary to the separate FIND and GET. Typically, it is the GET format which involves the whole sub-schema record type which is combined with the FIND.

Chapter 16

DML Updating Statements

16.1 Introduction

Having now gone through the FIND and GET statements at considerable length, we can move to the DML updating statements, which collectively are less complex than the FIND. It must be remembered that the FIND is the navigation statement. Its principal role is to update the current of run-unit indicator so that other DML statements can perform various actions on the record identified in the indicator. GET, MODIFY and ERASE all have one feature in common. They act on the record identified in the current of run-unit indicator. STORE acts on the record image in the record area for the record type named, and in that way STORE differs. There are certain rules which apply to all updating statements. It would be rather tedious to repeat them for each statement. In short, the realm or realms affected must have been successfully readied for update (see Section 14.2.1) before the updating statement can be executed. This applies not only to the realm to which records of the type named in the statement have been assigned (see Section 4.8), but also to any realms indirectly affected. Such realms might contain record types named in a hierarchical set selection criterion (see Section 8.6) or record types which are 'below' the record type named in the update statement.

We will consider each updating statement in turn in the order MODIFY, ERASE, STORE, CONNECT and DISCONNECT.

16.2 MODIFY Statement

A MODIFY statement has the effect of replacing the record identified in the current of run-unit indicator by the record stored in the record area. As in the case of the GET statement, it may reference the whole record or else some of the items. The DBTG's two formats for MODIFY are

Format 1

MODIFY [record-name] [USING db-id-1 [, db-id-2] ...]

Format 2

MODIFY record-name; db-id-3 [, db-id-4] ...

[USING db-id-5 [, db-id-6] ...]

The optional USING clause in the above formats is intended to allow for the situation where the programmer wishes to change the set to which the current record of run-unit is connected.

It is not clear when the option is of use to modify the current of run-unit under circumstances such that the record name may be omitted. Normally the MODIFY will include the record name. Occasionally it may be useful to use Format 2 to change certain items. If items are not named when Format 2 is used, then the values of these items in the data base are not changed.

The COBOL JOD proposes a modified form for the MODIFY statement, again with two formats.

Format 1

$$\text{MODIFY [record-name]} \left[\left\{ \begin{matrix} \text{INCLUDING} \\ \text{ONLY} \end{matrix} \right\} \left\{ \begin{matrix} \text{ALL} \\ \{\text{set-name-1}\} \dots \end{matrix} \right\} \text{MEMBERSHIP} \right]$$

Format 2

$$\text{MODIFY } \{\text{identifier-1}\} \dots \left[\text{INCLUDING} \left\{ \begin{matrix} \text{ALL} \\ \{\text{set-name-1}\} \dots \end{matrix} \right\} \text{MEMBERSHIP} \right]$$

Together, these two formats are more complete than those of the DBTG, so we will use them in the exposition which follows.

The purpose of this MODIFY statement is explicitly either to alter the values of one or more data items in a record, or to disconnect a record from one set and connect it into another, or both.

With both formats, the exclusion of the option in the square brackets implies that the sole purpose of the MODIFY is to alter the item values.

It must be noted that altering a record in the data base is a three stage process, as follows:

1. Retrieve the record to be modified from the data base.
2. Modify the item values in the record area using MOVE statements.
3. Replace the record in the data base with the modified image of that record which is in the record area.

The MODIFY statement is used *only* in the last of these three stages.

If an INCLUDING or an ONLY phase is included in the statement, then this means that the record on which the statement acts (namely that identified in the current of run-unit indicator) is to be disconnected from one set and connected into another. Since a record type can be a member in one or more set types, it is necessary to be able to specify the set types to which the statement applies with ALL being an obvious shorthand for all such set types.

It is necessary for the programmer to take into consideration the set selection criterion for each set type named explicitly or implied by the use of ALL. The set selection criterion may have been given in the Schema DDL (see Chapter 8) or in the Sub-schema DDL (see Section 12.12.3). It should be recalled that taking into consideration the set selection criterion at program preparation time implies one of the following for *each* set type involved.

1. Ensuring that the current of set name indicator is set.
2. Storing a data base key value in the item designated in the set selection clause.
3. Initializing items designated in the set selection clause with the values of the record type's CALC key.
4. Initializing a hierarchical path as designated in the set selection clause.

In Format 1, the difference between ONLY and INCLUDING is that ONLY means that set participation only is modified, that is to say, the values in the record in the data base are not changed. Presumably, in this case the content of the record area is irrelevant. Use of the INCLUDING option means that both the record and one or more of its set participation change.

Format 2 names one or more items or group items in the record and clearly, ONLY has no meaning in this context.

16.2.1 Possible Complications in a MODIFY

Complications can occur with a MODIFY if an item whose value is modified plays some specific role for the record type in the data base. Examples of such roles are

1. Calc key
2. Sort key (range key)
3. Search key

One may encounter implementations where it is not allowed to modify the value of calc key items. This means that the program must erase the record and store it again in its new form if it is desired to make such a change.

If the value of a sort key item is changed, then the position where the record is connected in the set has to be adjusted by the system.

If the value of a search key item is changed, then the search key index has to be updated accordingly.

In case of calc keys, sort keys, and search keys, any restrictions on duplicate values most not be contravened as a result of the MODIFY.

16.2.2 Data Base Exception Conditions

The DBECs which may be encountered in practice are the following:

1. Current of run-unit null.
2. Object record has been altered by a concurrent run-unit.
3. Current of run-unit record type does not correspond to type in statement.
4. New item causes duplicate calc key, sort key or search key values.
5. New item value of wrong type.
6. New item value does not satisfy CHECK clause.
7. Realm not readied for update (i.e. realm not available).
8. Space in realm exhausted.

In the case of changing from one set to another, the following may also be encountered:

9. No set satisfying set selection criterion.
10. Owner of set in realm not readied for update.
11. Owner of set is not included in sub-schema.
12. Change of set participation implied.

16.3 ERASE Statement

DBTG used the word DELETE in the statement used to wipe out a record from the data base. DELETE is in fact widely used in this context in DBTG based and non-DBTG based data base management systems. DBLTG decided to use ERASE rather than DELETE in the COBOL JOD because DELETE is a word which is already used in COBOL to remove a record from a mass storage file.

Both DBTG and JOD identify four options: one work horse, one of occasional value, and two semantically complex options which hopefully will disappear in the course of time.

DBTG identified their options as

$$\text{DELETE} \ [\text{record-name}] \ \begin{bmatrix} \text{ONLY} \\ \text{SELECTIVE} \\ \text{ALL} \end{bmatrix}$$

whereas in the same sequence, the JOD options are

$$\text{ERASE} \ [\text{record-name}] \ \begin{bmatrix} \text{PERMANENT} \\ \text{SELECTIVE} \\ \text{ALL} \end{bmatrix} \ \text{MEMBERS}$$

As indicated earlier, the ERASE operates on the record identified in the current of run-unit indicator. If record-name is included in the ERASE statement, then the type of the current of run-unit record must be that of record-name. If the record-name is omitted, then it does not matter.

In all the ERASE options, if the statement is successfully executed, the current of run-unit indicator is set to null—but not the others.

16.3.1 Simple ERASE

A simple ERASE, without any of the three option words appended, is the most useful. It causes the current of run-unit to 'disappear' from the data base if, and only if, it is not the owner of a non-empty set. If it is the owner of a non-empty set, then the record is not erased and a DBEC occurs.

When we discussed the chain linked to next in Section 5.5 and the chain linked to next and prior in Section 5.6, we indicated what can happen when a record is erased. The reader is encouraged to refer to these sections again.

16.3.2 ERASE ALL

The ERASE ALL is the option felt to be of occasional value. However, the programmer using it must know exactly what he is doing. If this statement is executed against the wrong record, half the data base could be wiped out.

ERASE ALL deletes the current of run-unit whether or not it is the owner in a non-empty set. Indeed, if it is the owner in a non-empty set, this option really comes into its own. All the members connected to the set are also erased. If any of these members happens to be connected to some other set of another type, this does not matter. Furthermore, if any of these members happens to be themselves an owner in a non-empty set, then their members in turn are erased—and so on down the hierarchy.

Each record affected by this vacuum cleaner action must be in a realm which has been readied for update. If any are not, the none is erased. This poses problems for the implementor because he more or less has to do a test pass through the hierarchy to ensure that it is all right to erase and then do a proper action pass actually performing the erase. It should be noted that if a record is to be erased is connected to a set of name type otherwise not affected by the ERASE ALL, the set must nevertheless be completely contained in realms which are both included in the sub-schema and furthermore have been readied for update. This is expecially important with multi-member set types.

16.3.3 ERASE PERMANENT

The two options described so far are reasonably straightforward semantically. The other two depend on the Removal Class which was discussed in Section 7.3. The reader may remember that each member in a set type must have a Removal Class of either permanent or transient. (DBTG used mandatory and optional respectively). It is in the execution of the ERASE PERMANENT that the Removal Class is taken into account.

The current of run-unit is erased as in the other options. If it is the owner in a non-empty set, then what happens to the connected member records depends on the Removal Class. Permanent records are erased; transient records are merely disconnected from the set and are left in the data base. It sound odd to say 'permanent records are erased', but it is the linkage which is permanent—not the record.

16.3.4 ERASE SELECTIVE

This option is essentially the same as ERASE PERMANENT with a difference in the way a record is treated if it is a transient member in the set whose owner is being erased. If the record is connected to some other set (necessarily of a different type), then it is not erased. If it is connected to any other set, then it is erased.

16.3.5 Data Base Exception Conditions

In presenting the data base exception conditions, we will continue the practice of giving the more likely conditions first followed by those which could occur only with the last three alternatives.

1. Current of run-unit is null.
2. Record type of current of run-unit not the same as that in statement.
3. Realm not readied for update.
4. Current of run-unit already erased by concurrent run-unit.

If the options which affect more than one record are used, then the following:

5. Record to be erased or disconnected is in a realm not readied for update.
6. Owner of record to be erased or disconnected is in a realm not readied for update.

16.4 STORE Statement

The STORE statement looks simple. In both DBTG and JOD it reads

<u>STORE</u> record-name [   ]

where the square brackets contain the same kind of syntax for suppressing the updating of currency indicators as is associated with the general format of the FIND statement.

The programmer builds up a record image in the record are in core. He then takes care of a few preliminaries and executes a STORE statement which causes the record to be stored in the data base. Most of the declarations made in the schema are tested during the course of execution of the STORE. This list includes the following:

1. WITHIN to determine which realms.
2. REALM-ID to determine which realm if more than one for record type.
3. LOCATION MODE to determine how within the realm.
4. Set type declaration to determine whether to create new sets.
5. Set type declaration storage class to determine whether to connect record into existing sets.
6. Set selection criteria to determine basis for selecting sets in which to connect record.
7. Set orders to determine where in each set record is to be connected.
8. Search keys to determine whether to update the index.

In addition, the various 'duplicates allowed' clauses on the values of calc keys, sort keys and search keys must be examined to see whether a 'duplicates not allowed' restriction may be violated.

Finally, if one of the set selection criteria requires it, the current of set name indicator is examined to determine which set of a given type the record is to be connected to.

The foregoing hopefully gives the reader an indication of the activity which can take place during the course of execution of a STORE. It could perhaps be mentioned here that some implementations provide device media control languages which do more than determine the device media to which a realm is assigned. They provide in addition for detailed control of the way records are stored in realms and possibly within the pages in a realm. Any such declarations are also taken into account by the system during the STORE, but normally this does not mean that the programmer has anything extra to take into account.

We will consider the effect of the various major factors in turn.

16.4.1 Effect of WITHIN Clause on STORE

If the data administrator's schema assigns all records of this type to one realm, then the programmer only has to ensure that the realm is readied for update prior to the execution of the STORE. However, if the data administrator decided to allocate several realms to the records of the type being stored (see Section 4.8.1), then the programmer must initialize the data items named in the REALM-ID clause to contain the name of the realm he prefers for the individual record being stored. He must, of course, take care that the realm has been readied for update.

16.4.2 Effect of LOCATION MODE

The programmer must always be aware of the location mode of the record he is storing. He may or may not be required to take some action depending on the location mode.

If the location mode is CALC, he must take care that the calc key items are correctly set in the record area. If duplicate values of the calc key are not allowed, he must be prepared to test for a DBEC which says that the key values of the record are the same as for a record already in the data base. On the positive side, the programmer should normally have no concern with the detailed aspects of the CALC algorithm—such as whether it is randomizing or indexed.

If the location mode is VIA SET, the programmer must make sure that the set selection algorithm is initialized. He may have to do this for other sets anyway if the record type is an automatic member in set type—irrespective of the location mode of the record type.

If the record type has a location mode of DIRECT, there is an item of type data base key (not necessarily in the record type) which he must initialize either with a null or with a valid data base key value (see Section 4.6.3). In the latter case, he may have retained the value from a record erased earlier in the program. Alternatively, he may have the knowledge to build up his own data base key values, a powerful idea but only for those who really know what they are doing, and probably not the intention of the DBTG. The safest alternative for the programmer is to initialize with a null value. This means that the system stores the record in a location which is convenient to the system. Since the system has no good reason to think ahead to retrieval, one can safely assume the STORE is executed as quickly as possible. This use of location mode DIRECT should be the same as location mode SYSTEM.

16.4.3 Effect of Set Type and Storage Class Declarations

The type corresponding to the record being stored can participate in an arbitrary number of set types either as owner or member. For each set type in which it participates as an owner, the system has to establish a new set occurrence. This is not necessarily a time consuming process.

For each set type in which the record type participates as a member, the system has to check the storage class. If the storage class is manual, then no further action is called for. In the case of each set type for which the storage class is automatic, the record being stored has to be connected into a selected occurrence. Which set occurrence and where are tasks which depend on other factors.

16.4.4 Effect of Set Selection

The set selection criterion (see Chapter 8) must be tested for each set type in which the subject record type is an automatic member. The following discussion applies to *each* such set type.

If set selection is based on the current of set name indicator, then set selection is a very rapid process. However, the programmer must have been careful to ensure that the indicator is set as it should be prior to the execution of the STORE.

If set selection is based on the location mode of the owner, then the programmer must have initialized the set selection items on which an implicit CALC based FIND (see Section 15.4.1) of an owner record is executed.

If the set selection criterion is the one we classed as hierarchical (see Section 8.6), then the programmer must initialize the whole path from the entry point down to the owner record in the set—a distasteful and error-prone business which is better avoided. Unfortunately, if the data administrator has chosen this option, the programmer using the STORE statement must live with it. This is not the case when using the FIND option which invokes the set selection criterion (see Section 15.4.2). In that case, the programmer can override it (see Section 15.5.4).

16.4.5 Effect of Set Order

For each automatic set type, the system has to connect the record being stored into a selected set occurrence. One of the most potentially time consuming parts of the STORE is the task for the system of finding where.

As discussed in Chapter 6, set order is one of the more complex of the schema declarations, in that there are so many different options which have such an impact on the execution time trade-offs.

Fortunately, the programmer does not need to get very involved with set order. Most of the time, there is no action called for at all prior to execution of the STORE. However, there are a few factors he may have to take into consideration.

In Section 6.2.2 we pointed out that set order was either a data administrator decision or a programmer decision. If the data administrator chooses to delegate the problem of set order, then the programmer is necessarily involved. However, the two programmer options mean that the record is connected into the set adjacent to the current of set name indicator. It should be noted that there would not be much sense with these set order options on basing set selection on anything other than the same currency indicator, although such folly is condoned.

The programmer options, INSERTION NEXT and INSERTION PRIOR (see Section 6.4.2), are such that the programmer can often ignore them to the same extent as he has to ignore the data administrator options. If he wishes to take advantage of the capability delegated to him to achieve some very special set order, then he must ensure that the current of set name indicator is adjusted to point to the appropriate record in the set so that the connection is made where he wishes it to be made.

One factor related to set order of which the programmer must be aware is the possibility of prohibited duplicates. According to the DBTG and the DDLC, this is a two-edged sword. The data administrator may prohibit duplicate values of the sort key in any of the sorted set types (see Section 6.7), and this option is frequently provided in commercially available systems, although it would not be used a lot. DBTG (page 131) and DDLC (page 3.70) also allow the data administrator to prohibit for a set type (sorted or chronological) duplicate values of certain items in a member record type. Such items need not be sort keys. This option will not be widely encountered in practice.

The programmer must be aware if duplicate values of any item (sort key or otherwise) are prohibited, because this creates a possible DBEC which he must test for after each STORE statement.

16.4.6 Effect of Search Key

It was pointed out in Section 6.10.3 that the search key is provided to facilitate retrieval, whereas an index for a sorted set is specified to facilitate update. That section also included a suggestion that these two be merged for the good of both.

As the specifications stand, the programmer does not need to be aware of an index at all. He does need to be aware of a search key only to the extent that yet again duplicate values of the search key item may be prohibited and he would need to take appropriate action if the DBEC arose, because of an attempt to connect a record into a set during the course of a STORE.

16.4.7 Effect of Set Mode

Set mode was a fairly fundamental factor in the DBTG report, as discussed in Chapter 5. As noted there, the DDLC removed the set mode clause from the Schema DDL ostensibly because the programmer did not need to know about the set mode. As far as can be ascertained, it does not help the programmer writing programs which use the STORE statement to know what the set mode is for a given set type. Hence, he can ignore it completely.

16.4.8 Data Base Exception Conditions

There are probably more DBECs possible during a STORE than during any other statement. In order to get an overview, we will break them down into three classes, preliminary, set selection and connection. Those in the third class are the same as those which might be encountered during the course of executing a CONNECT to be discussed later in this chapter.

The following DBECs may occur during the early phases of the STORE execution.

1. Realm not readied for update.
2. No space available in realm.
3. Calc key values null.
4. Calc key values contravene duplicates not allowed declaration.
5. User supplied data base key value already in use.
6. User supplied data base key value invalid.
7. Values of other items in the record are of wrong type.
8. Values of the items in the record are invalid with respect to a CHECK clause.

The following DBECs could occur during set selection either because the record type has a location mode of VIA SET or because it has to be connected into a set in which the record type is an automatic member.

9. No set satisfies set selection criterion.
10. Current of set name indicator is null when needed for set selection.
11. Owner record of set is in a realm not readied for update.
12. Hierarchical set selection criterion causes access to record type or set type not in sub-schema.
13. Hierarchical set selection criterion causes access to record in a realm not readied for update.

The following DBECs could occur during the course of connecting the record into a set (otherwise satisfactorily selected) in which the record type is an automatic member.

14. Sort key item values in record conflict with duplicates not allowed declaration.
15. Other item values in record conflict with duplicates not allowed rule.
16. Some record in the set is not the sub-schema.

17. Some record in the set is in a realm which has not been readied for update.
18. Current of set name indicator is null when needed to determine connection point.
19. Record is already connected to the set selected.
20. Set members cannot be stored in both permanent and temporary realms.
21. Search key item values in record conflict with duplicates not allowed declaration.

16.5 CONNECT Statement

Having just discussed the STORE statement, the CONNECT can be clearly identified as part of it. A CONNECT acts on a record which is already in the data base, and exactly which record is affected is determined by the setting of the current of run-unit indicator.

Execution of the statement causes the record to be linked into an occurrence of each set type named in the statement. Which set of each type is chosen, in the case of CONNECT, is determined exclusively by the setting of the appropriate current of set name indicator.

The meaning of DBLTG's syntax is fairly obvious

$$\underline{\text{CONNECT}} \ [\text{record-name}] \ \text{TO} \ \begin{Bmatrix} \text{set-name-1} \ [, \ \text{set-name-2}] \dots \\ \underline{\text{ALL}} \end{Bmatrix}$$

The option to include the name of the record type follows the practice already discussed in the case of FIND and GET, and the DBEC which can occur is the only one possible during a CONNECT but not during a STORE. Otherwise, the DBECs possible are those listed for STORE as numbers 14 to 21.

The effect of certain schema declared factors is identical to what happens during the course of a STORE. The specific factors of importance during a CONNECT are

1. Set Order (see Section 16.4.5)
2. Search key (see Section 16.4.6)

One further DBEC is peculiar to the CONNECT, and that is an attempt to connect a record into a set occurrence into which it is already connected. This cannot happen during a STORE since the record being considered in that case is 'brand new'.

One important effect of a successful CONNECT is that the current of set name indicator for each set type in the statement is updated to point to the current of run-unit.

16.5.1 Data Base Exception Conditions

The following DBECs may occur during the execution of a CONNECT. The first group includes only conditions which may occur prior to set selection.

1. Current of run-unit null.
2. Current of run-unit has been erased by a concurrently executing run-unit.
3. Current of run-unit record type does not correspond to type in statement.
4. Realm not readied for update.

The second group of DBECs may occur during the set selection process (for each set type named in the statement).

5. Current of set name null.
6. Owner of selected set in realm not readied for update.
7. Owner of selected set not included in sub-schema.

The final group of conditions may occur during the connection process (for each set type named in the statement).

8. Record is already connected to selected set.
9. Sort key items in record conflict with duplicates not allowed declaration.
10. Other items in record conflict with duplicates not allowed rule.
11. Record already in set is not in sub-schema.
12. Record already in set is in a realm not readied for update.
13. Set numbers may not be stored in both permanent and temporary realms.
14. Search key items in conflict with duplicates not allowed declaration.

16.6 DISCONNECT Statement

A DISCONNECT follows the CONNECT by acting on the current record of run-unit and allowing the possibility to disconnect from several sets in one statement, each selected by means of the current of set name indicator.

The DBLTG's syntax reads

$$\underline{\text{DISCONNECT}} \text{ [record-name] } \underline{\text{FROM}} \left\{ \begin{array}{l} \text{set-name-1 [, set-name-2]} \dots \\ \underline{\text{ALL}} \end{array} \right\}$$

If the record identified by the current of run-unit indicator is indeed linked into a selected set of a type referred to in the statement, then the effect of the DISCONNECT is to unlink it. The record remains in the data base, but it cannot be accessed by means of the set type relationship in which its record type participates.

Unlike a CONNECT, successful execution of a DISCONNECT does not affect any of the currency indicators. This could cause problems. If the current of set name indicator happens to be the same as the current of run-unit, then after the current of run-unit has been disconnected the setting of the current of set name indicator for the set type just affected will point to a record not connected to any set.

16.6.1 Data Base Exception Conditions

The following DBECs may occur during the execution of a DISCONNECT. The first group includes only conditions which are prior to set selection.

1. Current of run-unit null.
2. Current of run-unit has been erased by a concurrently executing run-unit.
3. Current of run-unit record type does not correspond to type in statement.
4. Realm not readied for update.

The second group of conditions can occur during the set selection process (for each set type named in statement).

5. Current of set name null.
6. Owner of selected set in realm not readied for update.
7. Owner of selected set not included in sub-schema.

The final group of conditions occur during the disconnection process (from a set of each type referred to in the statement).

8. Current of run-unit is not connected to the selected set.

Chapter 17

Other DML Statements

17.1 Introduction

This chapter is the final one on the subject of the DML statements and it covers all those not yet covered. They represent a rather miscellaneous collection and will be grouped together into classes and treated as follows:

Concurrency control	KEEP, FREE, REMONITOR
Set level	ORDER
Moving from systems location	ACCEPT
Conditional	IF
Exception conditions checking	USE

After we have reviewed these six statements, we shall have completed the presentation of the DML.

17.2 Concurrency Control

It is frequently asserted that the application programmer should not need to know about the kind of environment in which his program will be executed. DBTG and subsequently JOD took the point of view that he should know, especially if his program is to execute in an environment in which one or more run-units (including the one under consideration) are updating records.

The concurrency problems in a multi-programming environment where all run-units are retrieving are no different from those in a uni-programming batch environment. However, as soon as we allow one run-unit to be an updating run-unit, then problems arise. It must be noted that the CODASYL approach does not allow explicitly for the concept of a retrieving run-unit or an updating run-unit. Nevertheless, the meaning of these terms in a CODASYL context is hopefully unambiguous.

The DBTG introduced two statement types for use by programmers writing update programs. These are the KEEP and FREE. JOD later added the REMONITOR statement and we will look at each of these in turn.

17.2.1 KEEP Statement

In the DBTG report (page 237), the function of the KEEP statement was given simply as 'to advise the DBMS (i.e. DBCS) of the run-unit's intention to re-access the object record occurrence.'

In other words, the programmer is provided with a means of explicitly signifying his intent to 're-access' a record. Normally, such a re-access would be in the form of one of the update statements such as MODIFY, ERASE, CONNECT or DISCONNECT. By catering for the situation where one record may be processed two or more times during the execution of a run-unit, the programmer is allowed to make sure that the record is not changed by some concurrently updating run-unit between its own two retrievals.

The KEEP statement acts on the record which is identified in the current of run-unit indicator at the time of execution of the KEEP. It is important to note that there is an implicit KEEP in effect for a record during the time that it is in the current of run-unit.

The important rule governing the effect of the KEEP is phrased by the DBTG (page 237, Rule 5) in the following terms:

'While a KEEP statement which has been executed by the current run-unit on a record occurrence is still in effect, any attempt by that current run-unit to alter that record will be successful only if no concurrent run-unit has altered the record since the KEEP statement was executed.'

Essentially, the DBTG is proposing a system of warning the programmer (by means of a data base exception condition) that the record may have been altered by some other run-unit between the time that the run-unit under consideration executes the KEEP and the time it tries to execute its updating statement.

This approach was later modified and in order to appreciate the ideas in the COBOL JOD, it is necessary to understand what is meant by the monitored mode and extended monitored mode.

The essence of the modification is to introduce three states for a record with respect to a run-unit instead of the DBTG's two states. The states are as follows:

Normal
Monitored mode
Extended monitored mode

A record moves from normal mode to monitored mode automatically when it becomes the current of run-unit. The effect of executing a JOD KEEP is to change the state of the record from monitored mode to extended monitored mode. (The DBTG specification made no difference between these two states.)

An important aspect of the monitored and extended monitored mode is that only one record can be in monitored mode at any point in time, but several can be in extended monitored mode.

However, apart from introducing these two states for a record and the terminology to describe them, the JOD thinking follows that of DBTG. In other words, when the subject run-unit attempts an update of a record which is in one of these two states, then a data base exception condition may arise if a concurrently executing run-unit has updated the record since the most recent establishment of monitored mode or extended monitored mode for that record.

17.2.2 FREE Statement

The FREE statement is intended to cancel the effects of the KEEP. However, since it will often be useful to free several records in one statement execution, there are a number of formats, proposed. DBTG and JOD differ in the option provided.

DBTG proposes two formats as follows:

FREE
FREE ALL

The simple FREE statement acts on the current of run-unit which means that the programmer's logic would often have to find a record before it can be freed.

FREE ALL has the fairly obvious meaning of freeing all records to which an *explicit* KEEP applies. This is clearly meant to exclude the current of run-unit.

JOD takes away the simple FREE option and replaces it with a more useful

$$\text{FREE} \left\{ \begin{array}{l} \text{ALL} \\ \text{record-name-1 [, record-name-2] ...} \end{array} \right\}$$

This statement has the effect of selecting all records of the types named which are in extended monitored mode and returning them to normal state with respect to the run-unit. As in the case of FREE ALL, the current record of the run-unit is not affected.

With both DBLTG FREE options it must be possible to free all the records selected, otherwise none is freed. However, the specifications are strangely silent on the question of what kind of situations would make it impossible to free all the selected records and, furthermore, no data base exception condition is identified to identify what has happened to the executing program.

17.2.3 REMONITOR Statement

The REMONITOR statement was added to the DBTG's list of DML statements in the JOD. Its function (see page III–12–42) is as follows:

'The REMONITOR statement causes a monitored mode or extended monitored mode to be ended, followed immediately by the establishment of a new monitored mode or extended monitored mode for the same record.'

The general format of this statement is

$$\text{REMONITOR} \left[\begin{array}{l} \text{ALL} \\ \text{record-name-1 [, record-name-2] ...} \end{array} \right]$$

This implies three alternatives corresponding to the combined set of selection options in the DBTG and JOD FREE options. The simple REMONITOR acts on the current record of the run-unit. The REMONITOR ALL and REMONITOR record-name-1 act on all records of all types or on all records of the named types. In both cases, the current of run-unit is excluded.

The real purpose of this REMONITOR statement is not made clear. It does not affect the state of any record which is selected (or any record which is not selected). It is not clear when it would be necessary or even desirable to use this statement.

17.2.4 Summary of Concurrent Processing Statements

The DBTG and JOD proposals for allowing the programmer to control the interaction of his program's run-units with other run-units have not found favour among implementors. This is not surprising. The approach is based on placing records into a state (monitored mode) such that any change made to that record by another run-unit can be detected by means of testing for an exception condition next time the record is processed. The ideas would be clumsy for the programmer to use and the risk of errors because of conditions not being checked for is high.

It is interesting to note that Univac's DMS 1100 does provide statements called KEEP and FREE, but these are semantically different from those proposed by CODASYL. For one thing, the programmer needs to be aware that records are stored in pages where a realm comprises a number of equal sized pages. In effect, a KEEP on the current of run-unit is a way of advising the DBCS of the run-unit's intention to re-access (normally update) the current of run-unit. It makes sure that no other run-unit can access the record in any way by locking the page in which the record is stored.

It is noted that use of KEEP is unnecessary if the realm has been readied with a usage mode of EXCLUSIVE or PROTECTED (see Section 14.2.1). The Univac approach can cause some slight slow-down, but it is far safer than that proposed by CODASYL.

17.3 Set Level Statement

The only statement which acts on a whole set is the ORDER statement. It has not been implemented as far as can be ascertained, but nevertheless, it is an important concept and merits some attention.

The ORDER statement must be thought of in the same light as the COBOL SORT verb, the difference being that SORT acts on a file, whereas ORDER acts on a single occurrence of a named set type. The reason why implementors have avoided ORDER is surely that the programmer can achieve the desired effect with a SORT statement.

There have been some relatively minor changes in syntax and semantics from the DBTG's 1971 ideas to the JOD 1976 thinking. To avoid confusing the issue on a facility not widely encountered, we will restrict consideration here to the more recent proposals.

The complete syntax reads as follows (see page III–12–37):

$$\underline{\text{ORDER}} \text{ set-name } [\underline{\text{LOCALLY}}] \left\{ \text{ON} \left\{ \begin{array}{l} \underline{\text{DESCENDING}} \\ \underline{\text{ASCENDING}} \end{array} \right\} \text{KEY} \right.$$

$$\left. \left\{ \begin{array}{l} [\text{record-name-1}] \dots \underline{\text{RECORD-NAME}} \\ [\text{record-name-1}] \dots \underline{\text{DB-KEY}} \\ [\text{data-name-1}] \dots \end{array} \right\} \dots \right\} \dots$$

The effect of executing an ORDER statement is to select a set of the named set type, using the current of set name indicator and to order the member records connected to that set in some way. Use or omission of the word LOCALLY determines whether the ordering which is established is valid only for the lifetime of the run-unit or not.

If the named set type is sorted (see Section 6.3), then it is clear that the LOCALLY option must be used. The reason for this is that it would not be meaningful to allow the data administrator's declared set order to be changed from the programmer's program. However, if the programmer wants a set of a given type to be logically sequenced in some way in order to optimize some processing to be performed later in his own program, then that is acceptable.

If the named set type is chronological (see Section 6.4) or the set order has been declared as immaterial (see Section 6.5), then it is reasonable for the programmer to specify an order for a set of that type such that subsequently executing retrieval programs can take advantage of the order. However, any updating program, including the one containing the ORDER statement, will connect records into the resequenced set according to the criteria established in the Schema DDL and *not* according to the order declared in the ORDER statemement.

The large ON clause which appears in the format for the ORDER statement allows the programmer to specify sort keys with the same degree of flexibility as for sorted types in the SET ORDER clause (see Sections 6.3 and 6.7). As in the Schema DDL, multi-member set types introduce a complicating factor which the user would be prudent to avoid. Apart from that, a sort key may be any of the following three:

1. A record name.
2. A data base key for records of a named type.
3. A data item.

Use of a record name would not be meaningful in a single member set type. Use of data base keys as sort keys is felt to be of very marginal value. In the case of multi-member set types, it could be meaningful to be able to qualify an item name with a record name.

An examination of the JOD syntax shows that it goes a step further than DBTG by allowing the programmer to mix sort keys from any of the above three classes of key. Whether this facility will ever be implemented let alone used is another question.

17.4 Moving from System Location

It is sometimes necessary when writing a COBOL/DML program to be able to copy a quantity such as a data base key value into a location declared in the program. DBTG recognized this need and proposed extensions to the existing COBOL MOVE statement.

The MOVE in COBOL is intended for transferring data item values from one programmer declared area in core to another possibly at the same time making a format transformation. In the COBOL JOD, quite appropriately, which is more consistent with the philosophy of COBOL, ACCEPT is used rather than the MOVE. ACCEPT in COBOL is previously intended for transforming data from system locations such as the date and the time.

17.4.1 ACCEPT CURRENCY

The two data base quantities which one can transfer using an ACCEPT are currency indicators and realm-names. The format for the first of these is

$$
\underline{\text{ACCEPT}} \ \text{identifier-1} \ \underline{\text{FROM}} \ \begin{bmatrix} \text{record-name} \\ \text{set-name} \\ \text{realm-name} \end{bmatrix} \ \underline{\text{CURRENCY}}
$$

Since the value being stored in the data item identifier-1 has the format of a data base key, it is necessary for identifier-1 to be declared in the Sub-schema DDL as having a type of DB-KEY (see Section 12.12.2). It should be noted that it would be useful to allow items of type DB-KEY to be declared in the working storage section (as already discussed in Section 12.12.2).

If no record-name, set-name, or realm-name is included in the ACCEPT format, then the contents of the current of run-unit indicator is copied into identifier-1. If either record-name, set-name, or realm-name is included, then the contents of the corresponding currency indicator is copied instead.

This ACCEPT option can be useful for remembering records which have been found during the course of execution of a program and which will need to be refound later in the program. The usefulness of the facility must be assessed in conjunction with the FIND Format 1 (see Section 15.6.2) as the two facilities would normally be used in tandem.

The problem with ACCEPT CURRENCY coupled with the concomitant facility for defining items of type DB-KEY in data base record types is that it opens the door to storing data base key values in the data base itself. While this practice will often buy performance, it is fraught with risk, and should be avoided as much as possible.

17.4.2 ACCEPT REALM-NAME

The second data base oriented ACCEPT option is as follows:

$$
\underline{\text{ACCEPT}} \ \text{identifier-2} \ \underline{\text{FROM}} \ \begin{bmatrix} \text{record-name} \\ \text{set-name} \\ \text{identifier-3} \end{bmatrix} \ \underline{\text{REALM-NAME}}
$$

The function of this statement is to allow the programmer to copy the name of a realm in a location declared in his program. Which realm name is copied depends on the setting of currency indicators. The name is copied into the location designated by identifier-2 which could be declared in the Data Division of the program or in any data base record type. It must be an alphanumeric elementary data item.

If record-name is used, the realm name is that in which the record identified in the current of record-name indicator is stored. If set-name is used, the realm name is that in which the record identified in the current of set-name indicator.

If identifier-3 is specified, then it must reference a data base key item and the content of that item must identify some record in the data base. The realm in which this record is stored is the one whose name is moved to identifier-2.

The ACCEPT REALM-NAME option is another facility destined for only modest use. It must be recalled that it is possible to assign records of a given type to two or more realms (see Section 4.8.1). In the case where a record type is assigned to only one realm, then this ACCEPT REALM-NAME facility would not be used. With the record type in several realms, it can happen that a record is retrieved as a result of a FIND option and the programmer needs to know which realm it came from. He would then need access to the realm name and the ACCEPT REALM-NAME option allows him to get it.

17.5 Data Base Conditions

The IF statement is a very basic and important statement in any programming language. It allows the programmer to specify that the path of control to be followed by his executing program depends on the evaluation of some condition which may be either true or false.

The introduction of the Data Base Facility into COBOL calls for the existing IF statement to be extended to allow for the testing of three classes of data base conditions. These three classes are:

1. Tenancy
2. Member
3. Nullity

and each will be discussed in turn.

17.5.1 Tenancy Conditions

If a record is connected as a member or else is the owner of a selected set of a specified set type, then it is said to be a tenant in that set. Sometimes it is useful to be able to check the involvement of a record in a set type. In fact, the facility proposed allows more than simply checking tenancy as can be seen from its format.

$$\text{IF } [\underline{NOT}] \text{ [set-name]} \begin{Bmatrix} \text{OWNER} \\ \text{MEMBER} \\ \text{TENANT} \end{Bmatrix}$$

The DBLTG specifications state:

'If set-name is specified, only the set type referenced by set-name is considered in determining the truth value of the condition. If set-name is not specified, all set types considered in determining the truth value of the condition.'

It is noted that the DBLTG specifications (page III–12–10) omit to mention that the current of set type indicator for set-name is used to select which set of that name is being examined. However, the record is that identified in the current of run-unit indicator.

No provision has been made in the extension for selecting a path dependent on the record name of a record. Two of the FIND options do allow a record to be found without the record type being specified in the FIND statement (see Sections 15.4.3 and 15.5.1). In view of this, it would be useful to be able to check the record type of the found record using an IF statement. This is possible to some extent using the tenancy condition, but it seems a rather circuitous way of doing it.

17.5.2 Member Conditions

The name given in the JOD (page III–12–10) to this class of condition should not be confused with one of the options in the tenancy class of conditions.

A member condition is one in which a test is made on a selected set occurrence to see whether any member records (of any type) are connected to it.

The format is

IF set-name IS [NOT] EMPTY

When the NOT is omitted, the condition is true if the set (selected using the current of set indicator) has no members connected to it. If set-name happens to refer to a singular set type (see Section 3.4), then there is only one set occurrence and the system need not refer to the current of set type indicator.

17.5.3 Nullity Conditions

So far in this text we have avoided the complex question of null values. This is largely because the whole issue tends to have been glossed by the DDLC and the DBLTG. DDLC does identify (see page 3.8) an external form for a null literal constant, namely NULL, and there are frequent references in the various general rules to the possibility that the value of a data item might be null or even be set to null.

The problem is that existing programming languages such as COBOL and

PL/1 do not provide an implicit way of treating null values. This leaves the problem to the programmer who will solve it as he wishes. In a data base environment where several programmers are writing programs to process the same data, a consistent solution is called for.

The nullity condition in the JOD (page III–12–11) can be used to determine whether or not a data item has a null value or not. Its format is simply

IF identifier-1 IS [NOT] NULL

The Data item identifier-1 must be defined in a sub-schema.

17.5.4 Other Useful Conditions

Before moving on to discuss the USE statement, mention must be made of the use of the IF statement to check whether a DML statement has been successfully executed or not. This topic has been touched on earlier (see Section 13.5).

The best way to handle this situation is with a USE declaration to be discussed in the next section. However, most implementations do not support the USE which means that it is advisable to include an IF after every DML. An example of this would be

IF DB-STATUS NE 0

which would cause a transfer of control to a more detailed error checking paragraph when the DB-STATUS register (see Section 13.5) has a setting other than zero.

17.6 Exception Condition Checking

A USE statement existed in COBOL before the advent of the Data Base Facility. Its purpose was for specifying procedures for input–output label and error handling. USE procedures can also be defined in a COBOL program for other purposes.

The JOD now proposes the addition of two further classes of USE procedure (see page III–7–158). One of these is for handling data base exception conditions and the other is for specifying procedures to generate privacy keys. Since privacy has not yet been presented, we will defer discussion of this until Chapter 18.

The syntax of the USE statement designed to handle data base exception conditions is as follows:

$$\underline{\text{USE}} \text{ FOR } \underline{\text{DB-EXCEPTION}} \left[\text{ON} \begin{Bmatrix} \text{OTHER} \\ \text{literal-1} \dots \end{Bmatrix} \right]$$

A USE statement must always follow a section header in the declarative portion of the Procedure Division. It is followed by one or more procedural paragraphs which are executed only when certain conditions occur. In a given program there may be several USE statements, each with its associated USE procedure. The capability is best illustrated by an example.

Many of the exception conditions are genuine errors. In other words, if they arise, something is radically wrong and the only sensible course of action to program is an aborting of the run-unit. Other conditions are certainly not errors. For example, when an attempt is made to perform an out of the blue access based on the value of a calc key (see Section 15.4.1), it is quite possible that the FIND is unsuccessful simply because no record exists in the data base with the requisite key value. The last thing the programmer would want to happen is an aborting of the run-unit. According to the JOD (page III–12–6) a data base exception condition 0502400 would arise. (The first two digits identify the statement type FIND and the others the condition.)

If this condition is the only one for special treatment, then the USE statements might appear as follows:

```
USE  FOR  DATABASE-EXCEPTION  ON  0502100, 0502400
         do nothing

USE  FOR  DATABASE-EXCEPTION  ON  OTHER
         PRINT DATABASE-STATUS, DATABASE-RECORD-NAME,
         DATABASE-REALM-NAME, DATABASE-SET-NAME
END
```

The programmer must take care that all data base exception conditions which can occur in the program are catered for. Normally, there will be a few which call for special handling such as the two in the example above, and the others will require a printing out of the data base registers (see Section 13.5).

Some contrivance may be called for to write a USE procedure to do nothing. The JOD does not recognize this as a new requirement. The problem is that the DBCS will automatically transfer control to execute the USE procedure before it proceeds to execute the statement after the DML statement. It has at present no way of ignoring the presence of USE procedures simply because a DML statement is followed by an IF statement.

The solution to this problem will be to separate exception conditions from error conditions. Combining them together has caused obvious problems.

Chapter 18

Privacy System

18.1 Introduction

So far we have considered almost every aspect of the DBTG and DDLC reports which has been thought through by the various committees and task groups to the point that syntactic and semantic specifications are possible.

The one exception to this is the privacy system or to be more accurate, privacy sub-system. Privacy is not a topic one can meaningfully attack as part of the Schema DDL, the Sub-schema DDL or the DML. The problem of getting the 'big picture', for example from the DBTG report, is that the thinking and specifications on privacy are scattered throughout the document.

It is our aim here first to pull these pieces together and to explain what appears to be the intent, secondly to review the adequacy of the approach, and thirdly to suggest a modified approach which hopefully will meet the various requirements more fully.

18.2 Components of a Privacy Sub-system

Before presenting the details of the CODASYL approach, it is useful to identify the three parts of any privacy sub-system.

1. A means of defining privacy locks.
2. A means of defining privacy keys.
3. A means of comparing keys with locks.

We will further use the terms

1. Privacy lock definition time
2. Privacy key definition time
3. Comparison time

to refer to the times at which various tasks are performed.

It should be noted that there are different forms that lock and keys may take. The form of a key need not necessarily be the same as the form of the lock into which it fits. Furthermore, each lock and key has what could be called a 'range of applicability' which has nothing to do with the form it uses.

The range of applicability of a lock is just that—how much of the data base it covers. It could be one value (that is an item occurrence) or it could be the whole data base. It could be all the records of a given type or even all the sets of a given type.

The best understood form of a privacy lock is a password, and facilities in present day operating systems tend to be limited to such passwords. DBTG introduced the fascinating concept of much more powerful forms, but so far these ideas have yet to be adopted by implementors, partly because one of the new forms relies on the data base procedure facility which, as we have indicated, is yet to be provided by any implementor.

18.3 DBTG Ideas on Privacy

The DBTG approach to privacy has been modified, but not significantly in the DDLC and in the JOD. This is a pity, because there seems to be a good case for a fresh approach to the problem. This is not to imply that the DBTG ideas were bad, but they were certainly incompletely expressed. At the same time, their thinking is stimulating and must be regarded as an important stepping stone.

18.3.1 Schema defined Locks

Each entry in the Schema DDL, this is to say the Realm Entry, Record Entry and Set Entry (see Section 11.2), may also have a PRIVACY lock clause. There is a standard form for this clause as follows

$$
\left[\underline{\text{PRIVACY}} \ \text{LOCK} \left[\underline{\text{FOR}} \| \quad \| \right] \text{IS} \left\{ \begin{array}{l} \text{literal-1} \\ \text{lock-name-1} \\ \underline{\text{PROCEDURE}} \ \text{db-proc-1} \end{array} \right\} \left[\underline{\text{OR}} \left\{ \begin{array}{l} \text{literal-2} \\ \text{lock-name-2} \\ \underline{\text{PROCEDURE}} \ \text{db-proc-2} \end{array} \right\} \right] \dots \right] \dots
$$

The clause is always optional and it is always possible to define more than one lock for a given realm, record type or set type.

The vertical pairs of parallel lines enclose a list of DML statements which it is possible to perform on the kind of data being described, for instance, READY and FINISH for realms and ORDER, CONNECT and DISCONNECT for set types.

If the FOR option is omitted, that is the piece between the inner square brackets, then the lock is taken to apply to *any* operation performed on the realm, set type, record type or item.

The DBTG's privacy locks on data in the Schema DDL may be summarized as follows:

1. Realm level—READY FOR $\begin{bmatrix} \text{EXCLUSIVE} \\ \text{PROTECTED} \end{bmatrix} \begin{bmatrix} \text{RETRIEVAL} \\ \text{UPDATE} \end{bmatrix}$, and support functions
2. Record level—CONNECT, DISCONNECT, STORE, MODIFY, FIND, GET, ERASE, ERASE ONLY, ERASE SELECTIVE, ERASE ALL
3. Item level—STORE, GET, MODIFY
4. Set level—ORDER, CONNECT, DISCONNECT, FIND

There is some interesting inconsistency here—probably due to the fact that the different levels were handled at different times during the preparation of the report by different task group members. The general form of the privacy lock is indeed standardized across the Schema DDL. With two statements, namely the READY and the ERASE, it is possible to define a privacy lock on the *option* level rather than on the statement level. Before going on to discuss the implications of this, it is appropriate to note that DDLC's only marginal modification in their 1973 report was to take away the facility to define option level locks on the ERASE statement (DELETE).

In addition to the privacy locks on data in the Schema DDL, DBTG also catered for the definition of four schema levels locks which are as follows:

$$\underline{\text{PRIVACY}} \text{ LOCK} \begin{bmatrix} \text{FOR} \left\| \begin{array}{c} \underline{\text{LOCKS}} \\ \underline{\text{DISPLAY}} \\ \underline{\text{COPY}} \\ \underline{\text{ALTER}} \end{array} \right\| \end{bmatrix} \text{IS} \left\{ \quad \right\} \text{OR} \left\{ \quad \right\} \dots$$

where the lock forms in the curly brackets may be as on the data level.

ALTER, COPY, DISPLAY and LOCKS are called 'support functions'. (This is a new and possibly more dignified term for 'utilities'.) ALTER is a function to modify a schema, except the privacy locks, once it has been defined. DISPLAY is a function to print out (or possibly 'display' on a terminal device incorporating a CRT) all of the schema *except* the privacy locks. The lock on COPY is an important one, because this lock allows the data administrator to inhibit use of the schema—or to be more precise, it allows him to control the process of translating sub-schemas.

The privacy lock for LOCKS brings out a very important concept. The locks themselves must be 'locked up' and consequently the DBTG envisaged a support function which in their words 'allows the viewing, creating, or changing of the privacy locks'.

The individual who holds the key to the privacy lock for locks is indeed in a position of power.

18.3.2 Sub-schema defined Locks

In addition to schema defined locks, DBTG also allowed for sub-schema defined locks. It is extremely important to note that if there is a schema lock on a piece of data (realm, record type, etc.) and then a sub-schema lock is defined on the same piece of data, the sub-schema lock *replaces* the schema locks. This does not mean that the schema lock is erased in some way, but programs which use this sub-schema must provide the key to the sub-schema lock rather than to the schema locks. This means that the 'privacy lock for COPY' in the Schema DDL is an important one. It is the only lock which needs to be satisfied by whoever defines the sub-schema.

The DBLTG's syntax for defining the privacy key is

$$
\underline{\text{PRIVACY KEY}} \text{ IS } \begin{Bmatrix} \text{literal-1} \\ \text{implementor-name-1} \\ \text{routine-name-2} \end{Bmatrix}
$$

We will discuss the form of the key when we discuss the form of the locks.

In addition, the person defining the sub-schema may also define sub-schema level privacy locks. Since DBLTG modified the DBTG's approach somewhat significantly, we will quote both. DBTG's Sub-schema DDL syntax for what they called the Identification Division (page 155) is

$$
\underline{\text{SUB-SCHEMA}} \text{ NAME IS sub-schema-name of SCHEMA NAME schema-name}
$$

$$
\left[\underline{\text{PRIVACY LOCK}} \left[\text{FOR} \left\| \begin{matrix} \underline{\text{LOCKS}} \\ \underline{\text{DISPLAY}} \\ \underline{\text{COMPILE}} \\ \underline{\text{ALTER}} \end{matrix} \right\| \right] \text{ IS } \begin{Bmatrix} \text{literal-1} \\ \text{lock-name-1} \\ \underline{\text{PROCEDURE}} \text{ db-proc-1} \end{Bmatrix} \right.
$$

$$
\left[\underline{\text{OR}} \begin{Bmatrix} \text{literal-2} \\ \text{lock-name-2} \\ \underline{\text{PROCEDURE}} \text{ db-proc-2} \end{Bmatrix} \right] \cdots \left. \right] \cdots
$$

$$
\left[\underline{\text{PRIVACY KEY}} \text{ FOR COPY IS } \begin{Bmatrix} \text{literal-3} \\ \text{implementor-name-1} \end{Bmatrix} \right]
$$

It can be seen that the format of the privacy lock declaration is identical to that in the Schema DDL except for the fact that the word COPY is replaced by COMPILE.

A privacy lock on COMPILE in the sub-schema would have to be satisfied by a key in the application source program in order for *compilation* of that program to be possible.

Otherwise, the functions ALTER, DISPLAY and LOCKS fulfill the same role on the sub-schema level as the corresponding functions on the schema level.

The JOD (see page IV–4–4) made a number of modifications to the DBTG's ideas and we now have a Title Division instead of an Identification Division.

TITLE DIVISION

SS sub-schema-name WITHIN schema-name

$$\left[; \underline{\text{PRIVACY LOCK}} \left[\text{FOR} \left\{ \begin{array}{|l|} \underline{\text{INVOKING}} \\ \underline{\text{ALTERING}} \\ \underline{\text{LOCKS}} \end{array} \right\} \right] \text{IS} \left\{ \begin{array}{l} \text{literal-1} \\ \text{implementor-name-1} \\ \text{routine-name-1} \end{array} \right\} \cdots \right]$$

$$\left[; \underline{\text{PRIVACY KEY}} \text{ IS} \left\{ \begin{array}{l} \text{literal-2} \\ \text{implementor-name-2} \\ \text{routine-name-2} \end{array} \right\} \right].$$

The DISPLAY function has been dropped which is of fairly minor consequence, but more important, the privacy lock for COMPILE was replaced by a privacy lock for INVOKING. The DBLTG's rules state quite clearly that this lock must be satisfied 'in order to execute a run-unit containing this sub-schema'.

The lock on compiling and the lock on run-unit invocation both seem to have a role to play. It is not clear why the DBTG omitted the second and the DBLTG conscientiously threw out the first.

18.3.3 Program defined Keys

As indicated above, there is one privacy key which may be defined in the Sub-schema DDL. Privacy locks may be defined in both Schema DDL and the Sub-schema DDL.

The DBTG proposed that all other keys should be defined in a new paragraph of the COBOL program's Identification called, appropriately enough, the Privacy paragraph to appear before the other 'standard' COBOL statements for that division. The function of the privacy paragraph is

'to establish the program and run-unit authority to execute classified DML imperative statements in accordance with the locks declared in the schema or sub-schema'.

The syntactic form of the privacy key clauses is as follows:

$$\left[\text{PRIVACY KEY FOR COMPILE IS } \left\{\begin{array}{l}\text{literal-1}\\ \text{implementor-name-1}\end{array}\right\}\right]$$

$$\text{PRIVACY KEY} \left[\text{FOR} \left\|\begin{array}{l}\left[\begin{array}{l}\text{EXCLUSIVE}\\ \text{PROTECTED}\end{array}\right]\text{RETRIEVAL}\\ \left[\begin{array}{l}\text{EXCLUSIVE}\\ \text{PROTECTED}\end{array}\right]\text{UPDATE}\end{array}\right\|\right]\text{OF}$$

$$\left\{\begin{array}{l}\text{realm-1 [, realm-2] ... REALM}\\ \text{ALL REALMS}\end{array}\right\}\text{IS}\left\{\begin{array}{l}\text{PROCEDURE}\left\|\begin{array}{l}\text{proc-name-1}\\ \text{literal-2}\\ \text{identifier-1}\end{array}\right\|\\ \text{literal-3}\\ \text{identifier-2}\end{array}\right\}\ldots$$

followed by a similar **PRIVACY KEY** clauses for record types, items and set types.

This syntax requires explanation and some can indeed be gleaned from the various syntax and general rules given. First of all, it is interesting to note that if the same lock applies to a number of different record types (or even to all record types) in the schema, then it is necessary to include an identical privacy lock statement in the Record Entry for each record type. However, if the same key applies to several record types, then this fact can conveniently be stated in one privacy key clause. There is one rather interesting syntax rule as follows:

'Multiple PRIVACY clauses that differ only in the specification of the key are not permitted.'

We take this to be a precaution against the dishonest programmer who includes numerous key specification clauses in his program in the hope that one fits the lock.

The idea of a key being a procedure is also interesting. It must be noted that this must be a named part of the programmer's source program. A privacy lock could be a data base procedure. There are three different ways of identifying a 'procedure key'. One is explicitly using a literal in the key clause (e.g. literal-2) which means that the literal is an alphanumeric value corresponding to a procedure name. The second is to communicate the name of the procedure by the content of an item in the program. The third is to name the procedure explicitly in the key clause.

In the JOD, definition of all privacy key clauses was modified considerably with the exception of the PRIVACY KEY FOR INVOKE. This is specified in the so-called Sub-schema Entry in the COBOL Data Division. The Sub-schema Entry is the way of identifying the sub-schema which a COBOL program is to use. The syntax reads

DB sub-schema-name WITHIN schema-name

[; PRIVACY KEY IS literal].

A PRIVACY KEY must be specified if sub-schema-name has an invocation privacy lock and the key must of course fit the lock.

The JOD's approach to the other privacy keys is to extend the existing mechanism for declarative procedures, namely the USE clause (see page III–7–159).

The new format is very complex and appears as follows:

$$\underline{\text{USE}} \text{ FOR } \underline{\text{PRIVACY}} \left[\left[\text{ON} \left\{ \begin{bmatrix} \underline{\text{EXCLUSIVE}} \\ \underline{\text{PROTECTED}} \end{bmatrix} \begin{Bmatrix} \underline{\text{RETRIEVAL}} \\ \underline{\text{UPDATE}} \end{Bmatrix} \right\} \dots \right] \right.$$

$$\left. \text{FOR} \begin{Bmatrix} \text{realm-name-1 } [, \text{ realm-name-2} \dots \\ \underline{\text{REALMS}} \end{Bmatrix} \right] \dots$$

$$\left[\left[\text{ON} \begin{Vmatrix} \underline{\text{CONNECT}} \\ \underline{\text{DISCONNECT}} \\ \underline{\text{STORE}} \\ \underline{\text{ERASE}} \\ \underline{\text{ERASE PERMANENT}} \\ \underline{\text{ERASE}} \; \underline{\text{SELECTIVE}} \\ \underline{\text{ERASE}} \text{ ALL} \\ \underline{\text{GET}} \\ \underline{\text{MODIFY}} \\ \underline{\text{FIND}} \end{Vmatrix} \text{ FOR} \begin{Bmatrix} \text{record-name-1 } [, \text{ record-name-2}] \dots \\ \underline{\text{RECORDS}} \end{Bmatrix} \right] \right] \dots$$

$$\left[\text{ON} \begin{Vmatrix} \underline{\text{FIND}} \\ \underline{\text{ORDER}} \\ \underline{\text{CONNECT}} \\ \underline{\text{DISCONNECT}} \end{Vmatrix} \text{ FOR} \begin{Bmatrix} \text{set-name-1 } [, \text{ set-name-2}] \dots \\ \underline{\text{SETS}} \end{Bmatrix} \right] \dots$$

$$\left[\text{ON} \begin{Vmatrix} \underline{\text{GET}} \\ \underline{\text{MODIFY}} \\ \underline{\text{STORE}} \end{Vmatrix} \text{ FOR identifier-1 } [, \text{ identifier-2}] \dots \right] \dots$$

It is fairly obvious that one of the optional FOR phrases must be used if the USE FOR PRIVACY clause is included. Furthermore, if there are privacy keys on the data to be specified, then a USE FOR PRIVACY clause is the place to do it.

The DBTG's ideas on privacy keys seemed to leave in the air the question of when the keys are compared with the locks. DBLTG's approach is much more definite. Their rule states:

'The execution of any given privacy procedure is caused by the execution of a READY statement which effects any realms, record types, set types or data items with which that privacy procedure is associated.'

The JOD also introduces (see page III–12–3) a special register called DB-PRIVACY-KEY. It is the task of the declarative procedure following the USE statement to enter the value of a key into this register. The DBCS then automatically makes the necessary comparison. If the key does not fit in the lock, the READY is not executed and a data base exception condition arises (see Section 13.5).

The declarative procedure may of course be very simple. If the schema privacy lock on a record type reads

RECORD-A PRIVACY LOCK IS "SESAME"

which means that the lock is the simplest form, namely a literal or password SESAME, then the programmer might write

USE FOR PRIVACY FOR RECORD-A
MOVE "SESAME" TO DATABASE-PRIVACY-KEY.

When the realm containing the record type whose name is RECORD-A is readied, then the USE procedure is automatically invoked and the value of the special register set.

It should be observed that this is an example of a very unsubtle privacy control. Anyone reading the schema listing or the program source listing will see what the privacy lock is. This is a general weakness with literals. One of the immediate advantages with literals is that it is relatively easy to illustrate and to understand them. Let us now consider the other forms.

18.4 Forms of Locks and Keys

It can be seen from the syntax of the standard form for a privacy lock in Section 18.3.1 that DBTG envisaged three different possible forms for each lock. These are:

1. Literal
2. Lock-name
3. Data base procedure

18.4.1 Literal Lock Forms

A literal is exactly the same as the well understood password. For example, on the item level the data administrator might write

SALARY PRIVACY LOCK FOR STORE MODIFY IS "BETSY"
  PRIVACY LOCK FOR GET IS "CAMERA".

This means that the programmer who wishes to modify a value of the data item SALARY in some record or other would have to include two DBLTG USE procedures such as

USE FOR PRIVACY ON STORE MODIFY SALARY
MOVE "BETSY" TO DATABASE-PRIVACY-KEY

USE FOR PRIVACY ON GET SALARY
MOVE "CAMERA" TO DATABASE-PRIVACY-KEY.

We assume here that in order to modify the record in which the item SALARY is contained, we must first be able to get access to records of this type and hence would need the privacy key to GET as well.

In the JOD (page IV–4–15), there is no concept of specific forms for the keys (nor for the locks). The fact that a lock takes the form of a literal does not mean that the key *must* be declared in the way illustrated above. In an on-line system, it is more likely that the USE procedure would contain statements to communicate with the terminal from which the value of the privacy key could be requested. The USE procedure could then place this value into the special register.

18.4.2 Variable Lock Forms

If the Schema DDL contains a privacy lock declaration of the form

PRIVACY LOCK IS ITEM-NAME

then ITEM-NAME is the name of an item into which the value of the lock is to be placed. Since we have now entered the region of concepts which have not been implemented, some speculation is called for into what the specifications could mean and how they could be interpreted.

We should recall that DBTG and DDLC propose that we could write

$$\text{PRIVACY LOCK} \left[\text{FOR} \middle\| \quad \middle\| \right] \text{IS LOCK-NAME-1 [OR lock-name-2]}$$

They explain further (on page 87) as a syntax rule that

'By their appearance in a PRIVACY clause, lock-name-1 and lock-name-2 are implicitly declared as data items with implementor-defined characteristics.'

The only change DDLC made to this was to modify the writing slightly and make it a general rule which reads (page 3.15):

'By their appearance in a PRIVACY clause, lock-names are treated as data items with implementor defined characteristics.'

The intent is clearly the same from a privacy point of view. Instead of dealing with a constant or literal explicitly declared as part of the schema, the Schema DDL is now used to declare a location, possibly in the data base, possibly in core, in which the value of the lock is to be found at the time any program processing the relevant data is executing.

The main questions to be asked here are where the item is, and how the value of the lock is entered prior to the initialization of run-units which process the protected data. The answer to the first question must be that the item must be part of the object schema and hence has a permanent home in direct access storage. From then on, the treatment must be different depending on whether the lock applies on the schema level or whether it is a lock on the data in the data base. We should consider the second situation first as it is more common and we are talking about a lock which needs to be satisfied at execution time by an application program.

The value of such a lock must clearly be set by some kind of lock setting utility program which can be run by the data administrator every time it is necessary to set or reset any lock in the schema of this form. In the case of a literal, in order to change the lock value, it would presumably be necessary to modify the statement in the schema and repeat the process of schema translation.

Hence, in the case of a privacy lock which is a variable, its value must be stored in the object schema and it may be set or reset using a special utility. If a sub-schema contains the data which is protected by a privacy lock of this form, then any time a program processing the data in the sub-schema is initiated, the value of the lock is then available in core and accessible to the part of the privacy sub-system which performs the lock key comparison function.

In the case of a privacy lock on the schema level, the process is essentially the same, except that the lock key comparison must be made before the function starts to execute.

It is interesting to note the lack of definition of the LOCKS support here. In the above discussion, we identified a 'lock setting utility program'. It is not clear that these two are the same, and we must be careful to distinguish between identifying the fact that a given part of the data base is protected, which DBTG proposes to be done in a privacy lock clause in the schema, and setting the value of that lock if the form of the lock is a variable.

18.4.3 Procedure Privacy Locks

The final form of a privacy lock is a data base procedure. As we indicated in Chapter 10, data base procedures themselves represent a capability which is very much open to interpretation. When we superimpose the data base procedure on the privacy sub-system, we are very much in the realms of speculation.

Whereas a privacy lock which takes the form of a variable needs to be set using a special utility, presumably the privacy lock which takes the form of a data base procedure is set by the execution of the procedure. When is it defined and when is it executed? While the output parameter from the procedure is probably a lock value, how does the writer of the procedure know where to store this lock value? Does the procedure have any input parameters and, if so, how are their values initialized? If the generation of a lock value is performed procedurally behind the scenes, how can the programmer or parametric user know what key to enter?

Perhaps a more realistic approach to the concept of the privacy lock as a data base procedure is to regard the procedure as the mechanism which itself tests the validity of the key, rather than generating a lock value to be tested by some centralized comparison routine. In this case, one can see that the privacy key value is then input to the privacy lock procedure. The procedure may need some other input such as an identification of the person trying to access the data base.

This approach is compatible with the ideas in the JOD for a USE FOR PRIVACY clause as discussed in Section 18.3.3. The DBCS can easily test whether a lock is a literal, variable or procedure and take the appropriate course of action. However, if the privacy lock is a procedure, then it must be borne in mind that conceivably both the lock procedure and the key procedure could request further input from the parametric user at the terminal. Care must be exercised to ensure that *both* procedures do not request the poor user to give the same input, such as key value.

A final point about the privacy lock procedure is that it needs to be identified to the DBMS as a special kind of data base procedure. For one thing, the source code for such a procedure must itself be kept private, otherwise a clever programmer will soon learn how to generate keys to access confidential data. Another point is that the process of defining that a privacy lock is a process which is separate from that of defining the procedure. It would help if all privacy lock procedures were treated separately from other data base procedures.

18.5 Review of CODASYL Approach

Having completed the exposition of the CODASYL ideas for a privacy system and discussed somewhat speculatively the implications of these, it is now appropriate to review the overall approach and to indicate shortcomings.

The fact that the approach to privacy proposed by the DBTG has not been implemented indicates one of several things about the implementors' reactions.

1. Privacy is not necessary to make a DBMS commercially viable.
2. It is not clear how to implement the CODASYL approach.
3. Privacy could easily be postponed and added in a later version.
4. The host operating system already had some privacy control.
5. They understood and did not like the CODASYL approach.

For whatever reason, the currently available systems based on the CODASYL approach have only modest privacy facilities and nowhere is the full extent of the DBTG's thinking reflected.

In the remainder of this chapter, we will highlight four problems with the approach and then go on to suggest an alternative and hopefully cleverer way of handling the problem. The four problems are identified as follows:

1. Confusion of privacy with privilege.
2. Confusion on *who* is being controlled.
3. Interweaving privacy locks with Schema DDL statements.
4. The privacy lock for copy as a critical link.

18.5.1 Privacy and Privilege

The DBTG approach to a privacy system mixes in two very separable concepts which we will refer to as privacy and privilege. If data is private, this means that the authority to retrieve the data and the authority to change it is subject to control. It has nothing to do with *how* the data is retrieved or *how* it is changed—but *whether* it is retrieved and *whether* it is changed. The important distinction here is between the *whether* and the *how*.

For instance, if a person is allowed to change a record of a given type, this is a matter of his authority rather than his skill. As we will discuss in the next section, the changes may in fact be effected by a parametric user entering data item values from a terminal with no knowledge whatever of the application program (or even of the art of programming).

The fact that there is a good case for making a very clear distinction between update programmers and retrieval programmers ties in well with two classes of privacy authorization—allowed to retrieve and allowed to update.

On the other hand, whether they are updating or retrieving, some programmers will have more skill than others and can be entrusted to utilize correctly more difficult facilities of the DML. DBTG with its various options in the privacy locks on each level—particularly the record level—seemed to be recognizing this and providing the data administrator with a means of inhibiting use of various DML statement options using privacy locks. This facet of the DBTG privacy lock has very little to do with whether or not someone is entitled to see or change the data. For ease of reference, we will restrict the term 'privacy' to mean control of authority to see or change the data and introduce the term 'privilege' to refer to the control exercised by the data administrator over the programmer's use of various DML options.

It must be noted that in order to exercise privilege control fully, it is necessary to spell out a similar kind of clause on each realm, set type and record type depending on the level on which the privilege control is to be exercised. If the data administrator wishes to prohibit use of the ERASE ALL statement, and there are 13 record types in the schema, then he must write out 13 statements such as

PRIVACY LOCK FOR ERASE ALL IS lock-name-7

although all the locks can be identical.

The criticism of the DBTG's approach in this section is more directed at how the capability is presented than the nature of the capability. The effect is that the facilities to control the privacy of the data are buried in the facilities to control the use of various options. Both are certainly important, and it is felt that a more effective capability to support each can be achieved if the two are separated.

18.5.2 Whom Does Privacy Control?

The fact that the DBTG required the privacy keys to be specified in a paragraph of the program and checked at program compile time seems to indicate that they felt that it was the programmer who was *the* potential threat to the privacy of the data base. The JOD modifications at least made it clearer that the parametric user at the terminal is also a threat.

In fact, a good privacy system should allow the control of both programmers and parametric users. In a sense, control over the former is much harder to attain because the programmer has the skill to write programs to access the data in the data base. Nevertheless, it is implicit in the overall concept of the DBMS that the programmer's program is being written to be used by a potential multitude of individuals who merely invoke the program (in its object form after it has been debugged) and provide values to whatever input parameters the program may have. The fact that the output from this program may contain sensitive information means that the act of invoking the program must itself be controllable.

The question of privilege is discussed in the previous section clearly applies only to the programmer and not to the parametric user, while the question of privacy applies to both.

There is, however, another facet of this question which must be considered. Apart from the programmers and parametric users, there could be members of the data administration staff who would be responsible for using the Sub-schema DDL translator and the various utility programs or support functions which go to make up the complete DBMS. It is important that facilities be provided to allow control over the use of such functions. DBTG recognized this in their provision of schema level locks. However, it is not clear that the Schema DDL is the place to define such locks.

18.5.3 Interwoven Privacy Lock Declarations

As indicated earlier in this chapter, the DBTG specified that the privacy locks should be included in the entries of Schema DDL. This is useful for giving an overview of all the properties of a given realm, record type, item or set type. The question arises as to whether this is in the best interests of flexible processing and adequate privacy.

It is likely that the locks will change more frequently than the other schema declarations. As indicated in the discussion in Section 18.4.2 on variable privacy locks, the value of a declared lock will probably change even more frequently. The fact that the locks change more frequently than the structurally oriented Schema DDL declarations is an argument for taking the privacy lock declarations out of the Schema DDL. The fact that the values of a given lock should change is an argument for using variables rather than literals, although the latter argument is weakened if the lock declaration is not in the Schema DDL.

On the question of the privacy of the privacy lock declarations, we must accept that the source listing of the schema is something which will need to be passed around to programmers. It is the easiest way of telling them the names of the record types, set types and realms and of the communicating properties of these that the programmer needs to know, such as location mode of a record type, realm to which record assigned, and so on. Certainly, one can envisage Schema DDL translators which have an optional suppression of the printing of privacy lock statements, but one must still control the *input* to the Schema DDL translator.

Recent DDLC thinking favours grouping privacy lock statements into a separate 'category' of the Schema DDL. To solve the problems of flexibility and privacy, the privacy lock declarations should be handled in a separate language; separate, that is, from the Schema DDL which has its own translator. We will call such a language the Privacy Language and discuss this later in the chapter.

18.5.4 Privacy Lock for COPY

If the definer of the schema chooses to put a 'privacy lock for COPY' on the schema, then anyone wishing to define a sub-schema of that schema must be able to satisfy this privacy lock for COPY. If he can satisfy this privacy lock, then he has the chance to define the data in the data base which he wishes to process and to define his own privacy locks—to which he presumably has the keys. The DBTG decreed that when there is a lock in the schema on some piece of data and also a lock in a sub-schema on that same piece of data, then the sub-schema lock *replaces* the corresponding schema declared lock in programs which use that sub-schema.

The result is that if a 'data thief' wishes to break into a data base, then the privacy lock for COPY is without question the Achilles heel of the whole privacy system. He has to crack this one lock, and then define his own locks to cover everything and the whole data base is wide open.

Some commentators feel that the schema declared privacy locks should be regarded as defaults with the more important locks being defined in the sub-schema. This implies that the data administrator then has to be responsible for the definition of the sub-schemas. Nevertheless, it seems to complicate the privacy system unnecessarily without giving any discernible extra protection to the data base.

18.6 Fresh Approach to Privacy

To overcome the various problems discussed in this chapter, a number of changes are suggested which may be summarized as follows:

1. Separate out the following three roles for a 'privacy lock'
   —data administration staff privilege

　　　　　—programmer privilege
　　　　　—data privacy
and provide a separate language with its own processor for each.
2. Remove all privacy lock declarations from the Schema DDL and from the Sub-schema DDL.
3. Clarify the use of the variable lock form and the procedure lock form.

18.6.1 Privilege Control Utility

It is envisaged that the very first component of the DBMS which would be used at an installation would be the Privilege Control Utility in which the data administrator would define locks on the use of the various other components such as

1. Schema DDL Translator
2. Data Strategy Description Language Translator
3. Data Privacy Language Translator
4. Lock value setting utility
5. Sub-schema DDL Translator
6. Programmer Privilege Language Translator
7. Restructuring Language (DBTG's ALTER function)

This list of components includes some which have already been identified in this book and two (the Data Strategy Description Language and the Restructuring Language) which will be introduced in the next two chapters. The important concept is that of Privilege Control Utility which controls the use of components of the DBMS. It is not meaningful to be able to control the use of languages such as the Schema DDL, but it is meaningful to control use of the processors which translate specifications written in the language.

The locks defined using the Privilege Control Utility which controls use of the Data Privacy Language Translator and the Programmer Privilege Language Translator are together equivalent to the DBTG's Privacy Lock for Locks, ostensibly to be defined in the Schema DDL.

It must be noted that the form of the privilege locks defined in this first utility must necessarily be literals. The keys to the privilege locks must also necessarily be literals entered immediately after the string of characters which tell the DBMS to invoke one of the components which is in the class of privileged, such as those in the above list.

18.6.2 Data Privacy Language

When we take out all capability concerned with *how* data is changed or retrieved, we are left with a relatively simple set of statements which could use the following formats:

Format 1

SCHEMA NAME IS schema-name

PRIVACY LOCK [ON sub-schema-name] TO $\left\{ \begin{array}{l} \text{UPDATE} \\ \text{RETRIEVE} \end{array} \right\}$

IS $\left\{ \begin{array}{l} \text{literal-1} \\ \text{lock-name-1} \\ \text{PROCEDURE db-proc-1} \end{array} \right\}$

If the ON phrase is omitted, the lock applies to all data in the data base defined in schema-name.

Format 2

SCHEMA NAME IS schema-name

$\left\{ \text{PRIVACY LOCK ON} \left\{ \begin{array}{l} \text{realm-name-1 [, realm-name-2]} \ldots \\ \text{set-name-1 [, set-name-2]} \ldots \\ \text{record-name-1 [, record-name-2]} \ldots \\ \text{item-name-1 [, item-name-2]} \ldots \end{array} \right\} \text{TO} \left\{ \begin{array}{l} \text{UPDATE} \\ \text{RETRIEVE} \end{array} \right\} \right.$

IS $\left\{ \begin{array}{l} \text{literal-1} \\ \text{lock-name-1} \\ \text{PROCEDURE db-proc-1} \end{array} \right\} \left. \right\} \ldots$

Some discussion of these formats is necessary. One major problem which arises is whether a set type in fact should be regarded as containing data other than that in the owner record type and the member record types. Unfortunately (for other reasons), the fact that an occurrence of a member record type is connected to an occurrence of the owner can in itself represent information which is not contained in either of the records. What should this mean if there is a lock on retrieving from both the owner and the member to which the user has a key, but there is a lock of the set type to which he does not?

The approach to this kind of problem should always be to provide sufficient power to allow any kind of control to be exercised, but at the same time to avoid over-design which leads to the system being difficult to understand and hence to use. The answer to the specific question raised above would then be to regard a privacy lock on a set type as a privacy lock on all its constituent record types—a nice easy rule to remember, and the set name then becomes nothing more than a shorthand for the names of the participating record types. However, if the user has authority to access all the participating record types in a set type, he does not automatically have access to the set type. This is consistent with the interpretation used for the Sub-schema DDL (see Section 12.8.6). Any other approach rapidly becomes bogged down in incomprehensible semantics.

Another problem with set types stems from the requirements to update the member records. If a record type is a member in a given set type, then it is not sufficient to have access and authority to update the member record type; the user must have authority to update the whole set type.

To be consistent, the realm-name is a shorthand for all the record types in the realm and it is already fully accepted that a record name is a shorthand name for all the data items in the record type.

In a given use of the Data Privacy Language, one should either use Format 1 or Format 2, but not both. If Format 1 is used, all sub-schemas must belong to the same schema and the data base procedures must also have been defined for that data base. If Format 2 is used, then each item, record type, or set type may be 'covered' only once, irrespective of *how* it is covered (that is by naming the realm, set type or record type) in a single use of the Language.

Problems arise if we allow a part of the data base to be covered twice with different locks. Which lock must then be satisfied to process the data? The DBTG approach would be to treat the locks as disjunctively related. In other words, the user only has to open one of them. Hence, allowing duplicate coverage in fact weakens the privacy rather than strengthens it. It is certainly rather clumsy to allow multiple coverage and then require a key to *each* lock. This creates problems for all concerned.

18.6.3 Programmer Privilege Language

The reasons for wanting to control the privilege of using DML options are the following:

1. Bad practice to use a given option.
2. Option not called for because of way schema is defined.
3. Programmer not skilled enough to use option.
4. Control data independence.

The last of these introduces the major topic of user control of data independence which will be discussed in a later chapter. The important thing about the list is that none of the aims are likely to hold say for one record type in the data base, but not for the other record types.

Hence, privilege is a property of the level data structure, rather than of the types on each level. as was pointed out, this is a problem with the DBTG's approach. In the Programmer Privilege Language, it is suggested that the syntax might be as follows:

Format 1

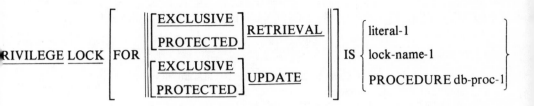

$$\underline{\text{RIVILEGE}}\ \underline{\text{LOCK}}\ \left[\text{FOR}\ \left\|\begin{array}{l}\left[\begin{array}{l}\underline{\text{EXCLUSIVE}}\\ \underline{\text{PROTECTED}}\end{array}\right]\underline{\text{RETRIEVAL}}\\ \left[\begin{array}{l}\underline{\text{EXCLUSIVE}}\\ \underline{\text{PROTECTED}}\end{array}\right]\underline{\text{UPDATE}}\end{array}\right\|\right]\ \text{IS}\ \left\{\begin{array}{l}\text{literal-1}\\ \text{lock-name-1}\\ \underline{\text{PROCEDURE}}\ \text{db-proc-1}\end{array}\right.$$

Format 2

$$\underline{\text{RIVILEGE}}\ \underline{\text{LOCK}}\ \left[\text{FOR}\ \left\|\begin{array}{l}\underline{\text{CONNECT}}\\ \underline{\text{DISCONNECT}}\\ \underline{\text{ERASE}}\\ \underline{\text{ERASE SELECTIVE}}\\ \underline{\text{ERASE PERMANENT}}\\ \underline{\text{ERASE ALL}}\\ \underline{\text{FIND}}\\ \underline{\text{GET}}\\ \underline{\text{MODIFY}}\\ \underline{\text{STORE}}\end{array}\right\|\right]\ \text{IS}\ \left\{\begin{array}{l}\text{literal-2}\\ \text{lock-name-2}\\ \underline{\text{PROCEDURE}}\ \text{db-proc-2}\end{array}\right.$$

Format 3

$$\underline{\text{PRIVILEGE}}\ \underline{\text{LOCK}}\ \left[\text{FOR}\ \left\|\begin{array}{l}\underline{\text{GET}}\\ \underline{\text{MODIFY}}\\ \underline{\text{STORE}}\end{array}\right\|\right]\ \text{IS}\ \left\{\begin{array}{l}\text{literal-3}\\ \text{lock-name-3}\\ \underline{\text{PROCEDURE}}\ \text{db-proc-3}\end{array}\right.$$

Format 4

It should be fairly clear that Format 1 is for statements on the realm level, Format 2 is for the statements on level of the record type and so on. The DBTG's decision to include all ERASE options is included, and there is also a good case for including all the FIND options as well. This means that each FIND option must be given a short name to include in the PRIVILEGE LOCK syntax.

A single use of the Programmer Control Language could include more than one lock declaration from each format, but again it is felt to be better to say that each DML option should be covered no more than once.

The keys to these locks should be included in the program in much the same way as proposed by the DBTG. In this case, it is clear that the key to lock comparison should be made at program compile time.

Chapter 19

Device Media Control Language

19.1 Introduction

We have now completed that part of the book which deals with capabilities which have been defined in reasonable detail by the CODASYL committees and can start to discuss a set of capabilities which have been 'left to the implementor'.

The term *device media control language* is one which occurs fairly frequently in both the DBTG and DDLC reports. A *device* is regarded as a disc drive and *media* refers to disc packs. Hence, a device media control language was originally a language to control the assignment of the data base to the storage media mounted on the various devices.

The DBTG report (pages 21–22) identified the role of the device media control language as 'the assignment of realms to devices and media space, and specifying and controlling buffering, paging, and overflow.'

The DDLC repeated this definition, but then gave a useful two page section (pages 2.13–2.14) on 'Facilities for Data Administration', which gives some useful insight into how this committee felt the DMCL fits into the overall picture of further tools for the data administrator.

In this text, we devote two chapters, this one and the next, to the matter of data administration aids and follow closely the thinking of the working group on data base administration, DBAWG, which was jointly sponsored by both CODASYL and the British Computer Society. Their 1975 report[1] to the CODASYL DDLC had something of the same role as the very first DBTG 1968 report to its parent committee. It was on the level of concept definition, but avoided language specification.

DBAWG felt that the term *device media control language* was somewhat restrictive and indeed it has not found favour among implementors of the CODASYL specifications. DBAWG introduced the term *Data Strategy Description Language*, DSDL, which was intended to embrace the old DMCL and to include many of the other aspects of assigning the data base (in whole and in part) to physical storage.

19.2 Relationship of DSDL to Schema DDL

The DSDL must be regarded, in a certain sense, as an extension to the existing Schema DDL. There are two ways in which this extension may be made. Possibly, the existing Realm, Record Type and Set Type Entries may each be extended to include the syntax of the DSDL. Alternatively, a completely separate language may be considered with its own translator so that the DSDL statements are *not* interwoven with the Schema DDL statements.

The interwoven approach offers the advantage that the reader of the source code (whoever he is) can see at a glance all the declarations for one realm, record type or set type and does not have to reference two source listings for this overview. However, the first advantage of the separate approach is that the applications programmer does not normally need to see the DSDL declarations; more significantly, only in rather specific situations can he profit (i.e. write better programs) from knowing these declarations. Another advantage of the separate approach is that it should be possible to modify the DSDL declarations without modifying those which belong to the Schema DDL. This is looking ahead to the restructuring capabilities to be discussed in the next chapter.

The idea of two separate languages, each with its own processor, is much to be preferred, although both approaches will be found in practice. With this in mind, it is important to consider the dividing line between the Schema DDL and the DSDL. To say that the first is logical and the second is physical is not felt to be a satisfactory way of defining this dividing line in view of the fact that the terms logical and physical are themselves ill-defined. Nevertheless, one can safely assert that the DSDL is 'more physical' than the Schema DDL.

We feel very strongly that the real dividing line can only be defined in terms of programmer cognizance. The clue to this comes from the DDLC's decision to remove the DBTG's set mode clause from the Schema DDL, as discussed in Section 5.5.2. (Since the DDLC had nowhere to move this clause to, they simply deleted it.) The argument in favour of this fairly radical decision was that the programmer did not need to know whether a set type was represented as a chain or as a pointer array. More important, even if he did know, the DML does not provide him with explicit facilities to take advantage of this knowledge—in terms of writing programs which would be more machine efficient. Carrying this argument further, the programmer does not need to know whether a set type is prior processable or not, but he can certainly profit from knowing, for instance by avoiding use of FIND PRIOR if the set type is not prior processable (see Section 15.5.1). Hence, the DDLC left the concept of prior processable in the Schema DDL.

This situation suggests the following classification for Schema DDL and DSDL statements.

1. Programmer needs to know.
2. Programmer does not need to know but could profit from knowing.
3. Programmer does not need to know and cannot profit from knowing.

Every statement or option in class 1 should be in the Schema DDL. Every statement or option in class 3 should be in the DSDL. This leaves a major problem with class 2. It is useful to note that examples of statements or options in this class include

1. Set type—prior processable and whether linked to owner
2. Set type—set order (if other than NEXT or PRIOR)
3. Set type—search key
4. Data item—whether virtual or actual
5. Record type—mapping inside each realm
6. Record type—location mode if not calc, then whether direct or via set

To support and explain one of these examples, consider the fifth item in the list which ties in with a DSDL option to be presented in this chapter. The relevant DML statement which was discussed in Section 15.5.6 is

$$\underline{\text{FIND}} \left\{ \begin{array}{l} \text{NEXT} \\ \text{PRIOR} \end{array} \right\} \left\{ \begin{array}{l} \text{RECORD} \\ \text{record-name} \end{array} \right\} \underline{\text{IN}} \text{ realm}$$

If the programmer does not know the DSDL intra-realm record mapping, he can use this statement intelligently only if he wishes to process all records (possibly of a given type) in the realm. If he does know the intra-realm record mapping, then he needs this FIND option to take advantage of his knowledge.

The outcome of this discussion is hopefully a basis for justifying whether a statement type be included in the Schema DDL or the DSDL—a decision which is more critical if the two definitions are translated into internal form by separate processors at separate times. The Schema DDL translation should always precede the DSDL translation, although the second and ensuing uses of the DSDL Translator could possibly nullify each preceding use of the DSDL. Translator for the schema named.

For the purposes of this discussion, Schema DDL serves as a point of reference, and no further attempt is made to suggest statements which would profitably be moved from the Schema DDL to the DSDL.

19.3 DSDL Facilities

The following facilities are identified in the same sequence as they might appear if they were interwoven with the Schema DDL statements, that is to say realm, record type, set type. It must be emphasized that these facilities are listed for expository reasons only. A given DBMS may or may not provide any of them, as will be discussed.

19.3.1 Realm Level Facilities

These could be as follows:

1. Partition a realm into a number of equal sized pages, where the page size could be either
   —fixed for the DBMS,

—chosen for the whole data base from a finite number of alternative page sizes provided in the DBMS,

—chosen for each realm from a finite number of page sizes provided in the DBMS.

2. Partition a realm into a number of page ranges (not necessarily of equal size).
3. Assign a realm or page range to a given device media type, exercising one of the following options:

—Whole realm or a page range to a specified location on specified volume.

—Whole realm or a page range to any (i.e. system decides) location on specified volume.

—Whole realm or a page range to a specified device media/type. (Further details left to system.)

—Whole realm near other realms.

—Whole realm avoiding other realms.

The problem of control over the wastage of physical storage space caused by a mismatch of the selected page size and that of the device type is regarded as inherent to the declarations for these two. Questions of overflow are regarded as record level facilities.

In addition, it is quite common to treat problems of logging and periodic dumping as a property of each realm. This means that each realm level specification might include a designation of whether or not changes to records in the realm are to be logged and if so where the log file is to be stored. If the log file has to be used at some subsequent time in order to reconstruct the realm to a correct version, then the reconstruction utility would be a separate component apart from the DSDL.

19.3.2 Record Level Facilities

These could be as follows:

1. Packing records of the same or different types into a page.
2. Where the length of a record may exceed the page size, control the physical contiguity of the pages needed.
3. Assignment of number of pages containing different mixes of record types (from 1 above) to specific page ranges.
4. For record types with a location mode of CALC, select or specify (referencing a data base procedure) the algorithm used (see Section 4.5.3).
5. Designate page range for CALC records (if not done in 1) and indicate specific pages or percentage of pages to be used for overflow or collision handling.
6. Selection of all or some items in the record type as compactable. (The compacting algorithm may be a data base procedure as in the ENCODING clause discussed in Section 10.6.3.)
7. Minimum, average and maximum number of records expected of a given type.
8. Declare procedure on which the assignment of records of a given type to two or more realms depends (see Section 4.8.1).

19.3.3 Set Type Level Facilities

These could be as follows:

1. Designate the storage mode of a set type as chain, pointer array (see Section 5.3).
2. Designate minimum, average and maximum number of member records expected to be connected to a set of a given type. For multi-member set types, this declaration applies to each member record type.
3. Designate a realm or page range to which the index for a sorted set type is assigned (see Section 6.3.2).
4. Designate a realm or page range to which a given search key for a set type is assigned (see Section 6.10).

19.4 Ways of Providing DSDL Facilities

The facilities listed above have been identified as some of the reasonable facilities to provide to a data administrator at the present state of the art. Each facility must be examined in the broader context of the following possible ways it may be provided.

1. Not necessary to implementor or data administrator. (This implies that no trade-off can be meaningfully controlled by the facility.)
2. Implementor defined; no data administrator decision possible. (This implies that the implementor either feels he knows best, or else wants to save implementation costs.)
3. Implementor defined default, but data administrator may override with a data base procedure. (This implies that the implementor must provide the data administrator with the capability to define data base procedures.)
4. Implementor defined default, but data administrator may override with DSDL statements.
5. Data administrator must decide; he may choose DSDL declaratives selecting an option or define his own data base procedure.
6. Data administrator must specify using DSDL declaratives.
7. Data administrator must specify using data base procedure.
8. Data administrator must delegate decision to programmer.

The ways in which a given DBMS may treat the various DSDL facilities are as follows. Each facility on each level is identified in the left hand column by the number in the above listing. Each column identifies one of the eight possible ways it may be met. A Y (for Yes) in the column indicates that the facility on that row may feasibly be provided in the way indicated by the number at the top of the column.

An asterisk preceding the Y indicates that the way which appears to be preferred in the DDLC's specifications. Only facilities which come within the scope of the DBTG's or DDLC's specifications have an alternative of this kind.

Level and number \ Alternative ways of providing facility	1	2	3	4	5	6	7	8
Realm level (Section 19.3.1)								
1		Y		Y		Y		
2	Y					Y		
3 (all)		Y				Y		
Record type level (Section 19.3.2)								
1		Y		Y		Y		
2		Y		Y		Y		
3	Y					Y		
4		Y	*Y		Y		Y	
5		Y		Y		Y		
6	Y	Y		Y	Y	Y	*Y	
7	Y					Y		
8		Y					Y	*Y
Set type level (Section 19.3.3)								
1		Y		Y		*Y		
2	Y					Y		
3		Y		Y		*Y		
4		Y		Y		*Y		

References

1. Data Base Administration Working Group, June 1975 report. Available from British Computer Society.

Chapter 20

Restructuring

20.1 DBTG Thoughts on Restructuring

Restructuring is a topic which both DBTG and DDLC mentioned only in passing. DBTG commented at three different places in its 1971 report. The first under the heading of 'System Support Functions' on page 21 claimed.

'... the specifications for a complete DBMS should include description and language specification for ...

... a language which permits modification of a schema or sub-schema and causes the changes to be reflected in the data base itself. Without such a language, changes to the schema can only be made by developing an entirely new schema and restructuring the data base in accordance with the new schema.'

It is appropriate to comment on a couple of points here. Firstly, it does not seem relevant to mention modifying sub-schema in the context of restructuring. Secondly, the idea of 'restructuring the data base in accordance with the new schema' needs careful interpretation. When a DBMS does *not* provide a restructuring facility, the data administrator has to take a very roundabout approach to restructuring. He may have to dump the old data base to sequential storage. He then translates his new schema. Finally, he must load the data so that it forms a data base conforming to the new schema. For this latter step, he would probably need an application program which is different from the one used to load the data base initially with the old schema.

The next DBTG comment on restructuring is found on page 23 under the heading of 'Reorganizing'. (We will delay for the moment a discussion of the difference between *restructuring* and *reorganizing*.) The comment reads

'As a result of information gained through his monitoring, or because of new information required in the data base, the Data Administrator may have to reorganize the data base. He may:
· Reassign realms to different devices/media (part of Device/Media Control Language).

· Change the schema and/or attributes of elements of the schema.
· Change the data base to reflect the changes in the schema (Restructuring).
· Remove 'dead' records and compact space ('garbage collection').

In the third point here, the DBTG's parenthetic reference to restructuring is consistent with the use of this term in the earlier quote on page 21. In other words, 'change the schema' is one act, 'restructuring the data base' is another, and the two are mutually exclusive. However, it is not meaningful to do one without the other, and therefore in this chapter we shall use the term *restructuring* to connote the combined effect of both actions. Where it is necessary to refer to the above two actions separately we shall use the terms *changing the schema* and *re-loading the data* or *adding the new data*. These matters will be discussed in more detail.

The final comment from the DBTG is on page 75 when the ALTER operation is introduced. It is stated:

'This operation permits the alteration of all of the schema with the exception of the privacy lock clauses.'

As mentioned in Section 18.3.1, DBTG and DDLC both suggest that it should be possible in the Schema DDL to define a privacy lock on this operation.

20.2 DDLC Thoughts on Restructuring

DDLC have added very little to the DBTG's earlier thinking on restructuring. It is noticeable that the above quote from DBTG page 23 has been amended to read (page 2.14):

'This requires the Data Administrator to
· modify the schema and compile the changes into the object version of the schema,
· modify the data base to reflect changes in the schema,
· remove inaccessible records and compact re-usable storage space (garbage collecting),
· reassign data to different devices and media (using a DMCL) based on time/space requirements,
· edit portions of the data base.'

This represents a useful clean-up of the DBTG's wording without adding any new penetrating insight into the problem.

20.3 Restructuring and Reorganization

It is first important to exclude from the consideration of restructuring any action which can normally be regarded as updating. Updating consists of changes to item values, records or sets in a data base which are specified in an application program using statements such as STORE, MODIFY, ERASE, CONNECT, DISCONNECT (see Chapter 16).

However, if the schema is changed, then it may be necessary to write an update or load program to carry the job through. (A load program is merely a special kind of update program.) It depends very much on the nature of the change to the schema.

It is not only the schema which may be changed. In the preceding chapter, we mentioned the Data Strategy Description Language. It is also possible that the declarations made for a given data base may need to be modified.

Finally, there is a class of restructuring which does *not* involve modifying declarations made earlier by the data administrator, but nevertheless causes some adjustments to be made to the physical placement of the data in the data base. The classical and possibly only example of this class of restructuring is the well known 'garbage collection' mentioned in the quote from the DBTG report.

For convenience, it is useful to break down restructuring facilities into the following three classes:

1. Schema level restructuring
2. DSDL restructuring
3. Re-organization

Hence, if a change is made to a declaration written using the Schema DDL, it is in the first class. If a change is made to some control declaration using the DSDL, it is the second class. Other kinds of change to the physical placement of the data is called simply a re-organization and is in the third class.

This means that a change which in one DBMS is a DSDL restructuring could be classed as a re-organization in another DBMS, simply because the second DBMS provides no DSDL level control to the data administrator (see Section 19.4).

20.4 Specifying Schema and DSDL Restructuring

There are two main approaches to specifying schema and DSDL restructuring. These can be identified as the replacement approach and the incremental approach.

With the replacement approach, the data administrator completely respecifies the whole schema. The DBMS component processing this new schema has to compare the new with the old to discover the differences, decides whether they are valid, and then perform the restructuring accordingly.

With the incremental approach, the data administrator may specify the changes to the old schema using a language which could be called Schema Restructuring Language (alias the DBTG's ALTER support function). The translator for this language has merely to assess whether the changes are valid with respect to the old schema; if so, they may be performed accordingly. These two approaches are equally valid with the DSDL restructuring.

20.4.1 Specifying Re-organization

In the case of the physical re-organization, the two approaches possible are different from those for the other two. Either the data administrator could be given a utility with very declarative languages aids, for example

COLLECT GARBAGE IN area-7
COAGULATE record-name-5 IN area-3

The alternative might be to use a special physical level manipulation language which would enable the data administration staff to write special procedural programs to perform the physical re-organization.

20.5 Performing the Restructuring

Restructuring and re-organization are all best performed when the machine or at least the data base can be completely dedicated (exclusive update usage mode) to the process being performed. If it is *never* convenient to dedicate the data base to restructuring or re-organization, then another approach must be found. If the data base is small enough with respect to the storage space available, it is possible to perform the restructuring on a dedicated copy, roll forward the restructured copy and then switch over processing the new copy. If this is not possible, then restructuring must take place in situ probably with realm level lock out. It would then help to have small realms.

20.5.1 Effect of Restructuring

The possible effects of performing a restructuring could be any combination of the following four:

1. Modify the object schema only.
2. Cause changes to be made to the internal tables built up as a result of translating the DSDL.
3. Modify the value content of the data base.
4. Modify the physical placement of the records in the data base.

20.6 Schema Restructuring

It is useful to classify changes to the schema as additive, subtractive and modificational, and we here present schema changes in this order with the 'minor sort key' being the sequence in which they would be included in the Schema DDL.

20.6.1 Additive Restructuring

For each change itemized, a mention is made of the section in this book where the initial Schema DDL definition is discussed. Furthermore, the probable impact is listed, using the four alternatives presented in Section 20.5.1 above.

No.	Additive Changes	Section	Possible Effects			
			1	2	3	4
1	New realm	11.4	Y	Y		
2	New record type	11.8	Y			
3	New item in existing record type	9.9	Y		Y	
4	New actual source item in existing record type	9.7	Y		Y	
5	New virtual source item in existing record type	9.7	Y			
6	New actual result item in existing record type	10.6.2	Y		Y	
7	New virtual result item in existing record type	10.6.2	Y			
8	New set type comprising existing record types	11.6	Y		Y	
9	Add index to sorted set type	6.3.2	Y			
10	New search key to any set type	6.10	Y			

It can be observed that in certain cases, an additive restructuring could affect the physical placement of the data in the data base as the records are expanded to create slots for new items or the physical representation necessary to cater for the participation in a new set type. Only the addition of a new realm would affect the DSDL tables and no additive change would affect the value content of the data base.

20.6.2 Subtractive Restructuring

The layout and sequence of the previous sub-section is followed.

No.	Subtractive Changes	Section	Possible Effects			
			1	2	3	4
1	Remove realm	11.4	Y	Y	Y	
2	Remove record type	11.8	Y		Y	
3	Remove item from existing record type	9.9	Y		Y	
4	Remove actual source item from existing record type	9.7	Y		Y	
5	Remove virtual source item from existing record type	10.6.2	Y			
6	Remove actual result item from existing record type	10.6.2	Y		Y	
7	Remove virtual result item from existing record type	10.6.2	Y			
8	Remove set type retaining constituent record types	11.6	Y			Y
9	Remove index from sorted set type	6.3.2	Y			
10	Remove search key from any set type	6.10	Y			

From the above analysis, it is clear that a subtractive schema restructuring will sometimes affect the value content and sometimes not. Removing a realm, it would affect both the object schema and the DSDL internal tables. The value content would be affected only if records were still in the realm.

This introduces one of those philosophical questions which permeate the whole topic of restructuring. Is it appropriate to allow the removal of a realm to be a convenient shorthand for erasing all the records it contains, or would this be a dangerous practice to allow? Most DBMS would surely prefer to play safe here and require that a realm can only be removed if and when it is completely empty.

Different arguments would apply in the case of removing a set type but retaining the constituent record types. Whether or not the value content of the data base is affected depends on the set selection option which has been chosen. In the case of a set item approach (see Section 8.8), the value content of the data base is not affected. In the case of the older and more established CODASYL options, such as that based on 'current of set', the fact that a member occurrence is connected to a set conveys information and represents value content. If the set type relationship is removed, the connection would also be taken away and this surely represents a modification to the value content of the data base.

Continuing with the interesting case of removing a set type from the data base, the fourth possible effect is that it may cause the physical placement of the records in the data base to be modified. This is possible both for the chain mode for set representation and for the pointer array. In fact, there are only two reasons for wanting to remove a set type without removing the constituent records. One is to save storage space and the other is to save update time. In the former case, it would be pointless to remove the set type if it did not result in a concommittant space saving.

In conclusion, it should be mentioned that subtractive restructuring is likely to be less common than additive or modificational restructuring. Data base structures tend to expand rather than contract and the tuning process results mostly in modification to various aspects of the data definition.

20.6.3 Modification Restructuring

Modificational restructuring includes the following facilities:

No.	Modificational Changes	Section	Possible Effects 1 2 3 4
1	Change name of realm	11.4	Y Y
2	Change name of record type	11.5	Y Y
3	Change name of item	9.9	Y
4	Change name of set type	11.6	Y
5	Change name of index	6.10.1, 11.6	Y Y
6	Change record to realm assignment	4.5.1	Y Y Y

No.	Modificational Changes	Section	Possible Effects	
7	Change calc key but retain location mode	4.4.1	Y	Y
8	Change location mode for a record type	4.3	Y	Y
9	Change item from actual to virtual	9.7	Y	Y
		10.6.2		
10	Change item from virtual to actual	9.7	Y	Y
		10.6.2		
11	Change set order for a set type	6.7	Y	Y
12	Change set mode for a set type	5.6	Y Y	Y
13	Change set selection criterion for a member	8.6	Y	Y
14	Change storage class for a member	7.4	Y	Y
15	Change removal class for a member	7.4	Y	

Changes 1 to 5 are all name changes. It is unlikely that such changes would be frequent after the data base is loaded. If the Sub-schema DDL has a renaming capability (see Section 12.8.3), then it would be unnecessary to modify programs as a result of name changes within the schema. It would, however, be necessary to modify the sub-schemas which used the old names and then to retranslate them.

Changes to the location mode raise interesting problems. The most significant kind of change is from a CALC location mode, because this would probably necessitate program modifications. A change to a CALC location mode would probably imply program modifications in order to take advantage of the CALC key—otherwise why make the change. A change of CALC key (item 7 in the above list) is an unlikely event, but it would fairly certainly cause program modifications.

Changing the set order for a set type is not likely to affect the physical placement of records in the data base, but we have noted it as a possibility. A more interesting question again is the effect on programs written to process the data base under its former schema. For a program to take advantage of knowledge of the set order, it is not enough to use a FIND statement which includes a reference to the set type (see Sections 15.5.1 and 15.5.4). It depends on how the statement is used. It is quite possible to use these statements in an 'order insensitive' way so that changes to the set order will not affect the semantics of the program.

A change to the set selection criterion is another interesting case which could merit a chapter of in-depth analysis in its own right. Suffice it to say here that the effect of a change is related to the storage class of a member which may or may not be changed in the same restructuring class. This is specially true if the storage class is or becomes automatic, which means that after the restructuring has taken place every occurrence of the member record type whose set selection is being changed *must* be connected into a set occurrence. If the change is made into one of the set selection options where the semantics of the updating program effectively determines which set is selected, then the restructuring cannot be achieved by a simple non-procedural declaration. This probably represents one of the most complicated problems to be faced in restructuring. Referring back to the discussion on set selection (see Section 8.9), the best advice which can be given is to choose a set item approach for as many set types as possible and avoid ever changing it.

20.7 Conclusions

The preceding discussions of restructuring have hopefully shed some light on a problem which is often mentioned but never analysed in detail. The CODASYL work until the publication of the DBAWG 1975 report has been very much limited to mentioning the problem.

Unfortunately, too many arguments and hypotheses on the goal of data independence have been predicated on the kind of restructuring which is most unlikely to be undertaken.

Chapter 21

The TOTAL Approach

21.1 Major Components

We now leave the CODASYL approach to data base management and take a look at two other widely used approaches. The first of these is represented by Cincom's TOTAL, a commercially marketed system available for an impressively wide range of hardware. TOTAL is the proprietary name of this system and it does not represent an acronym. As in the case of the CODASYL approach, details of specific implementations will be avoided, the aim in this text being to indicate the major data base management provided in each approach. For the record, however, implementations are currently available for Burroughs, Control Data, DEC, Harris, Honeywell, IBM, ICL, Interdata, NCR, Siemens, Univac and Varian machines.

In presenting the system, we shall, where possible, follow the sequence of this book, giving references to where the corresponding capability is discussed earlier for the CODASYL approach. The description of a capability in this chapter does not mean that it is available for each and every implementation.

The TOTAL components corresponding to those identified in Chapter 2 are the following:

Schema DDL	Data Base Definition Language, DBDL
Data Manipulation Language	Data Manipulation Language, DML
Data Base Control System	DATBAS (IBM OS users only)

DATBAS is the name of the small interface module which is called. The main execution time module is usually referred to as TOTAL. There is no Sub-schema DDL although some of the capability can be achieved. There is no Device Medium Control Language (see Chapter 18), although the Physical Environment Entries provide a little of its flavour.

21.1 Implementation of DML

The DML in TOTAL is also an extension to existing programming languages, consisting of a series of CALL statements each with its own parameter list. Most CALL statements take the form

CALL 'DATBAS' USING operation, status, file, reference, linkage-path, control field, element list, record-area, end-of-parameter list,

where the first parameter in the list, namely 'operation', is the name of the statement type which will be executed. Certain parameters, for example 'reference' and 'linkage-path' are only used in certain situations.

Using this CALL statement interface, it is possible to support more than one host language (see Section 2.5.2) and indeed COBOL, PL/1, FORTRAN and Assembler are all equally usable for this role.

21.3 Basic Structuring Concepts

The structure of a TOTAL data base relies largely on inter-record structures (see Section 3.3) with a set type (see Section 3.4) referred to either as a 'relationship' or sometimes as a 'linkage-path'. It is important to note that all set types in TOTAL are single member ones and many problems are avoided for both implementor and user by avoiding the very marginal value multiple member set type (see Section 3.4). However, there is a special capability in TOTAL which effectively allows the user to define multiple member set types by use of an intra-record structure technique. This will be described later.

For reason which should soon become clear, there are no system owned set types, another capability of somewhat minimal value.

21.3.1 Inter-record Type Structures

The way in which the set type relationship may be used to build up a data base structure is very similar in TOTAL to the CODASYL approach, but there is one very major restriction. In TOTAL it is *not* possible for a record type to be an owner in one set type and a member in another set type. Fortunately, it is possible for a record type to be a member in several set types and consequently there is a way for a TOTAL data base designer to get around this somewhat nasty problem.

In Figure 21.1 (a repeat of Figure 3.11), a simple three level hierarchy is

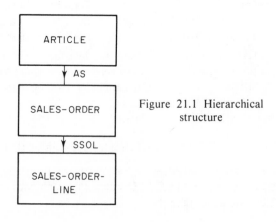

Figure 21.1 Hierarchical structure

depicted. This kind of structure would present no problems in either a CODASYL system or, as will be seen, in IMS, but in TOTAL it is necessary to introduce a fourth record type which results in the kind of structure in Figure 21.2.

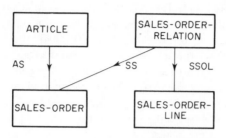

Figure 21.2 Typical TOTAL two-level
structure

Each time a new occurrence of SALES-ORDER is added to the data base, the programmer must ensure than an occurrence of SALES-ORDER-RELATION is also created and stored. This fourth record type would normally only be quite small. Furthermore, the extra set type relationship SS is in effect a one to one relationship. In other words, there is exactly one occurrence of SALES-ORDER for each occurrence of SALES-ORDER-RELATION. This should be contrasted with the other two relationships in Figure 21.2 which correspond to those with the same names in Figure 21.1. For these two, namely AS and SSOL, there may be zero, one or more occurrences of the member for each occurrence of the owner.

It must be noted that TOTAL places no restrictions on the number of set type relationships which may be defined between any two record types. Figure 21.3

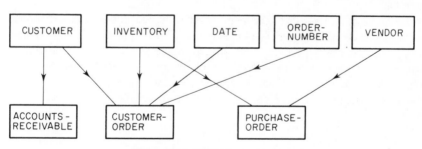

Figure 21.3 TOTAL data base

illustrates a typical TOTAL data base structure, in fact taken from the sample problem in the TOTAL reference manual, but with the record types renamed and the structure redrawn according to the conventions used in this text. This illustrates the two level nature of the permitted TOTAL data base structure more clearly.

TOTAL requires that each record type is given a four character name and that each data item be given an eight character name such that the first four characters of the item name are equivalent to the name of the record type containing the item. Each set type must be given an eight character name of the format mmmmLKxx.

The convention used with TOTAL to illustrate graphically the structure of a data base uses a different symbol, namely a hexagon, to represent a member record type. It is inherent to the whole idea of TOTAL that a record type in the data base can play either the role of owner or else the role of member, but never both. The term used to refer to an owner is *single entry* or *master*, while a member record type is called a *variable entry*. The collection of all records of a given type is called either a *single entry data set* or a *variable entry data set*. The term *data set* is a widely used IBM operating system term. In some places, the literature on TOTAL uses the word *file* instead of *data set*.

21.3.2 Intra-record Type Structures

There is a special intra-record type facility in TOTAL, which is unlike any capability proposed by CODASYL. It is referred to as the *record code concept* and is really a formalization of a trick with sequential files sometimes used by COBOL programmers.

When the data base is defined, any member record type may be divided into two parts called the base data and redefined data. The base data must be the first part of the record type, and there are clear rules about which items must be included in this base part. The redefined part may have two or more completely different definitions, and each definition is distinguishable by a two character 'record code'. Furthermore, each coded record (essentially a 'record sub-type') can participate in set type relationships distinct from other coded records in the same file.

The length of all records of the member record type is the same, independent of which record definition a redefined part follows. The implication is clearly that all record occurrences require as much storage space as the longest definition in a given record type, and the records which follow one of the shorter definitions contain blank unused space. When the lengths are widely divergent, then it would be advisable to define different record types (that is to say different TOTAL variable entry files).

21.4 Mapping Record Types to Storage

The only control a data designer can exercise over how a record type is mapped to storage is when he decides whether it is to be an owner or a member. There is no explicit concept of location mode (see Section 4.3) in TOTAL. However, it is useful to think of all owner record types as having a location mode of CALC (see Section 4.5), but with duplicate values not allowed (see Section 4.5.1). In other words, each owner record type must have a unique prime key item whose value is used as a basis for the built-in randomizing technique used to store occurrences of the record type. All owner record types in any TOTAL data base use the same randomizing algorithm and collisions (see Section 4.5.2) are handled automatically.

While it is possible to suggest that owner record types have a location mode of CALC, the most appropriate location mode for member record types is SYSTEM (see Section 4.6.2) which implies that the system decides how the records of that type are to be stored and there is nothing the data base designer can do to influence the process. A member record type cannot have a prime key without defining an extra record type specially for this purpose.

The ability to allow a member record type to have an unlimited number of owners (as in CODASYL but not IMS) in fact solves several problems. A data base designer can, in fact, let a member record type have several keys by the simple expedient of defining an owner record type which contains the item from the member record type which is to serve as a key. There will be only as many occurrences of this owner record type as there are different values for the key item. The key item is a unique prime key to the owner record type, but it serves as a non-unique access key to the member record type. The application programmer who will write programs to process this part of the data base must be fully aware of the fact that keys to the member record type are provided in this way and will have to go through the process of retrieving an owner record and then a member record.

The realm concept provided in a CODASYL system (see Section 4.8.1) has the effect of placing records of *different* types close to each other, where 'close' in this case probably means on the same disc pack. The location mode of VIA SET (see Section 4.7) allows member records to be placed as close as possible to others in the same set and also to the owner of the set. Such control over physical placement of records is not provided for in TOTAL apart from the facility to control the number of logical records per block and hence per track. However, the 'coded record' concept (see Section 21.3.2) allows some control over the physical contiguity of two or more record set types.

21.5 Mapping of Set Type to Storage

All set types in TOTAL are represented in storage as chains linked to next *and* prior (see Section 5.6). There is no other option available to the data base designer. As in the case of a CODASYL system, this implies that there are two pointers stored in each owner and member record (see Figure 5.4). However, in TOTAL the person preparing the data base definition must allocate eight bytes of space in a record type for each relationship in which the record type participates, whether it is an owner or a member. (In a CODASYL system this allocation of space is implicit in the definition of the set type and where appropriate the set mode (see Section 5.3).)

This restriction to one set mode only is not a bad decision from the data base designer's point of view. The trade-offs for the different CODASYL options concern the usual processing time versus storage space and are not always easy to evaluate accurately. Allowing only one possibility saves the possible agony of deciding which alternative would be right in the case of each set type.

21.6 Set Order

It is not possible for the designer of a TOTAL data base to specify an order for a set type (see Section 6.2). To find what happens when a new record is connected into a set, it is necessary to examine the semantics of the TOTAL equivalent of the STORE statement (see Section 16.4). In TOTAL this is called the ADD statement (see Section 21.12.3). Although it is somewhat premature to consider the DML in detail, it is relevant to note that a different statement needs to be used to store a member from that used to store an owner. Furthermore, there are three different options available in the case of storing a member.

The impact of this is that the order of any set type is firmly in the hands of the programmer who writes the update programs. If there is more than one such programmer, then hopefully they will agree what the set order is to be. It may be recalled that in a CODASYL system (see Section 6.2.2), the data administrator may delegate the decision on set order to the programmer (see Section 6.4.2). The TOTAL approach is in effect close, but not identical, to this CODASYL option.

21.7 Search Keys

TOTAL does not support the older kind of intra-set type search key (see Section 6.10) proposed by CODASYL. Again, this is not felt to be a very significant omission. A more interesting kind of search key is that referred to (see Section 6.10.3) as a global search key. This is a property of a record type in the same way as its location mode and provides a capability to define secondary keys.

In the case of a member record type in TOTAL, the technique of using an extra owner record type to fulfil the task of a prime key can equally well be used for other search keys. The use of an extra set type to simulate a secondary index has long been recognized by CODASYL. The DBTG probably felt that this was a reasonable justification for not providing global search keys originally.

21.8 Storage Class and Removal Class

No options are provided for these two concepts in TOTAL. A member record type is necessarily an automatic member of any set type. The implications of this approach are best illustrated by examples. In the case of the example given earlier (see Section 7.1), one approach would be to include an extra item in the ARTICLE record type (see Figure 21.4) which indicates that the article is a back-order. Another example is illustrated in Figure 21.5.

If it is required to cater for the situation where an employee does not have to be assigned to a department, then it would be necessary to store a DEPARTMENT record in the data base to represent a dummy department. It would need to have a dummy department number, and employees who are not in any real department

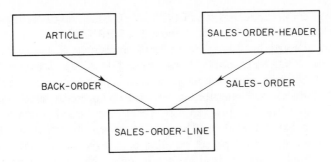

Figure 21.4 Automatic storage class only

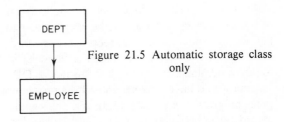

Figure 21.5 Automatic storage class only

would need to be connected to this record. This represents extra work for the programmer, but it is not clear that it is necessarily much more than is called for in the case of a set type with manual storage class.

Removal class (see Section 7.2) concerns the semantics of the ERASE statement (see Section 16.3). In TOTAL this is called DELETE, and as with the STORE there are different formats for owners and members. It would not be meaningful to ascribe either of the two possible CODASYL removal classes to TOTAL.

21.9 Set Selection

Anyone reading the reference literature on TOTAL will not find the term *set selection* or even anything remotely akin to it. Nevertheless, the problem (see Section 8.2) exists in any DBMS supporting inter-record type relationships, and the solution in TOTAL is absurdly simple.

In an owner record type, there must be for each set type one item (or group of items) which serves as a control field. In the member record type of the set type, there must be an item which corresponds in length to the control field in the owner record type. The value of this item in the member record type must be the same as the value of the 'control field' in one of the owner records already stored in the data base.

The approach can be illustrated using the example in Figure 21.5. Assuming that the item, DEPT-NO is the prime key in the record type DEPT, then there must be an item in the record type EMPLOYEE which takes the same value as DEPT-NO. It does not need to have the name DEPT-NO.

It should be noted that this approach corresponds quite closely to that recently added to the CODASYL specifications by the DDLC (see Section 8.9). At the expense of duplicating an item in two record types, the unnecessary abstruseness of the CODASYL set selection is avoided. It becomes clear that in the CODASYL approach, the programmer specified set selection (see Section 8.3) ties in with manual storage class. The TOTAL approach with all storage classes automatic and only the simple set selection option gives less control over some rather obscure trade-offs and is at the same time much easier conceptually.

21.10 Sub-schema

As indicated earlier, there is no Sub-schema DDL in TOTAL. One of the aims of the sub-schema is to allow the programmer to limit his view of the data base and bother only about the record types which he intends to process in his program. In a CODASYL system each such 'limited view' would be defined by the data administrator using a Sub-schema DDL (see Section 12.2). Each sub-schema would have a name, and all the programmer has to do is to use the name in his program (see Section 13.3), and one significant effect of this would be that a record area (see Section 12.4) would be reserved for use by each executing instance of that program.

With TOTAL, the programmer must define record areas in his program for each record type he wishes to process. Any record type not of interest may be omitted. This approach satisfies the 'limited view' aspect of the Sub-schema DDL concept, but it does not give the data administrator control over who is allowed to process which part of the data base. This may be achievable by judicious use of the COBOL library facility.

21.11 Data Manipulation Language Concepts

As indicated earlier in this chapter (see Section 21.2), all accesses to the data base from the host language (see Section 13.2) must be made by means of a CALL statement. The first parameter in the list always indicates the operation to be performed. The second is called simply 'status' and it identifies a location in the calling program's working space where a status condition is set to indicate what happens each time the CALL statement is invoked. We can think of the status variable as a kind of data base register (see Section 13.5).

The TOTAL literature makes no reference to the convenient concept of currency indicators (see Section 13.6), but this is in clear agreement with the fact that it does not mention data base keys (see Section 4.2) either. Examination of the semantics of some of the DML statements indicate that the concept of several currency indicators could well be introduced. This should become clear when the various DML statements are presented.

21.12 DML Statements

We have already indicated in passing (see Section 21.6) that there are different DML statements for owner record types and member record types. The most convenient way to review the DML statements is to look at three categories in turn.

1. Record type independent
2. Owner record type
3. Member record type

It is not the intent here to give a detailed definition of how each statement works, but merely to indicate sufficient for a comparison with the CODASYL approach to be made.

The following table summarizes the possible statement types in each of these three categories and gives the equivalent CODASYL statement for comparison.

CODASYL equivalent	Owner record types	Both	Member record types
READY	OPENM	SINON OPENX	OPENV
FINISH	CLOSM	SINOF CLOSX	CLOSV
FIND/GET	READM	RDNXT RINDX	READV READD READR
STORE	ADD-M		ADDVA ADDVB ADDVR
ERASE	DEL-M		DELVD
MODIFY	WRITM		WRITV

There has been a recent trend towards the statements which apply to both owners and members. This means that, while statements such as OPENM and OPENV are still valid in order to retain compatability with earlier versions, the latest manual describes OPENX and omits the other four OPEN statements.

21.13 DML Statements Valid for Owners and Members

21.13.1 SINON, READY and FINISH

The first TOTAL statement included in an application program written to process a TOTAL data base must be a SINON. In some senses this is akin to a

CODASYL READY, but since there is an OPEN as well, it is appropriate to examine the differences.

A given installation may have several TOTAL data bases, which means more than one 'Data Base Description Module' is in some kind of catalogue or library. The SINON statement parameters are different from those for the other statements and include one called 'access' which is analogous to usage mode (see Section 14.2.1). The four options among which the programmer must choose include retrieval, update and recovery. This last option enables use of a special DML statement (WRITD) which will not be described here.

In addition to specifying a usage mode, the SINON statement has another parameter in which the programmer specifies whether or not logging is required, and if so the details of how and where.

The next statements which are independent of the role of the record type involved are those for opening and closing several files using one statement. The statements have the operation codes OPENX and CLOSX respectively. The parameter 'status' in this case must be able to accommodate one status code for *each* file to be opened. The programmer is responsible for testing each of these status codes.

There is no concept of exclusive or protected processing (see Section 14.2.1) in TOTAL, and all processing is assumed to take place in unprotected mode (see Section 14.2.4). Whether it is for retrieval or for update is referred to as 'acess mode' and is specified in SINON. If we assume that each record type in TOTAL is assigned to one realm and that there is hence a one to one relation between realm and record type, the OPENX is then equivalent to (see Section 14.2).

READY [realm-name-1] ... ; USAGE MODE IS RETRIEVAL

and CLOSX is the same as

FINISH [realm-name-1] ...

A SINOF (sign off) is used for task termination.

21.13.2 Multi-purpose READ

A comparatively recent addition to the list of statement codes is the RDNXT or READ NEXT. This supercedes the older statement SEQRM (or SERIAL READ MASTER) and can be used with either owners or members. However, the distinction is only partially eradicated because the use of the parameters in the CALL statement vary depending on the 'role' of the record type.

With suitable parameter settings the programmer can achieve a number of different CODASYL FIND options. The critical parameter for this statement is called the 'qualifier'. For an owner record type (i.e. master file) there are three alternatives:

1. BEGN
2. KEY=kkk ... kk
3. rrrr

while for a member record type (i.e. variable file), there are a further five:

4. BEGN ƀƀƀƀ SERIAL
5. rrrr ƀƀƀƀ SERIAL
6. BEGN ƀƀƀƀ mmmmLKxx
7. rrr ƀƀƀƀ mmmmLKxx
8. mmmmLKxx KEY=kk ... kk

Although these may seem somewhat cryptic, each has a reasonable explanation as follows:

1. The BEGN option is for initializing a search and it is to all intents and purposes the same as

   FIND FIRST record-name-1 IN realm-name

   (see Section 15.4.3). If the statement is executed successfully, then a record is placed in the record-area referred to in the CALL statement parameter list, thus giving the TOTAL RDNXT the same effect as a combined FIND and GET. In addition, the content of the parameter field whose name is given in the parameter list as 'qualifier' is also changed. It is set to the 'internal reference point' (essentially the data base key value) of the record found. The reason for this will be clear from the description of the third option.
2. The KEY=kkk ... kkk option is the 'out of the blue' FIND option using a value of the unique prime key which every owner record type must have. It is therefore equivalent to

   FIND ANY record-name

   (see Section 15.4.1). The data base key of the record found is placed in the first four bytes of the 'qualifier' (thereby overwriting KEY=).
3. The rrrr option is equivalent to

   FIND NEXT record-name-1 IN realm-name

   (see Section 15.5.6). A data base key value is assumed to have been stored in the first four bytes of the 'qualifier' as could have been done by *either* of the first two options. This value is incremented by one and the record physically next to the one whose data base key value is stored in 'qualifier' is found and the contents of 'qualifier' incremented further.
4. The BEGN SERIAL option is equivalent for a member record type to alternative 1 for an owner.
5. The rrrr SERIAL option is equivalent for a member record type to alternative 3 for an owner.
6. The BEGN mmmmLKxx option has no exact equivalent in CODASYL although the closest is perhaps

   FIND FIRST record-name-1 IN set-name-1

   (see Section 15.5.1) with the essential difference being in how the set occurrence is selected. Bearing in mind that a member record type can participate in several set types, the purpose of the second part of 'qualifier', namely mmmmLKxx, is to specify which set type (or linkage path) is of interest. What TOTAL does is to perform a serial search from the beginning of the realm looking for a record which is FIRST in one set or the other of the set type designated. (TOTAL calls this the 'head of the chain'.) As in the case of the options available for owner record types, the data base key value of the record found is placed in the first four bytes of 'qualifier'.

7. The rrrr mmmmLKxx option is the same as the preceding one with the single difference that the search starts at the record whose data base key value is given in rrrr.

8. The mmmmLKxx KEY=kkk . . . kk option is another variant of

> FIND FIRST record-name-1 IN set-name-1

with the set being selected by means of selecting the owner whose prime key value is kkk . . . kk.

An analysis of these eight alternatives given for RDNXT shows that there are three steps for each as follows:

1. Starting point
2. Path followed
3. Condition satisfied by record sought

There are three starting point options:

A. FIRST IN realm
B. DB-KEY value in 'qualifier'
C. Record selected by out of blue access to an owner

There are two path options:

D. Serially through realm
E. No path

There are three possible conditions which the record sought must satisfy

F. NEXT IN realm
G. FIRST IN set
H. No condition

Permuting these three steps gives 18 conceivable alternatives of which the eight allowed are the following:

1. A, E, H
2. C, E, H
3. B, D, F
4. A, E, H
5. B, D, F
6. A, D, G
7. B, D, G
8. C, E, G

21.13.3 Boolean FIND

A recent extension to the retrieval facilities is provided in the FINDX which in some ways can be regarded as a modification of RDNXT.

Having explained RDNXT it is convenient to present FINDX in similar terms.

FINDX has the same parameter 'qualifier' as RDNXT. The eight alternative settings for this parameter are identical. In addition, FINDX has a further parameter called 'argument', which must be set to point to a list containing the search criterion. This criterion consists of a number of relational conditions on items in the record type sought. These conditions are ANDed together, which means of course that all conditions must be satisfied for the search criterion to be satisfied. One of the well known six relational operators, EQ, NE, GT, GE, LT, LE, must be used in each condition.

Bearing in mind the three steps in RDNXT, namely

1. Starting point
2. Path followed
3. Condition satisfied by record sought

it is convenient to use the same steps for FINDX and to note the slightly different options for the last two. The three starting point options are identical and we will again call them A, B, and C.

The two path options are rather more complicated and can be identified as follows:

D. Serially through realm
E. Serially through realm, then sequentially round chain

The conditions which the record sought must satisfy is given through the parameter 'argument'. Hence, the eight alternative forms of FINDX are as follows:

1. BEGN. Start from FIRST in realm, searching serially through the realm for a record satisfying the search criterion.
2. KEY=kkk .. kk. Start from record with unique prime key as specified in parameter, searching serially through the realm for a record satisfying the search criterion.
3. rrrr. Start from record whose data base key value is as given, search serially through the realm for a record satisfying the search criterion.
4. BEGN ... SERIAL. This is the same as 1, but for a member record type.
5. rrrr ... SERIAL. This is the same as 3, but for a member record type.
6. BEGN ... mmmmLKxx. This starts from FIRST in realm and searches serially through. Records which are FIRST in the set type named are tested against the search criterion.
7. rrrr ... mmmmLKxx. This is the same as 6, but starts from the record whose data base key value is as given.
8. mmmmLKxx KEY=kkk ... kk. This starts from the owner record whose unique prime key value is as specified. The FIRST in set is retrieved and tested

against the search criterion. If it fails, the search proceeds through the set (that is to say round the chain) with the search criterion evaluated against each member.

This option is almost identical to the following CODASYL option (see Section 15.4.2)

FIND record-name-1 WITHIN set-name-1
USING db-id-1 [, db-id-2] . . .

in the case that the items in the USING clause do not represent a search key or a sort key.

21.14 Owner Record Type DML Statements

Firstly, we must mention the OPENM and CLOSM statements which stand for OPEN MASTER and CLOSE MASTER. This use of the term MASTER is probably some old TOTAL terminology which has subsequently been replaced by 'single entry', but it still pervades the operation codes. OPENM and CLOSM refer to one owner record type only. They have been essentially superceded by OPENX and CLOSX (see Section 21.13.1).

21.14.1 Retrieval Statements

The older TOTAL manual describes some retrieval statements which have subsequently been embedded in RDNXT. Although extra capability was provided at the same time, the negative aspect is that the reader and maintenance programmer must dig more deeply into the parameters of the CALL statement to determine what a given statement does.

As an example of this situation, the 'out of the blue' FIND for an owner record is READM, READ MASTER. This is equivalent to alternative 2 of RDNXT. It works in the same way as the CODASYL option for finding a CALC record (see Section 15.4.1), except that in TOTAL the prime key is unique and there is no question of being able to retrieve duplicates as well (see Section 15.5.2). The corresponding CODASYL syntax would be

FIND ANY record-name

READM in fact combines the effect of the GET (see Section 15.8) and moves selected items into a designated record area.

The older FIND option for owner record types was the 'serial retrieval function' SEQRM, SERIAL READ MASTER. This is equivalent to alternatives 1 and 3 of RDNXT which must be preferred in new programs. This statement appears to be very close to the CODASYL option (see Sections 15.4.3 and 15.5.6)

FIND $\left\{ \begin{array}{c} \text{FIRST} \\ \text{NEXT} \end{array} \right\}$ RECORD IN realm-name bearing in mind that there is only one type of record in each realm. In order to be able to do a FIND FIRST, it was necessary in TOTAL to use a special operation called RESTM, RESTORE MASTER, which in the words of the reference manual 'will reset the master serial reference record counter of the DML to zero, so that the next execution of the SEQRM function will retrieve record one of a file.'

This 'serial reference record counter' clearly did the job of the 'current of realm-name indicator' (see Section 13.6). The job is now done by one of the parameters of FINDX and RDNXT, namely the rrrr in 'qualifier'.

21.14.2 Update Statements

New owner records may be added to the data base using the operation ADDM, ADD MASTER, which corresponds fairly closely (see Section 16.4) to the CODASYL

STORE record-name

in the case of a CALC record type which is not a member in any set type.

Existing owner records may be modified using the statement WRITM, WRITE MASTER, which in fact works rather differently from the CODASYL

MODIFY record-name [item-name] . . .

which acts on the current record of run-unit (see Section 16.2). The TOTAL statement WRITM in fact embodies the READM operation discussed above. The items to be modified must be listed in an array specified in one of the CALL parameters.

The TOTAL operation DEL-M, DELETE MASTER, is semantically similar to the CODASYL simple ERASE (see Section 16.3.1) in that only owner records with no member records connected to them may be deleted.

21.15 Member Record Type DML Statements

For member record types known in TOTAL as 'variable entries', there are special OPENV and CLOSV operations which correspond closely to OPENM and CLOSM presented for owner record types.

21.15.1 Member Retrieval Statements

In reviewing the options for retrieving member records, it is important to note the role of one of the parameters which is referred to as 'reference'. To process round a set occurrence in the way which is fairly clear in a CODASYL system (see Section 15.5.1), it is necessary to initialize the processing by using a special setting of 'reference'. The operation REDV, READ VARIABLE FORWARD, will then execute in somewhat the same way as

FIND FIRST record-name IN set-name

However, there is a subtle difference between CODASYL and TOTAL again based on the way TOTAL performs set selection. Another parameter in the CALL statement identified as 'control field' must be set to contain the appropriate value of the owner's prime key in the set type being used.

When it is required to execute the equivalent of

FIND NEXT record-name IN set-name

the parameter 'reference' will have a different setting. However, executing a READV itself causes this parameter to be modified to point to the record retrieved. This reference parameter can be seen to be playing the role of the CODASYL current of set name indicator.

The capabilities implicit in READV are in fact identical to those provided in alternative 6 of RDNXT and alternative 8 of FINDX, in the latter case with a dummy search criterion which every record tested will satisfy.

There is a statement called READR, READ VARIABLE REVERSE, which has no equivalent in RDNXT and FINDX, but it works in an analogous way to READV.

The third statement for retrieving a member record is READD, READ VARIABLE DIRECT, and again its semantics depend upon the setting of the 'reference' parameter. If this parameter contains the number of a record in the data base, then that record is retrieved. In TOTAL the number referred to is called the 'Relative Record Location'. This option can be compared with the CODASYL 'FIND based on data base key' (see Section 15.6.2).

Another use of READD is more subtle and has no direct parallel with CODASYL. The role in TOTAL of this kind of READD was originally explained as the following:

'. . . re-direct the linkage path for subsequent variable entry functions.'

In other words, this option would be used when it is required to initialize a search at a point previously identified in the program. It is then possible in a subsequent statement to proceed round any chain to which the record belongs.

21.15.2 Member Updating Statements

The STORE statements for member record types in TOTAL also offers a number of interesting options. The reason for the options is that it is the programmer, not the data administrator, who determines the set order for a given set type. When the record is stored in the data base, the option used determines where the record is to be connected in the set occurrence which is being followed. The three options available and the position in CODASYL terms are as follows:

ADDVC ADD VARIABLE CONTINUE   (end of set)
ADDVB ADD VARIABLE BEFORE   (prior to current record of set)
ADDVA ADD VARIABLE AFTER   (next to current record of set)

A semantic problem arises with ADDVA and ADDVB when the record type under consideration is a member in two or more set types. The parameter 'reference' for the statement contains either a data base by value (internal reference point) or else a set name. If a set type is named, then it is in an occurrence of this set type that the record being stored is positioned (before or after). In sets of other types to which the record must be connected, it is automatically connected at the *end* of the chain.

There has also been confusion with the use of the term 'primary linkage path' to refer to the set in which the record is to be connected with a ADDVB or ADDVA. This term has also been used at definition time with 'coded records' (see Section 21.3.2) to refer to a set type in which *all* record set types are members. These two uses are not necessarily the same.

The ADDVC option was intended to allow the addition of the record to the end of a set irrespectively. In recent TOTAL manuals, ADDVC has been dropped and it now defaults to a form of ADDVA on translation.

There are two options for modifying member records already in the data base. One of these is called ADDVR, ADD VARIABLE REPLACE, and one might be forgiven for thinking it is in some way associated with the other three ADD statements. The association is in fact that the programmer gets involved again with linkage paths, but this does not seem to justify the similarity of operation name. ADDVR should be used when changing the value of a 'control field'. This will of course have the effect of disconnecting the record from one set and connecting it to another, and is analogous to the CODASYL statement (see Section 16.2)

MODIFY record-name ONLY set-name MEMBERSHIP

If it is desired to change the value of an item other than a 'control field', then a different statement, namely WRITV, WRITE VARIABLE, must be used. It should be noted that WRITV cannot be used to change the content of 'control fields'. WRITV acts on the most recently read record (alias the current record of run-unit) and is hence different from the WRITM which itself finds the record it is going to change. WRITV is therefore much more akin to the CODASYL MODIFY (see Section 16.2), apart from the fact that WRITV cannot change a record from one set to another of the same type.

Finally, the DELVD, DELETE VARIABLE, is a fairly straight forward (simple ERASE' (see Section 16.3.1) which acts on the most recently read record.

21.16 Summary of TOTAL

The TOTAL approach to data base management does bear a number of interesting similarities to the CODASYL approach. The main structuring difference is clearly in the fact that TOTAL in restricted to flat networks. As a consequence of this, it makes sense to require a standard location mode of CALC for all owner records, although it would have been a useful advantage to allow it with member records.

The TOTAL DML is not as elegant as the corresponding CODASYL facility.

Programs with numerous CALL statements containing complex parameter lists will be harder to read and maintain than those with narrative DML statements. The semantics of the STORE and MODIFY statements may cause programmers trouble.

On the other hand, TOTAL is a much simpler system for the data base designer than a CODASYL system. He has less decisions to make and less concepts to grasp when he is new to data base management. This must surely account for TOTALS's measure of commercial acceptance.

Chapter 22

The IMS Approach

22.1 Major Components

IMS stands for Information Management System. This approach to data base management was originated by North American Rockwell in the mid-sixties. It was adopted by IBM around 1967 and has been considerably extended since then. However, some of the more central data management aspects can undoubtedly be traced back to the original system.

It is important to note that IMS is not simply a data base management system. It is, in IBM's own terminology, a 'Data Base/Data Communication System'. In other words, a good half of what is implied in the acronym IMS is a communications management facility and discussion of this is outside the scope of the present text. The data base management part of IMS is sometimes referred to as DL/1, Data Language 1, which is in fact the original name from North American Rockwell. In this chapter, we shall use the more widely recognized abbreviation IMS, noting that IMS uses DL/1 to identify what in the CODASYL approach is called the Data Base Control System (see Section 2.6).

The word 'schema' is not used in IMS, but a broadly equivalent function is provided by one or more control blocks, each known as a Data Base Definition or DBD.

The sub-schema capability (see Section 2.4) is well supported in IMS on the inter-record, but not on the intra-record, level. A sub-schema is defined by means of defining a set of Program Communications Blocks, PCBs, which are collectively called a Program Specification Block, PSB. As with the DBD, the PSB source language is in fact a set of IBM System 360 Assembler Language macro statements.

22.2 Implementation of DML

The normal DML for IMS is similar to that of TOTAL, in other words, it is a CALL statement interface. However, the name of the module to be called varies from one host language to another. For instance, from a COBOL program, one must write

> CALL 'CBLTDLI' USING parameter-count, function, PCB-name,
> I/O area, SSA-1, . . . , SSA-n.

The meaning of the parameters in this statement will be explained later in the chapter.

22.3 Basic Structuring Concepts

As in the case of CODASYL and TOTAL, the structure of an IMS data base relies on inter-record type structures (see Section 3.3) and as with TOTAL, a set type (see Section 3.4) is called a *relationship*. The meaning of the term *data base* in IMS differs from that in the other two approaches and indeed in IMS there are two different kinds of data base. The meaning of the term *record type* is also rather obscure in IMS, but we shall endeavour to clarify these two points before proceeding.

The term *segment type* in IMS has been used historically to convey the structural concept which we understand by *record type* in CODASYL and TOTAL. There are, however, references in the IMS literature to an *IMS record* and to appreciate what this implies, it is necessary to comprehend the meaning of an *IMS data base.*

It is well known that IMS depends completely on hierarchical structures. In fact, an IMS data base is just that—a hierarchical structure. Each of the Figures 22.1, 22.2, 22.3 and 22.4 illustrates a valid structure for an IMS data base.

In each of these four hierarchical structures, there is one record type at the top of the structure. In IMS terms this is called the *root segment type*. An *IMS record* is one occurrence of this root segment type together with all the occurrences of the low level records which are directly or indirectly connected to it. Figure 22.5

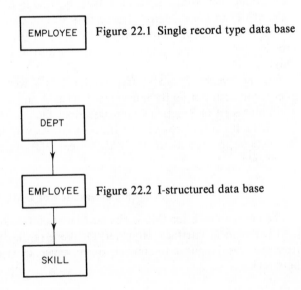

EMPLOYEE   Figure 22.1 Single record type data base

DEPT

EMPLOYEE   Figure 22.2 I-structured data base

SKILL

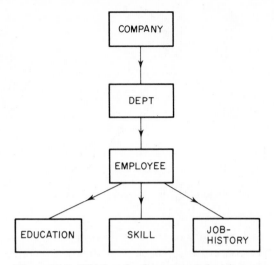

Figure 22.3 'Chicken foot' structured data base

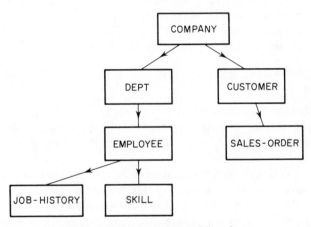

Figure 22.4 Full tree structured data base

shows an IMS record for the I-structure of Figure 22.2. Since the representation of a set type has yet to be presented, no significance should be attached to the lines connecting the record occurrences or to the lack of arrows on these lines. For the time being, it can be asserted that the eight record occurrences in Figure 22.5 collectively comprise one *IMS record* of the data base depicted in Figure 22.2. There is a measure of 'togetherness' for these eight records which is not found in CODASYL or TOTAL, which hopefully will become clear.

22.3.1 Intra-record Type Structuring Concepts

In the earlier versions of IMS, it was necessary for all occurrences of each record type to be of the same length. The most recent version of IMS, namely

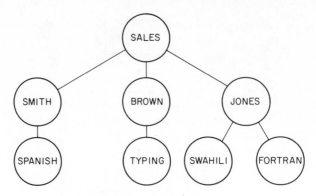

Figure 22.5 IMS record occurrence

IMS/VS, allows each record type to be of fixed or variable length. Apart from this, IMS does not concern itself much with the intra-record structure. When preparing a Data Base Description (alias schema), it is not necessary to name *all* the items in each record type. The length of each record type must be given, however, so that the system knows how much space to reserve for each record occurrence. The most recent version of IMS (IMS/VS) allows a variable length record type on any level in a hierarchical data base.

22.3.2 Set Types

Having explained the emphasis on hierarchies in IMS, it is appropriate to return to the set type concept in order to clarify the role this structural concept plays in an IMS data base. In fact, it is very different from that played in CODASYL and TOTAL.

In a hierarchical structure, it should be clear that any member record type can have at most one owner. As a result of this, it has not been found useful by the designers of IMS to introduce a naming convention for set types. A set type is defined in a data base by the simple expedient of stating the name of another record type in a record type declaration. IMS uses the term *parent* rather than the CODASYL term *owner* and the term *child* rather than *member*.

Every record type in an IMS hierarchical structure has one and only one parent except, of course, the *root segment type*. The latter must always be defined first for each hierarchical structure.

The earliest versions of IMS were completely limited to these hierarchical structures, each of which, as was mentioned earlier, constitutes a data base. It is permissible to define several such data bases at one time and, furthermore, an application program may process several of them. (In CODASYL and TOTAL one talks of *the* data base and a program processes the data in the data base. The fact that IMS allows a program to process several of what it calls *data bases* is a necessity rather than a strength.)

In 1970, IBM realized the inherent weakness in their purely hierarchical approach and introduced a major enhancement into IMS/2. This allowed each member record type to be related to two owner record types. The idea of defining a series of hierarchical data bases was necessarily perpetuated. However, it became possible for a second relationship to be defined between a record type in one hierarchy and another record type which could be in a different data base.

To distinguish between the two owners now possible, the one in the same data base as the record type being considered is called the *physical parent* and the other is called the *logical parent*. Furthermore, a data base *as defined* is called a *physical data base*. When we introduce the IMS sub-schema concepts, the concept of a logical data base will be clarified.

Figure 22.6 illustrates two physical data bases with a logical relationship

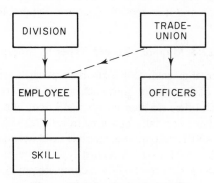

Figure 22.6 Logical relationship

between them. Each record type can have one physical parent and no more than one logical parent. A useful IMS convention is to represent the physical relationship with a continuous line and the logical relationship with a dotted line. (This must never be confused with the CODASYL storage class (see Section 7.1) which uses a dotted line for manual membership and a continuous line for automatic.) By means of the hierarchies structures and the logical relationships, network structures can be represented.

Before concluding our remarks on logical relationships, it is useful to quote the IMS/VS DB Primer on the topic.[1]

'Rules for defining logical relationships in physical data bases.
<u>Logical child</u>
1. A logical child segment must have one and only one physical parent segment and one and only one logical parent segment.
2. A logical child segment is defined as a physical child segment in the physical data base of its physical parent.
3. In its physical data base, a logical child segment cannot have another logical child as its immediate dependent.

Logical parent

1. A logical parent segment can be defined at any level of a physical data base including the root level.

2. A logical parent segment can have one or multiple logical child segment types.

3. A segment in a physical data base cannot be defined as both a logical parent and a logical child.

4. A logical parent segment can be defined in the same or a different physical data base as its logical child segment.

Physical parent

1. A physical parent of a logical child cannot also be a logical child. (This is the same as Rule 3 for the logical child.)'

In addition, it should be noted that there are interactions between the definition of logical relationships and how record types are mapped to storage.

22.4 Mapping Record Types to Storage

Having ascertained that each IMS data base consists of a hierarchical structure, the next issue of interest is how such structures are mapped to storage. Unlike TOTAL which offers no alternatives, IMS does offer several, but they are very different from those normally provided in a CODASYL system.

Firstly, in a CODASYL system, it is possible (and necessary) to choose a location mode (see Section 4.4) for each record type in the data base. In IMS, it is necessary to select one access method for a complete physical data base. The four access methods are the following:

HSAM	Hierarchical Sequential Access Method
HISAM	Hierarchical Indexed Sequential Access Method
HDAM	Hierarchical Direct Access Method
HIDAM	Hierarchical Indexed Direct Access Method

When making comparisons with the CODASYL approach, these four access methods seem to have a few aspects in common. The root segment type can be thought of essentially as a record type with a location mode of CALC, where CALC does *not* necessarily mean randomizing (see Section 4.5). The other lower level record types in a data base can all be thought of as having a location mode of VIA SET (see Section 4.7) because there is a clear implication of storing records of the same type as close as possible to each other and to their owner (or parent), although the closeness to each other depends on the access method used.

HSAM is intended principally for a data base stored on magnetic tape and in that sense it is different from the other three access methods. Updating an HSAM physical data base is different from updating any of the other three and, furthermore, it does not make sense to allow record types in an HSAM data base to have a logical parent or to be a logical parent. Furthermore, HSAM has no logging facilities and it is not generally used.

HISAM makes use of the well known indexed sequential access method using an item in the root segment type as the prime key. It is also possible with HISAM to involve the record types on the second level (that is the children of the root segment type). The effect is that the second level key is concatenated with that in the root to form the ISAM key and it is hence possible to retrieve records on the second level directly.

In HDAM, root segments are stored in a location determined by a user supplied randomizing algorithm which could well be of the kind discussed for a CODASYL system (see Section 4.5). In HIDAM, root segments are stored in approximately ascending sequence of their key and retrieved using a separate index. In both HDAM and HIDAM, each lower level segment is stored and retrieved using pointer chains from its owner (parent). The lower level records are stored according to a rather complex chaining algorithm. The same technique for storing lower level records is used with HIDAM, but the root segment type only is stored using an ISAM technique rather than randomizing.

One of the aims of IMS is to give some control over trade-offs and at the same time allow the user to change the access method used for a data base from one to another. While one might change *from* HSAM, a user is less likely to want to change *to* it. Hence, the programmers who write programs to process the data in an IMS data base do not need to know whether it is HISAM, HDAM or HIDAM. If the program is a retrieval program, the programmer would not need to know whether or not it was a HSAM data base. However, experience has shown that the choice of access method can be critical and that there are considerable differences in execution time between the right one and the wrong one in a given situation.

22.5 Mapping a Set Type to Storage

The way a set type in IMS is represented in storage could be a property of a complete physical data base or else of a single set type as in the CODASYL approach. There are several options in IMS, unlike TOTAL which makes exclusive use of bidirectional chains (see Section 21.5). The options are quite different from the CODASYL ones (see Sections 5.4 and 5.8), although it must be recalled that the latest CODASYL thinking is that this is a matter for the implementor since the programmer does not *need* to know at the time he writes his programs. Since the various IMS options have no equivalent in CODASYL, we will use the IMS terminology to refer to them.

Each option makes use of pointers, and the options are identified by the kind of pointers which are stored in the various records in a data base. Not all options are available with all three access methods using direct access storage, and the choice depends on how the lower level records in a structure are stored. This topic was not discussed in the preceding section, but hopefully it can be appreciated that the choice of access made and pointer option combinations can be rather critical, because a program may function correctly but not efficiently with several combinations.

There are two basic alternatives to IMS pointers. The first alternative consists of a pointer from each owner to the first member in the set (in IMS terms *first child*) and a pointer from each record to the *next* (*forward twin*). This latter pointer is also included from one root segment occurrence to the *next*. In Figure 22.7 this alternative is depicted for the logical structure shown in Figure 22.2. It is

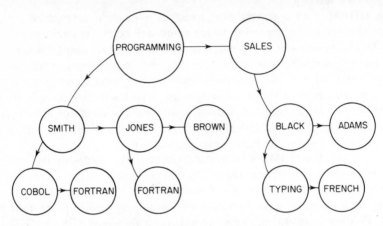

Figure 22.7 First child—forward twin

possible to add further pointers when this alternative is used. The additions comprise the following three:

1. Last child
2. Backward twin
3. Parent

and any combination or selection of these three may be added to the basic two. For this alternative, it is possible to choose the pointers per relationship, but it is

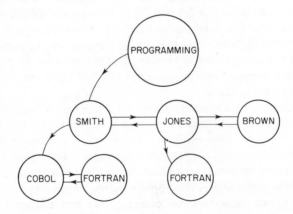

Figure 22.8 First child—twin forward and backward

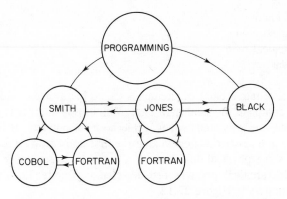

Figure 22.9 First and last child—forward and backward twin

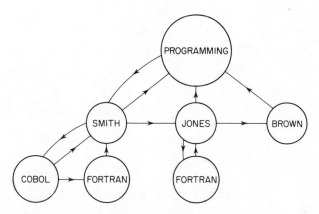

Figure 22.10 First child, forward twin and parent

far more common to choose them for a complete physical data base. Examples of
the basic two pointers plus some of the more useful option extras are shown in
Figures 22.8, 22.9, and 22.10 for a single physical data base.

It is important to note that the pointers in this alternative can be defined for
both physical and logical relationships. In fact, it is normal to use the words
physical and logical to qualify the class of pointer, giving for example

first physical child
forward physical twin
backward physical twin
physical parent

and for logical relationships

248

first logical child
forward logical twin
backward logical twin
logical parent

The other alternative class of pointer is called hierarchical and these may be defined for a complete physical data base. Within this alternative, there are two options—called one way and two way hierarchical pointers. It is important to note that there are restrictions on mixing the first and second alternative pointer classes in the same physical data base.

One way hierarchical pointers are depicted in Figure 22.11 and two way hierarchical pointers in Figure 22.12.

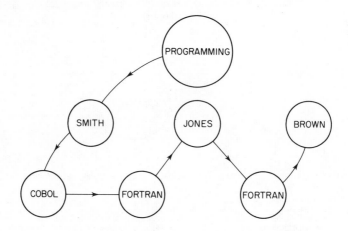

Figure 22.11 One -way hierarchical pointers

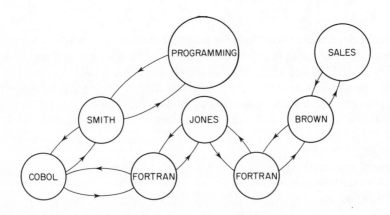

Figure 22.12 Two-way hierarchical pointers

A number of comments are called for regarding these various pointer options. The default definition is First Child—Forward Twin (Figure 22.7) which indicates the implementor's opinion that this is the most useful option. The hierarchical pointers may seem somewhat strange unless one appreciates how one of the FIND options (GET NEXT) works.

22.6 Set Order

At the time of Data Base Definition, the data administrator may select an item in each lower level record type to play the role of *sequencer*. Bearing in mind that each lower level record type is a member (in IMS terms *child*) in one and only one set type, it can be seen that this *sequencer* is in effect what in a CODASYL system would be called a sort key (see Section 6.3). As in the case of CODASYL, IMS allows the data administrator to choose whether the sort key is unique or not, with the former being the default.

This IMS sequencer plays a fairly major role in the semantics of several of the DML statements as will be seen later in this chapter. For the time being, it is interesting to note that the CODASYL, TOTAL and IMS approaches provide radically different solutions to the matter of set order. In the case of a CODASYL system, it was suggested (see Section 6.3.1) that one should have good reason for making a set type sorted.

22.7 Search Keys

The older versions of IMS did not support any kind of secondary indexing, but the most recent version, namely IMS/VS has introduced a relatively powerful and complex secondary indexing facility. This is more akin to the very recent CODASYL idea of a global search key rather than the other 'intra-set type search key' (see Section 6.10).

In IMS, either a root segment type or a dependent may have a secondary index. In the latter case, there is an interesting extension. It is possible to use an item in a member record type to index the owner record type. The owner must be the *physical parent* and not the *logical parent*.

The secondary index table is itself an IMS physical data base. It should be noted that this fact fits in with the fact that in IMS/VS lower level record types may be variable in length.

22.8 Storage Class and Removal Class

The concept of storage class (see Section 7.1) is not provided for in IMS, which is another way of saying that each member record type is an automatic member in the one or two set types in which it participates. The way of avoiding problems is exactly the same as in the case of TOTAL (see Section 21.8).

Removal class (see Section 7.2) concerns the semantics of the ERASE statement (see Section 16.3). In IMS this is called DELETE and works in the same way as ERASE ALL (see Section 16.3.2). In other words, when a record is deleted, any dependents below it in the physical data base are also deleted. If the record deleted is a parent in a logical relationship, there is added flexibility—and complexity.

22.9 Set Selection

There are no options for set selection in IMS, and it works differently from the nice simple approach of TOTAL. In effect, the IMS solution is one of the lesser used CODASYL options referred to as *hierarchical set selection* (see Section 8.6). However, in IMS the path down the hierarchy always starts from the root segment and is defined in terms of the *sequencer* discussed in connection with set order (see Section 22.6).

The effect remains the same as in most of the CODASYL options, namely that the onus is on the programmer to define the path. This should be contrasted with the TOTAL approach (see Section 21.9) which relies on the replication of data items in the member record types.

22.10 Sub-schema

In IMS, the schema view of the data is the network defined by one or more physical hierarchies possibly linked by logical relationships. The definition of a sub-schema view is a two stage process.

The first stage is to reduce the network defined in the schema to one or more hierarchies which are referred to as logical data bases to distinguish from the physical data bases initially defined in the schema. The root segment of each logical data base must be the root segment of a physical data base or possibly a segment which can be accessed directly using a secondary index. The dependent segments in a given logical data base must lie along the paths defined in the schema (in other words, they must be related using physical or logical relationships).

A logical data base may include segment types from two or more physical data bases. Usually, one logical data base is defined for each physical root segment type.

The second stage is to define the sub-schema views to be seen by a particular program. This is done using a Program Specification Block or PSB, and each of these contains one or more Program Communication Blocks, or PCBS. Each PCB defines part of a hierarchy defined as a logical data base.

Some IMS terminology relevant to the sub-schema concept is the following. A segment type is said to be *sensitive* to a program if it is included in a PCB with the program uses, hence the phrase *segment sensitivity*. There is one problem which arises when a program is sensitive to a segment type but not to its dependents. If the program deletes a segment of the type to which it is sensitive, then all dependent segments, sensitive *or not*, will also be deleted.

One interesting feature of the PCB definition is that it is necessary for *each* sensitive segment type to state one or more processing options. For instance, if a program is to be allowed to retrieve segments of a given type, then the processing option G (for Get) is assigned. Any attempt to delete or replace a segment of this type would be unsuccessful. One extension of this processing option concept is the alternative K (for Key) which implies that the program is sensitive only to the key item in the record type.

22.11 Data Manipulation Language Concepts

As indicated earlier in this chapter, all accesses to the data base from the host language (see Section 13.2) are normally made by means of a CALL statement. However, two preprocessors have recently been announced called COBIMS and PLIMS, which will allow the programmer to write IMS statements in a narrative form in COBOL and PL/1 programs. We will restrict consideration here to the CALL statement.

The CALL statement format for COBOL has the following form:

CALL 'CBLTDLI' USING parameter-count, function, PCB-name,
I/O area, SSA-1, . . , SSA-n

In this list, 'function' indicates the name of the statement type being called. Examples of valid function codes are GU, GN, GNP, ISRT, DLET and REPL. The first three present different GET options, and the last three are the basic up-date options—insert, delete and replace.

The 'PCB-name' refers to a storage area which must be included in the Linkage Section of the program's Data Division as well as having been defined during a sub-schema definition phase (in IMS called PSBGEN). The storage area in the program contains a number of important parameters, including the following.

1. Name of data base
2. Status code (for communication to calling program)
3. Segment name (also for feedback to the calling program)
4. Length of feedback key
5. Key feedback area

Most of this so-called 'PCB mask' is in fact for feedback from the system to the program.

The 'I/O area' parameter in the list designates where in the program a record occurrence is placed following successful retrieval or where it is to be found in the case of an insert or replace. The I/O area fulfils the same role as the CODASYL record area (see Section 12.4). In IMS, however, it is user defined.

The parameters SSA—1, . . . , SSA-n designate areas in core in which the programmer has stored his so-called segment search arguments, SSA. The segment search argument concept represents a very major part of the semantics of the IMS DML and therefore some explanation is called for.

22.11.1 Segment Search Arguments

Any IMS CALL statement may have one or more SSAs, in which case it is called *qualified* or it may have no SSA at all, in which case it is regarded as *unqualified*.

There are three classes of format for an SSA as follows:

1. Segment name
2. Segment name, item name, relational operator, reference quantity
3. Segment name, item name, rel.op., ref.quan. [Boolean connector, item name, rel.op., ref.quan.] . . .

where the relational operator may be any of the standard six and the Boolean connector may be either of the usual two. We will restrict consideration to the first two classes here.

It is important to note that these segment search arguments are areas in the application program and it is hence possible for the programmer to modify the content of the areas by moving values of interest into them. This provides a rather powerful capability to the enterprising programmer.

The meaning of the segment search argument varies somewhat depending on the function with which they are used, as will be indicated.

22.11.2 Retrieval Statements

The IMS GET statement is a combination of the CODASYL FIND (see Section 15.2) and GET (see Section 15.8). After an IMS GET has been executed successfully, a record is to be found in the area designated in 'I/O area' in the parameter. Which record this is depends on the GET option used and the presence and value of the segment search arguments.

GET UNIQUE, abbreviated GU, is the IMS 'out of the blue' FIND (see Section 15.4). The segment search arguments can be used to define a path from the top to a lower level in the hierarchy. The actual record type retrieved is necessarily on the lowest specified level of the path.

GET NEXT, GN, is the simpler of the two 'relative' FIND options in IMS (see Section 15.5). GET NEXT would often be used without segment search arguments to gain access to the record in the hierarchy which is 'next' to the one most recently found (current of run-unit).

It is interesting to compare this IMS GET NEXT with the CODASYL FIND NEXT IN SET (see Section 15.5.1). The latter stops at the end of a set occurrence. The IMS statement is capable of carrying on through to the last record in the data base. Its path is best illustrated in Figure 22.11. GET NEXT follows the hierarchy processing rule top to bottom, left to right. If there is no segment search argument at all (that is to say it is unqualified), it will go down one level and retrieve the first record there. When a record is the owner of two members, the sequence in which the members were defined in the PCB is followed. When the current record has no dependents, the next record of the same type is sought and failing that the next record of the parent.

The other relative FIND option is GET NEXT WITHIN PARENT, GNP, which is useful for processing sequentially through a sub-structure underneath a given record occurrence. The IMS documentation discusses the interesting sounding problem of 'setting parentage'. This is always done during the successful execution of a GET UNIQUE or a GET NEXT. It is important to observe that this 'parentage' once established is not modified by any subsequent GNP statement. Only another GU or GN will have this effect.

Before moving on to discuss update statements, the role of the HOLD option must be presented. In order to replace or delete a record in a data base, the program must first find it successfully. In order to be able to update it, it is necessary that the programmer incorporates a HOLD option into the GET. This HOLD is a way for the programmer to tell the system that an update to that record is to be made. Instead of using the function codes, GU, GN and GNP, he uses GHU, GHN or GHNP. The detailed semantics of these options in a concurrent processing mode are again quite complex, but the programmer does not need to be aware of such semantics.

22.11.3 Update Statements

The three update statements are the following:

DLET Delete
REPL Replace
ISRT Insert

The DLET statement acts primarily on a record which has been successfully retrieved with one of the GET and HOLD statements. Unlike TOTAL (see Section 21.12.2), the effect of executing an IMS delete is to delete all the children and grandchildren and so on as in the case of the CODASYL ERASE ALL (see Section 16.3.2). This is valid whether or not these dependents are of a type to which the executing program is sensitive. Furthermore, it may also have effect across logical relationships. One saving grace appears to be that the appropriate processing option must have been defined in the PCB for the top record type being deleted. Another is that the DLET statement is not allowed to be specified with segment search arguments.

The REPL statement also acts on a record which has been successfully found, using a GET and HOLD. The modification to this record must be effected in the I/O area before the REPL is executed. It is not possible to modify the value of the *sequencer* (see Section 22.6), which is a rather disturbing restriction not found in the TOTAL MODIFY statement (see Section 21.12.3) because there is no such sequencer, but also not found in the case of CODASYL sorted sets. To get around this problem in IMS, it is necessary to delete the record and then insert it with its new sequencer value. The programmer must take steps to handle any substructure he wishes to preserve, and this may cause a potentially complex situation outside the scope of this discussion.

The ISRT statement must not be confused with the other and widely found form of the CODASYL CONNECT (see Sections 13.8 and 16.6). The IMS ISRT could rather be compared to the CODASYL STORE statement (see Section 16.4). The full semantics of ISRT are again very complex and a simplified view of some of the possibilities will suffice here.

ISRT is used for initial load and for subsequent update. It cannot be used to update an HSAM file for fairly obvious reasons. The segment search argument facility is normally used in the case of an updating ISRT to specify the complete hierarchical path from the root segment to the place in the hierarchy at which it is to be inserted. However, on the level of the segment to be inserted, it is the value of the *sequencer* in the record area which determines the position. Special rules and options apply in the case where duplicate values of a sequencer are allowed or where no sequencer is present.

22.11.4 Other DML Statements

One important feature of IMS is that there is no OPEN or READY statement (see Chapter 14). In effect, a data base is opened for a program automatically when the program starts to execute. The difference between the two processing modes of update and retrieval (see Section 14.2.1) is obtained effectively by the specification of the processing option in the PCB. As with TOTAL, the concurrency mode is effectively UNRESTRICTED, but it is also possible to specify the equivalent of 'exclusive' on a per segment type basis.

22.12 Summary of IMS

IMS can be seen to provide a very different approach to data base management from that of CODASYL and TOTAL. It is easy to construe TOTAL as a modest simplified sub-set of the CODASYL proposals, but IMS is about as different as is possible.

The emphasis on defining hierarchical structures and processing only hierarchical structures gives the approach a superficial aura of simplicity which is soon dispelled when one delves into the semantics of the DML together with the powerful but complex use of segment search arguments.

On the data definition side, a decision that set types must be sorted would have the same effect on performance with large sets as with a CODASYL based system.

The DML is full of potential traps for the unwary. There are all too many factors of which the programmer does not need to be aware in order to write correctly functioning programs. Nevertheless, he can profit from an awareness of these factors if he wishes to write a program which would function more efficiently.

References

1. IMS/VS-DB Primer. IBM document No. S320–5767.

Chapter 23

The ADABAS Approach

23.1 Major Components

One system which is not quite so widely used as those discussed in the two preceding chapters, namely IMS and TOTAL, is nevertheless having a growing impact on the user fraternity world wide and therefore merits attention. There are, at time of writing, two implementations of ADABAS available, for the IBM 360/370 hardware and for the Siemens 4004.

The ADABAS components corresponding to those identified in Chapter 2 are the following:

Schema DDL   Control cards for LOADER utility

Data Manipulation Language   ADABAS commands

There is no Sub-schema DDL, although it is the normal practice for the programmer to describe in his program only the record types which he needs to process in his program. Some of the LOADER utilities control card formats contain some of the kind of capability included in a DMCL.

23.2 Implementation of the DML

The DML in ADABAS is an extension to existing programming languages such as COBOL and PL/1 and Assembly Language. Each so-called ADABAS command is a two character code embedded in a control block referred to in a CALL statement which has the following kind of format.

CALL 'ADABAS' USING control-block, format-buffer, record-buffer,
                     search-buffer, value-buffer, ISN-buffer

Irrespective of which DML statement type is being used, the CALL statement has the same format. The programmer must have one or more areas defined in his Working Storage Section for each of the six parameters in the CALL statement.

There is a specific list of contents defined for the 'control-block'. One of the parameters is often called 'COMMAND-CODE'. This defines which DML statement is being invoked. The role of the areas indicated in the other parameters and the other parts of the 'control-block' are dictated by this code.

23.3 Basic Structuring Concepts

ADABAS relies more heavily than any of the other three approaches on the use of intra-record type structures, but it also uses inter-record type structures in an interesting and instructive way quite radically different from CODASYL, IMS and TOTAL.

ADABAS is similar to CODASYL in permitting a full network capability, the only constraint of interest arising if one of the two quite distinct ways of handling inter-record type relationships is used.

23.3.1 Intra-record Type Structures

Whereas the intra-record type structuring facilities in other approaches tend to be dictated by the capability established in the host languages used, ADABAS has its own rather unique capability which is incompatible with that of COBOL and PL/1. The reason for this is possibly that when the system was first being designed, the trend was towards it being a self-contained system. The shortcomings in this class of system were recognized and it became a host language system, but the non-standard intra-record type structure was perpetuated.

The capability allows for one or more variable repeating groups at the top level, that is to say zero, one or more occurrences of the group for each record occurrence. Furthermore, it is possible to define fixed repeating groups. In addition, fixed and variable size vectors can be defined either on the top level or within a repeating group. In ADABAS terminology, a vector is a *multiple value field* and a repeating group is a *periodic group field*.

23.3.2 Inter-record Type Structures

There are two ways of handling inter-record type structures. However, both depend upon the concept of what in ADABAS is called a *descriptor*, basically a CODASYL record level search key (see Section 6.10.3), but not a unique search key. In fact, the only way to achieve uniqueness in one of these search keys is by writing the necessary checks into the programs which update records of the type for which a unique key is required.

There may be one or more of these search keys defined for a record type. (In ADABAS terms, there may be one or more descriptors for any file, a file being all the records of a given type in the data base.) In order for there to be a meaningful relationship between two record types, there must be search keys for each record type. Furthermore, it must be possible to match a value of one search key with a value of the other and get equality.

The two ways of handling the relationship come about as follows. There is an explicit facility called *coupling* which can be defined (using control cards) as part of the data base load process. When this facility is used, the two files are said to be coupled, and the coupling is represented in storage using indexing techniques. Furthermore, a special multi-record FIND statement makes use of the coupling if a conditional expression is used, which includes conditions on search key items in both record types. Because this usage is an implicit one, that is to say the relationship is not named explicitly in the FIND statement, there is no naming requirement in the Schema DDL. The effect of this is obvious, namely that there may be only *one* use of this coupling feature between any two files in the data base.

User experience with ADABAS has shown that this coupling feature is not entirely satisfactory, for reasons of storage space used and performance. However, since the search key facility is based on indexing techniques, then if there are search keys defined for two record types and if, as before, it is possible to match the values and obtain equality, then a relationship between the two record types exists and no further action need be taken. This situation is best explained by two examples.

Figure 23.1 shows two record types, DEPT and EMPLOYEE. Supposing that

Figure 23.1 ADABAS relationship—unfortunately many to many

DEPT has a search key DEPT-NO and EMPLOYEE has a search key EMP-DEPT-NO. These names are deliberately different, but the permitted value set for each is the same; in other words, the values are matchable. This example has been chosen because normally one would like to have DEPT-NO as a unique key. As indicated, there is no way this can be defined in ADABAS. On the other hand, EMP-DEPT-NO would not be a unique key, because there would be several employees in any given department.

It is possible to pick out all the employees in a given department (namely the set occurrence owned by a given department record) if the value of DEPT-NO is known, and it can be established that there is an equal value of EMP-DEPT-NO.

On the other hand, a mistake could occur and there could be two occurrences of DEPT with the same value of DEPT-NO in the data base. This would cause problems.

The second example in Figure 23.2 shows a many to many relationship

Figure 23.2 ADABAS relationship—usefully many to many

between PERSON and MACHINE. The record type PERSON contains a search key with name MACHINE-TYPE-CAN-OPERATE. This means that for each person there will be one or more machines which he can operate. The record type MACHINE contains an item called MACHINE-TYPE defined as a search key. For each value of MACHINE-TYPE there are several occurrences of PERSON containing the same value of MACHINE-TYPE-CAN-OPERATE.

This provides a fairly realistic example of a useful many to many relationship. A person can operate several machines, namely those of a given type. A machine can be operated by several persons, namely those able to operate that type.

In ADABAS, there is facility available to handle an extra level of complexity by combining the intra-record structuring facilities with the inter-record facility.

For the sake of illustration, the above example could be extended by assuming that a person could operate machines of several types. The effect is that MACHINE-TYPE-CAN-OPERATE is in a vector, but it is still a search key. With a stretch of imagination one could similarly say that a given machine has assigned to it one or more type codes. This means that MACHINE-TYPES is in a vector within the record type MACHINE. It can also continue to be a search key in that record type.

Although it is not particularly relevant to the analysis of ADABAS, it is illuminating to see how this situation would be handled using TOTAL or a CODASYL based system. This is depicted in Figure 23.3.

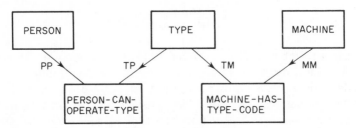

Figure 23.3 Structure needed in CODASYL or TOTAL to handle ADABAS problem

Nevertheless, it is fair to indicate that the semantics of any manipulation are independent of the specific structuring technique involved.

23.4 Mapping Record Types to Storage

In ADABAS, there is no concept of location mode, so one can essentially regard each record type as having a location mode of SYSTEM. In this sense, it is fair to assert that the user exercises no control over how a record type is mapped to storage.

There is no concept of a realm, so one should hence assume that all occurrences of each record type are stored in one realm. This in turn means that there is no control exercisable over the physical contiguity of records of different types. Nevertheless, users often wish to store member records close to the owner, and the way to do this in ADABAS is often to make use of the intra-record structuring facilities. Needless to say, using these facilities calls for a different approach to manipulating the relationship from that used with an inter-record type relationship.

23.5 Mapping of Set Types to Storage

The use of an indexing technique to support non-unique search keys, coupled with the requirement to duplicate the item in the related record type together make up the ADABAS approach to representing set type relationships in storage.

The technique illustrates clearly the analogy between a set type and a search key in CODASYL terms. It also illustrates the extra flexibility provided by indexing over that of randomizing.

For the purpose of comparison, one could say that ADABAS uses a variation of what CODASYL calls a pointer array. ADABAS certainly has something close to the CODASYL concept of a data base key, but in ADABAS it is termed an Internal Storage Number, ISN. The difference between the two concepts is that an ISN must be qualified by a file number to be unique within the data base. Otherwise it is only unique within a file.

23.6 Set Order

There is no concept of set order in ADABAS. Noting how the system represents set types in storage, that is to say using search key indexes, it appears that the CODASYL equivalent of set order for ADABAS would be either LAST or IMMATERIAL.

23.7 Search Keys

As already indicated, search keys are a cornerstone of the ADABAS approach. The capability has been introduced already in order to explain the way inter-record type structuring is handled. In addition, it can be added that a search key can consist of far more than just a single elementary item. It can be a vector (as explained already), or an item in a repeating group. Multiple component search keys are also possible. This means that a search key can include up to five components where a component can be an item, a part of an item, a group item, an item in a repeating group or a vector. These multiple component search keys referred to as 'super descriptors' can be very useful in ad hoc retrieval programs.

23.8 Storage Class and Removal Class

As in the case of IMS and TOTAL, there are no equivalents for either of these concepts in ADABAS. The way of handling any problem this may create is exactly analogous to that described for TOTAL (see Section 21.8).

23.9 Set Selection

As in the case of TOTAL, there is no concept of set selection in ADABAS. However, TOTAL is similar to CODASYL in that it works exclusively in terms of one to many relationships and the question arises of which owner to connect a member to when the member is first stored in the data base.

Because of the complete orientation towards many to many relationships, the question does not even arise in ADABAS. The fact that a record type has a relationship with some other record type in the data base is of no importance. The concept of a M to N relationship accepts zero to many, many to zero, one to zero and so forth on a completely equal basis.

23.10 Sub-schema

The comments on a sub-schema facility which were made for TOTAL (see Section 21.10) all apply exactly for ADABAS.

23.11 Data Manipulation Language Concepts

All access to the data base from a host language (see Section 13.2) must be made by means of a CALL statement. The first of the six parameters identifies a control block and one of the items in the control block contains a code value identifying which operation is to be performed. Another item in the control block is what in ADABAS is termed the *response code* which is exactly equivalent to the CODASYL data base status register (see Section 13.5).

ADABAS does not have any explicit concept of currency indicators, in the sense that these are system provided data items which the system uses to keep track of which record (of a given type, in a given set type or a given realm) the run-unit last retrieved or stored. ADABAS requires the programmer to include items in the control blocks which can accommodate a data base key value (ISN). Such items have the role of currency indicators.

The command-id may be used to keep track of logically related calls, for example when a series of 'relative' FINDS (see Section 15.3) is interrupted by one or more 'out of the blue' FINDS.

23.12 DML Statements

Each DML statement type is known by a two digit command code. The code is an abbreviation for the German term for the operation concerned and hence may seem slightly odd to English speaking users.

A hangover from the earlier versions of ADABAS necessarily retained for compatibility is that several of the command codes have two forms, one for programs to be executed in a uni-programming environment and the other for programs executing in an environment where two or more programs (actually run-units) may access the same data base at the same time. The multi-programming version now works equally well in a uni-programming mode.

Level	DBLTG Name	ADABAS Name	Code
Realm	READY	OPEN	OP
	FINISH	CLOSE	CL
Record only	FIND	FIND	Several
	STORE	ADD	N1
	ERASE	DELETE	E1/E4
Record and item	GET	READ	Several
	MODIFY	UPDATE	A1/A4
Concurrency	KEEP	HOLD	H1
	FREE	RELEASE	R1

(E1 and E4 and A1 and A4 are examples of two forms for the same code)

Figure 23.4 ADABAS DML statements

The ADABAS DML statements may be summarized as in Figure 23.4.

The best way to present these statements is somewhat similar to that used for the CODASYL DML statements as follows:

1. Retrieval
2. Update
3. Other

where the third category includes the READY statement which is the most significant.

23.12.1 DML Retrieval Statements—FIND

Although ADABAS has two retrieval statements, named FIND and READ, the division of roles between these two is subtly different from that between the CODASYL FIND and GET. In ADABAS, the FIND is a multi-record statement and the result of a successful execution is a list of data base key values in the control buffer. The READ acts on one record only and delivers it to the calling program.

The three FIND formats are identified as follows:

FIND NORMAL   S1/S4
FIND AND SORT   S2
FIND COUPLED   S5

The first two of these can be considered together, and the only difference is that in the second statement the list of data base key values is sorted according to some specified sort criterion. It is asserted with good reason that the FIND NORMAL is the main FIND option used in any ADABAS program.

The programmer must build up a conditional expression in an area in the control block called the search buffer. This expression consists of a number of conditions based on the search keys in the record type being sought. In addition, such conditions may be expressed on the search keys in related record types. A related record type is one which is directly related to the record type being sought. Conditions on the value of any one search key may be disjunctively connected.

As noted above, several records may satisfy the conditional expression. The system uses the search key indexes to evaluate the expression, and records in the data base are not accessed for that purpose. Of the records whose data base key values are included in the list, the first is actually retrieved and stored in an area in the control block called the *record buffer* (analogous to the CODASYL record area but not implicitly provided). The way the record is stored in this record area is dictated by yet another part of the control block called the *format buffer*. This allows the programmer to specify which parts of the record are required and how they are to be formatted. A count of how many records satisfy the condition is also stored in the control block.

The FIND COUPLED is really a shorthand for a capability which could be expressed approximately using FIND NORMAL. In CODASYL terms, it is a way of retrieving a set occurrence. The set occurrence is selected by means of the data base key value of an owner record. In this sense it is different from the FIND NORMAL, because if FIND NORMAL is used to do the same job, it would be necessary to express a condition on the search key item which is used in both record types. Another difference is that FIND COUPLED does not make any record available to the calling program.

It is important to observe that both of these FIND options only work if the relationship between two record types has been explicitly defined (see Section 23.3.2). This is relevant to the FIND NORMAL if it is required to base the condition on a related record type as well as on the record type being sought.

In conclusion, it is clear that these three formats do not correspond to any of those provided in the CODASYL approach.

23.12.2 DML Retrieval Statements—READ

The five READ formats in ADABAS are as follows:

READ FIELD DEFINITIONS	LF
READ ISN	L1/L4
READ PHYSICAL SEQUENCE	L2/L5
READ LOGICAL SEQUENCE	L3/L6
READ VALUES	L9

The READ FIELD DEFINITIONS has no equivalent in CODASYL. It provides a facility for reading the object schema at program execution time. Because of the feature in the FIND NORMAL with which the programmer may define the format of a record as it is to be stored in the programmer's record area, it is therefore often useful to be able to read the object schema at execution time.

The READ ISN is analogous to a CODASYL GET. It is normally used in conjunction with FIND NORMAL and makes the whole record available to the calling program. As with the CODASYL GET, it may also be used to make some part of the record available to the calling program.

The READ PHYSICAL SEQUENCE is analogous to the CODASYL format

$$\underline{FIND} \; \begin{Bmatrix} \underline{FIRST} \\ \underline{NEXT} \end{Bmatrix} \; record\text{-}name \; \underline{IN} \; realm\text{-}name$$

(see Section 15.4.3). The FIND FIRST option is achieved by setting to zero the parameter in the control block which holds data base key values. One successful execution of the statements sets this parameter to contain the data base key value of the record then found. A FIND NEXT is executed if the parameter contains such a value.

The READ LOGICAL SEQUENCE has no complete equivalent in a CODASYL system, largely because CODASYL systems have this historic leaning towards the use of randomization techniques (see Sections 4.4.1 and 15.4). One of the search keys defined for a record type must be specified in the control block. It is possible to specify a start value for this search key in another part of the control block. It is also possible to start with the lowest value of the search key.

The closest CODASYL FIND option to this ADABAS facility is the following:

$$\underline{FIND} \; \begin{Bmatrix} \underline{ANY} \\ \underline{DUPLICATE} \end{Bmatrix} \; record\text{-}name \; \underline{USING} \; item\text{-}name\text{-}1, \ldots$$

(see Sections 15.4.1 and 15.5.2). In CODASYL style, the ADABAS facility would have the format

$$\underline{FIND} \; \begin{Bmatrix} \underline{FIRST} \\ \underline{ANY} \\ \underline{NEXT} \end{Bmatrix} \; record\text{-}name \; \underline{USING} \; item\text{-}name\text{-}1$$

where item-name-1 is a search key or a calc key.

Finally, the READ VALUES also has no equivalent in a CODASYL system. It is a more typical self-contained DBMS feature and must be used to generate a list of all the values which a given search key for a given record type may take, and the number of times each is used in a record of the file. The list generated need not start with the lowest value of the search key, but a value can be specified. The list will then start with this value or the next higher value to this. One execution of the statement generates one value and a count of the number of its occurrences. If the statement is built into a loop, successive values can be produced.

23.12.3 DML Update Statements

The ADABAS updating statements provided are the usual three, STORE, MODIFY and ERASE. Because of the different nature of the relationships handled, the semantics of STORE and ERASE are somewhat different from the other DBMS discussed here.

When a record is first stored, there is no need for the system to check for an owner to which to connect it. The record is stored in the appropriate file, normally with a new ISN (the major part of the data base key value) and any search key indexes are updated. Relationships with other record types are involved only if any explicit relationship with another record type (the coupling facility) is defined.

Similar considerations arise when a record is erased. A record can be erased from the data base without the system bothering whether it is an owner in a non-empty set. What this really means is that if there exists conceptually a one to many relationship between two record types, then the semantics of the program updating the data base must take care of that which the system takes care of automatically in other systems.

The MODIFY is very similar to CODASYL, but there are some special rules which the programmer must remember when modifying data in data aggregates. As in a CODASYL system, it is necessary to retrieve a record before it can be modified. Unlike CODASYL, there is no question of changing the record from one set occurrence to another as a result of the modification.

23.12.4 Miscellaneous DML Statements

The ADABAS READY is called OPEN and requires the programmer to state explicitly whether a file is to be opened for update or for access, where the latter means retrieval only.

The OPEN statement in ADABAS is important because it forms part of the rather powerful privacy facility for the system. The control block used by an OPEN statement contains provision for an eight byte security password. It is the programmer's responsibility to ensure that this is set before any part of the data base is opened. He may do this by setting it himself or causing the value to be read in from a terminal. The password in this role is a privacy key. Associated with each privacy key is a range of applicability or an authority to process a part of the data base in a given way.

The ADABAS HOLD statement would usually be used implicitly in the FIND and READ statements. Where the two character codes were shown, the higher code implies that a HOLD is also performed. However, it is possible to program a free standing HOLD statement. The RELEASE is very analogous to the CODASYL FREE statement (see Section 17.2.2).

23.13 Summary of ADABAS

The ADABAS approach to data base management is interesting because it is so different from the CODASYL approach, although one could reasonably claim that ADABAS does provide full network capability by means of the implicit rather than the explicit relationships. As indicated, users seem to prefer the former class for host language applications. It should be noted that the user of the self-contained facilities provided must use the coupling facility.

The use of many to many relationships rather than one to many relationships is not necessarily a strength, but it is interesting because it gives a lead on how many to many relationships could be provided. The approach would be stronger if it supported *both* classes of relationship rather than only many to many. Although the discussion in this chapter has not covered this aspect, the many to many relationship is more meaningful when ad hoc queries are involved.

The designer of an ADABAS data base does not have many decisions to make. He may use the intra-record structure to handle some one to many relationships and he must predict the search keys needed, although it is possible to add new search keys later if required. The chief advantage of the system comes from its reliance on indexing techniques rather than radomization, although once again a good system would provide the choice for all record types in the data base.

Chapter 24

Relational Approach

24.1 Background

The approaches described in the three preceding chapters are commercially viable and in wide use among commercial installations all over the world. In this chapter we turn attention to an approach to data base management which is being widely studied among the academic fraternity and among the more research oriented in government and commercial organizations.

The relational approach evolved in a series of papers by Codd[1,2] in 1971, although the number of papers on this topic which have been published is quite vast. For a good comprehensive overview of what relationalism is all about, a recent book by Date[3] is recommended.

It must be emphasized that the relational approach is essentially a theory on which a number of experimental systems have been based. Rather than select one of these systems for presentation, we shall in this chapter present the elements of the theory in such a way that comparison with the CODASYL approach is facilitated.

There are no 'components' of the relational approach as is the case of the other three approaches we have considered. There is no data definition language per se, simply a way of looking at data. There is, however, a data manipulation language which Codd calls a *data sub-language*. In fact, this term is felt to be a better term than *data manipulation language*. It conveys the implication of an extension to an existing programming language so much more effectively. Codd's data sub-language is called ALPHA.[2]

24.2 Relational Terminology

The first task is to equate the terminology used in discussion of the relational approach with that which we have presented in connection with the CODASYL approach. It says something about the state of comparative understanding of these two approaches when one considers that even a terminology equivalence table can be contentious. Bearing this in mind, we present in Figure 24.1 the equivalences to be used herein, and then discuss each in turn.

Relational	CODASYL
attribute	data item
value	value
domain	—
relation	record type
tuple	record (occurrence)
table	file
inter-relation dependency	set type
degree of a relation	number of items in record type

Figure 24.1 Terminology equivalences

24.2.1 Attribute, Domain and Data Item

The word domain comes from classical set theory. It implies that in a mathematical set there may be a number of elements and in a given situation some of these may be collectively referred to as a domain. It is also useful to think of a domain as a value set, such as M and F in the domain SEX. This idea of a predefined value set is not one which is implied in the term *data item* (specifically an elementary item) widely used in all commercial data processing.

Before leaving this topic, it is useful to repeat what Codd[4] writes on the topic of domains and fields (i.e. items):

'It is the attribute concept rather than domain which is in close correspondence with field. The domain concept is missing from traditional data processing including the CODASYL DBTG approach.

When a relational data base is defined, one of the first steps is to identify the underlying domains: that is, the semantically distinct pools of non-decomposable data items from which tuples may be dynamically created. . . . If attributes A, B . . . take their values from a common domain, then it is semantically permissible to compare values of A, B for equality. . . .'

As an example, we could have a domain called NAME-OF-PERSON and two attributes, CUSTOMER-NAME and EMPLOYEE-NAME. These two attributes are probably distinct and separate, but if they are not, it would be possible to test whether a given customer is also an employee.

This kind of precise thinking is not inherent in the use of the term *data item* and the concept of a domain as distinct from an attribute is one which should be promulgated. The solution to the unfortunately loose thinking which surrounds the term *data item* is not to change the term, but rather to encourage recognition of the importance of defining the domain of values for an item prior to specifying the record types to which the item belongs.

24.2.2 Relations and Record Types

One major problem in conventional data processing terminology stems from the imprecise use of *record type* and *record*. Nine people out of ten will use *record* when they mean *record type*. In conventional data processing, this did not matter so much. In a data base oriented environment, it can cause communication and comprehension problems.

If the problem in the use of conventional data processing terminology is avoided, then *relation* and *record type* can be seen to be equivalent.

24.2.3 Tuples and Records

The word *record* in early FORTRAN carried an implication of a contiguous string of stored data—a very physical meaning. In COBOL, it has a far more logical meaning (see Section 3.2) and there seems to be no inherent problem with equating record to tuple. It should be noted that tuple is an abbreviation for 'n-tuple'.

24.2.4 Tables and Files

A collection of tuples of a given relation is called a *table*. The word *file* in COBOL has a broader meaning in that it embraces the concept of multiple record type files and also it implies something which is stored on secondary storage, even though the CODASYL COBOL Journal of Development glossary defines a file quite simply as *a collection of records*.

The CODASYL data base specifications, rightly or wrongly, avoid the word file. Perhaps if the specifications had been built on the terminological base of a file instead of a set occurrence, some of its concepts might have been easier to grasp by those with experience in conventional techniques.

The word *table* (which has an intra-record type meaning in COBOL) is used in relational theory to refer to a collection of tuples of a given relation. There are rules which these tuples must adhere to, but these are some of the facets of the theory.

24.2.5 Set Type and Inter-relation Dependency

We are now entering into some of the more tricky aspects of a comparison between relational theory and the CODASYL approach, and it is appropriate to postpone discussion of this particular equivalence until the aspects of the theory have been presented.

24.2.6 Degree of a Relation

The degree of a relation is the count of the number of domains or attributes in the relation. Since some writers use *domain* and some use *attribute*, it is not clear whether the difference is important. However, it would be convenient in terms of the association with everyday data processing terminology and practice to require a difference, such that the degree is the number of attributes, whether one or more attributes (even in the same relation) can take their values from the same domain.

24.3 Exposition of Relational Theory

Although relational theory is based on mathematical set theory, the literature does not yet appear to present the theory as a cohesive set of propositions. It therefore seems useful to attempt to list the necessary propositions inherent in the theory. This is done using relational terminology and (for comparison) the terminology of everyday data processing. It must be emphasized that all statements in both terminologies apply to relational theory. There is no attempt to compare the relational approach with that of CODASYL.

We will number each statement and classify each as a definitional lemma or a propositional lemma. A lemma is an assumed or demonstrated proposition used in argument or proof. Since there is nothing to prove here, the exposition is only to clarify argument.

For clarity, the lemmas are presented in a form which facilitates lemma by lemma comparison. All terms used with a special meaning are in italics.

RELATIONAL TERMINOLOGY DATA PROCESSING TERMINOLOGY

DEFINITIONS

1. An *attribute* is a nondecomposable element of named data.

An *elementary data item* (also called an *item*) is a nondecomposable element of named data.

2. A *domain* is a collection of values which may be associated with one or more *attributes*.

A *domain* is a collection of values which may be associated with one or more *items*.

3. A *relation* consists of a number of *attributes*.

A *record type* consists of a number of *items*.

4. The *degree* of a *relation* is the number of *attributes* in the *relation*.

The *degree* of a *record type* is the number of items in the *record type*.

5. The definition of a collection of *relations* constitutes the definition of a *data base*.

The definition of a collection of *record types* constitutes a *data base schema*.

6. A *tuple* is one set of the values of all *attributes* in a *relation*.

A *record* is one set of the values of all *items* in a *record type*.

7. The collection of all *tuples* for a *relation* is called a *table*.

The collection of all *records* of a *record type* is called a *file*.

PROPOSITIONS

1. The order of *tuples* in a *table* is immaterial.

   The order of *records* in a file is immaterial.

2. The ordering of the *attribute* values in a tuple must correspond to the ordering of the attributes in the relation.

   The ordering of the item values in a record must correspond to the ordering of the items in the record type.

3. Each *relation* must contain one or more *attributes* which collectively serve as a unique primary key.

   Each *record type* must contain one or more *items* which collectively serve as a unique primary key.

4. When a dependency exists between any two relations, one relation is the parent and the other is the subordinate.

   When a set type relationship exists between two record types, one record type is the owner and the other is a member.

5. For a dependency to exist between two relations, an attribute or attributes which serve as a primary key in the parent must also be present in the subordinate.

   For a set type relationship to exist between two record types, the item or items which serve as a primary key in the owner must also be present in the member.

6. If a relation in the subordinate in one dependency and the parent in another, then the primary key of the parent of the first dependency must be propagated through the subordinate of the second dependency.

   If a record type is the member in one set type and the owner in another, then the primary key of the first set type's owner must be propagated through its member to the second set type's member.

24.4 Constraints in CODASYL Terms

A careful study of these propositions indicates that relational theory implies a fairly rigid set of constraints in a relation data base. It is useful to summarize these constraints in CODASYL terms.

1. Each record type contains only elementary data items.
2. Each record type must have a unique prime key.
3. To be able to define a set type, the prime key of the owner must also be in the member.

It is further useful to list several CODASYL Schema DDL concepts which are explicitly prohibited in a relational data base.

1. Repeating groups.
2. Control over physical contiguity of records of the same or different types.
3. Predefined set order.
4. Definition of search key.
5. Multi-member set types.
6. Storage class and removal class.
7. Set selection algorithms.

With specific reference to IMS and TOTAL, it is important to understand that relational theory does not call for either of the major restrictions noted for these two systems. There is no assertion in the theory that a record type may not have more than two owner record types, which is felt to be a major problem with IMS (see Section 22.3.2). Furthermore, relational theory does not dictate that a record type cannot serve as an owner in one set type and a member in another set type at the same time. This is the main problem with the structuring facilities in TOTAL (see Section 21.3.1).

24.5 Relational and CODASYL Networks

There has been considerable debate on the relative merits of the relational approach and the CODASYL approach.[5] Interestingly, the CODASYL approach is invariably identified as 'the network approach' in the literature. A quote from one of Codd's early papers[6] may explain this.

'It may be argued that in some applications, the problems have an immediate natural formulation in terms of networks. This is true of some applications, such as studies of transportation networks, power-line networks, computer design and the like. We shall call these network applications. . . . The numerous data bases which reflect the daily operation and transaction of commercial and industrial enterprises are, for the most part, concerned with non-network applications. To impose a network structure on such data bases and force all users to view the data in network terms is to burden the majority of users with unnecessary complexity.'

This kind of unfortunate thinking tends to convey the impression that there is something inherently undesirable about networks. It was Date however[3] who identified the CODASYL approach as 'the network approach' in the same paper comparing it with the 'relational model'.

Taking the writings of Codd and Date together, one could be forgiven for concluding not only that networks were undesirable, but also that the relational approach does not cater for them. Nothing could be further from the truth.

It is unfortunate that the simple little examples used to illustrate the principles of relational theory tend to be based on two or three record types such as those depicted using Bachman diagrams in Figure 24.2.

It is also unfortunate that the papers on relational theory have, for one reason or another, not used Bachman diagrams (or any other graphic formalism) for depicting the structure of a data base.

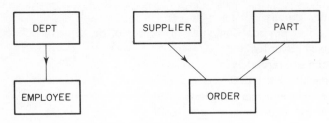

Figure 24.2 Simple data bases

In fact, a study of the extensive writing on relational theory leads to the following assertion.

The logical data structure which may be represented in a relational data base may be of the same degree of complexity as that allowed for in the CODASYL proposals for a data base management system—with the sole exception of the CODASYL facility to represent cyclic structures. This assertion cannot be made for IMS or TOTAL.

24.6 Use of Keys

Relational theory *requires* each record type in the data base to have a unique prime key. The CODASYL approach merely allows this as a possibility. It is achieved by giving the record type a location mode of CALC (see Section 4.4.1) with 'DUPLICATES NOT ALLOWED' option declared. It must be recalled that the latest CODASYL thinking is to remove any connotation of randomizing from the use of the term *calc*.

It must be noted that it is not possible to assign a prime key to each record type in a TOTAL data base or in an IMS data base. Actually, one can achieve the objective of a prime key for every record type in both of these systems at the cost of *not* using set type relationships. Few users would consider this a worthwhile price to pay.

CODASYL allows the definition of search keys or secondary keys. These are explicitly not catered for in relational theory.

24.7 Set Types and Heir Properties

The set type capability is buried deep in the prose of the writings on relational theory. The term *inter-relation dependency* does not appear to be used, but Date[3] uses the term *intra-relation dependency* and also the term *inter-relation consistency*.

24.7.1 Defining a Relationship

What happens in the three commercially viable approaches, CODASYL, IMS and TOTAL, is the following. Two record types, A and B, are defined, and then in a separate piece of syntax a relationship between A and B is defined. In

CODASYL and TOTAL there may be one or more relationships between A and B, and it is therefore necessary to name them. In IMS, there may not be more than one relationship between A and B, and no naming of the relationship is allowed.

In relational theory, record types are defined, but any relationship between them is implicit in the attributes in each record type. For instance in the simple case of departments and employees, the record types may be as follows:

DEPT
  DEPT-NO
  DEPT-NAME
  MANAGER
  LOCATION

EMPLOYEE
  EMPLOYEE-NUMBER
  EMPLOYEE-NAME
  DEPT-NO
  SALARY

The repetition of the data item DEPT-NO in both record types coupled with the fact that DEPT-NO is the prime key of the record type has the effect of defining a set type relationship between the two record types. In other words, the definition of a set type relationship in a relational data base is implicit in the items defined in the record types as opposed to being explicit.

It is of great significance that TOTAL uses exactly this method to handle set type relationships with its control items (see Section 22.9), whereas IMS does not even allow it as an option.

It is also noteworthy that the early CODASYL specifications did not cater for this kind of approach, and hence commercially available implementations tend not to support it. However, the most recent CODASYL specifications do permit this as an alternative (see Section 8.9).

24.7.2 Set Order

One of the more contentious properties of a set type is the set order. There is no concept of set order in relational theory. In fact, in his initial paper,[1] Codd affirms:

'Those application programs which take advantage of the stored ordering of a file are likely to fail to operate correctly if for some reason it becomes necessary to replace that ordering by a different one.'

One cannot argue with this truism. However, the evil lies not in defining an order, but in taking advantage of it. Using *reductio ad absurdum* arguments, one could assert that an application program should not take advantage of any factor defined in the data definition because in theory it might change. Where does one draw the line?

However, relational theory had its impact directly or indirectly on the CODASYL proposals for set ordering. The set order clause was not removed, but the option for the data administrator to define a set order immaterial (see Section 6.5) was added. This option allows the capabilities proposed in relational theory to be achieved in a CODASYL system.

24.7.3 Storage Class

Finally, the CODASYL concept of storage class must be examined. Relational theory does not admit of such a concept, which is another way of saying that the storage class is always automatic. A relational system would in effect behave in the same way as TOTAL. When a member record is stored, the value of the set item for any set type in which it participates must correspond to that in one of the owner records in the data base.

24.7.4 Set Mode

We have deliberately left set mode until last. The references to chains and pointer arrays in the early CODASYL papers gave rise to some of the early criticism that the proposals were unnecessarily involved with questions of how the data should be stored. The DDLC reacted well to such comments and the set mode clause (see Section 5.3) was removed from the Schema DDL. In fact, the chain concept had tended to dominate the early image of the CODASYL proposals. Now it is realized that the important capability is that of defining 1:M relationships between record types rather than the techniques for representing such relationships in direct access storage.

Relational theory steps back even further from the explicit definition of the relationship, calling in effect for an implicit definition in terms of the data items in the record types. Nevertheless, supporters of the relational approach have been heard to admit verbally that some kind of set mode must be provided behind the scenes. As in the case of the set order, it should not be a factor which is defined explicitly so that the application programmer can take advantage of it.

24.8 Practicality of Relational Theory

Three aspects of relational theory can be examined in terms of their impact on the practitioner. These are

1. Unique prime key for every record type
2. Means of representing set type relationships
3. Propagation of prime keys down structure

Before discussing these aspects, the rationale for them must be analysed. It is purely and simply a question of data independence and the design of a data manipulation language which will maximize that data independence. The question to be asked is whether these rigid rules are in fact justified in order to achieve the data independence.

24.8.1 Unique Prime Key

Relational theory calls for every record type to have a unique prime key. In most cases this is justifiable and no one could argue against it. There are a few instances where it appears contrived. One example is depicted in Figure 24.3.

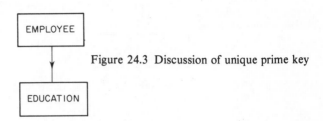

Figure 24.3 Discussion of unique prime key

Employees normally have employee numbers and a prime key in the record type EMPLOYEE is perfectly acceptable. However, in the other record type, namely EDUCATION, a unique prime key seems to be rather contrived. It is unlikely that any use of this modest data base would call for an access to an EDUCATION record independent of the EMPLOYEE record to which it belongs.

Insisting on a unique prime key is a good idea most of the time. Certainly, it is important to *be able to* define such a key for any record type in the data base (not possible in TOTAL and IMS), but to *have* to do so seems unnecessary.

24.8.2 Representation of Set Type Relationships

The relational way of handling set type relationships is simple and effective. It is achieved at the expense of duplicating an item (and therefore its concomitant values) in two record types. The approach is easy to understand and to use. It is without question commercially viable as it is the only way allowed in both TOTAL and ADABAS.

By contrast, the CODASYL approaches to this problem are provided in the plethora of set selection options, and only recently has one of these corresponded to that espoused by relational theory.

We have no hesitation in endorsing the relational approach in this respect as being preferable in almost every case. It is perhaps the second major disadvantage of IMS that this kind of facility is not provided in that system.

24.8.3 Propagation of Prime Keys

The illustration of this practice is shown (Figure 24.4) in an example borrowed from Codd's initial paper.[1] In subsequent papers on relational theory, the examples chosen are all two level ones.

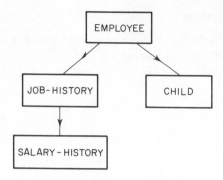

Figure 24.4 Three-level structure

If the four record types were to adhere to relational theory, they would be in the following form:

EMPLOYEE (<u>EMPNO</u>, NAME, BIRTHDATE)
JOB-HISTORY (<u>EMPNO</u>, <u>JOBDATE</u>, TITLE)
SALARY-HISTORY (<u>EMPNO</u>, <u>JOBDATE</u>, <u>SALARYDATE</u>, SALARY)
CHILD (<u>EMPNO</u>, <u>CHILDNAME</u> BIRTHDATE)

This way of specifying the record names and the items belonging to each is widely used in papers on relational theory. The underlining of an item name is the recognized way of indicating that this item serves as the prime key in the record type, or as part of the prime key. These record types are collectively expressed in what relational theory refers to as third normal form—a term so far not introduced into this chapter although its implications have been taken into full account.

This kind of representation is a very inherent aspect of relational theory. In essence, what is happening is that constraints are being placed on the items to be contained in the record types in a data base structure with the aim of being able to manipulate this structure in such a way that the application programs are somewhat more independent of changes to the data structure than they otherwise would be. What is happening is again that the relationships between record types are implied in the data items in those record types.

While endorsing wholeheartedly the practice of propagating prime keys down one level, it seems very contrived to do this down two or more. The requirement to include the item EMPNO in the SALARY-HISTORY record type merely to satisfy the semantic needs of a specific manipulation language is hard to support.

24.9 Data Sub-languages (DML) for a Relational Data Base

There is no single DML defined for a relational data base. Instead there are to approaches which are based on relational algebra and relational calculus. Date[3] summarizes the difference between these rather succinctly.

'There are at least two ways in which we might allow the user to do this: (1) he could actually specify the sequence of relational algebra operations to be performed to produce the desired result; (2) he could simply state a definition of the desired result in terms of the relational calculus leaving the system to determine which operations are necessary. The difference between the two approaches is analogous to the difference between (1) actually constructing a set by performing a sequence of set operations (union intersection, etc.) and (2) simply stating the "defining property" of a set in the form of a predicate; in other words the difference between procedurality and non-procedurality.'

24.9.1 Relational Algebra

A relational algebra operation refers to one or more record types and naming yet another record type as the result of performing the operation. The two main operations are referred to as *projection* and *join*.

A *projection* acts on one record type only and produces one with less items. To be precise, the operation does not act on a record type, but on all the records of the type named. The effect of executing a projection is to generate a collection of records, all of this new record type. These are regarded as being stored in what relational theory calls a workspace.

A workspace differs from a CODASYL user working area in two major respects, the first being that it is essentially open ended and the second that there is no restriction which states that it accommodates only one record of each type.

In COBOL, records which are generated during the course of execution of a program would normally correspond to a record type defined in the Working Storage Section. In addition, the application programmer would have to declare the space needed for storing the file produced as a result of executing the projection.

The other major statement is usually referred to as a *join*. If two record types have an item which is in both and the values of the item are in both cases selected from the same domain of values, then it is possible to perform one of these join operations on the common item. The effect is to generate a collection of records of a new type which contains all items from both record types, but the common item only once. If a value in the common item appears in the collection for a record of one type and not for *any* record of the other type, then the record containing this value does not participate in the join.

In fact, the join is nothing very novel. It will be recognized by those with experience in the processing of tape files as a merge operation. Nevertheless, the project and join together seem to provide a powerful relatively non-procedural way of manipulating files.

One could argue that it is necessarily heavy on storage space compared with the record at a time logic of the commercial systems in use today. Its advocates point to the much reduced number of statements required to specify any given transaction.

24.9.2 Relational Calculus

The relational calculus is different from the relational algebra in the way already indicated. The data sub-language ALPHA[2] is the best known example of this approach. Just as the FIND statement (see Chapter 15) is the cornerstone of the CODASYL DML, so is a powerful GET statement the most important statement in ALPHA.

The general format of a GET statement might be as follows:

GET workspace target-list WHERE condition

The parameter workspace refers to the storage space in which the set of records generated as a result of the statement are stored. It is an important aspect of ALPHA that the programmer does not need to know whether the workspace is in direct access storage or not. The target list consists normally of a list of item names (possibly qualified by record names), and record names alone. Finally, the condition could be of full Boolean complexity rather like compound conditionals in COBOL.

In addition to the GET, there are a number of other statement types such as PUT (i.e. STORE), UPDATE (MODIFY) and DELETE.

24.10 Summary of Conclusions

A number of conclusions can be made from the analysis of the relational approach. They are as follows:

1. The relational approach requires a data definition process which contains a number of restrictions.
2. Two of the restrictions—unique prime key and the way of defining set types—are felt to be quite acceptable. Propagating prime keys from the top to the bottom of a deep structure is questionable.
3. The relational approach permits the definition of network structures as complex as those proposed by CODASYL (with the exception of cyclic structures).
4. The CODASYL approach fits far more closely with relational theory than does either IMS or TOTAL.
5. The requirement to propagate prime keys through the structure is needed to support the semantics of the data sub-language suggested for a relational data base.
6. The CODASYL single record at a time DML could manipulate a relational data base.

Finally, it must be stated that much of the debate 'relational versus network' was contrived to draw people's attention away from the deficiencies in such systems as IMS. In fact, the relational approach and the CODASYL approach have quite a lot in common. The DDLC decisions during the period 1972 to 1976 indicate that relational theory has indeed been having an impact on the CODASYL thinking, and rightly so. Relational theory on the other hand has had no impact whatever on IMS.

References

1. E. F. Codd, 'A relational model of data for large shared data banks', *CACM,* **13,** No. 6, 377–387 (June 1970).
2. E. F. Codd, 'A data base sub-language founded on the relational calculus', *Proceedings of ACM SIGFIDET Workshop on Data Description Access and Control*, 35–68.
3. C. J. Date, *An Introduction to Data Base Systems*, Addison–Wesley (1975).
4. E. F. Codd, 'Understanding relations', *FDT*, **6,** No. 4, 18–22 (1974).
5. Workshop on Data Description Access and Control—Data Models: Data Structure Set Versus Relational (Debate Proceedings), Part of Proceedings of ACM SIGMOD Workshop held May 1974.
6. E. F. Codd, 'Normalized Data Base Structure; A brief tutorial', *Proceedings of ACM SIGFIDET Workshop on Data Description Access and Control*, held November 1971, pp. 1–16.
7. C. J. Date, 'Relational Data Base Systems: A Tutorial', published in Information Systems COINS IV, 1974, Plenum Press, pp. 37–54.

Chapter 25

Concluding Comments

25.1 Recapitulation

In the first 18 chapters of this text we have attempted to present the major concepts provided in the CODASYL approach to data base management. This was done with emphasis on explaining what each capability is all about. No attempt was made to present the capabilities as a rigorous definitive book of law. This task should be done by the formal specifications, which make them hard to read. A subjective weighting mechanism was applied and features which would be widely found in commercial implementations are given much more weight.

Chapters 19 and 20 touch on two aspects of a DBMS which were identified in the DBTG and DDLC reports but not defined in detail. The presentation in these chapters on a Data Strategy Definition Language and a restructuring facility follow to some extent the work of the UK based Data Base Administration Working Group.

Finally, Chapters 21, 22 and 23 look at three competitive commercial approaches, and Chapter 24 analyses the widely advocated relational view as seen from the context of the CODASYL approach.

25.2 Criticisms of the CODASYL Approach

There are few who would claim that the CODASYL approach to data base management is utterly without blemish. Throughout the course of this text we have tried to point out weaknesses in the appropriate chapters and sections where the capability is discussed. The author's view on some of the major flaws was given in a paper[1] presented at a conference sponsored by IFIP Technical Committee 2. This conference was dedicated to a review of the Schema DDL and the papers by Nijssen,[2] Waghorn,[3] Kay,[4] Earnest,[5] Gerassimenko,[6] and Steel[7] are relevant to many of the topics in the present text.

The following list contains aspects of the approach discussed in earlier chapters which may be encountered in practice, which it is felt should be changed in the specifications (if not already done so).

1. Implication that CALC implies randomization (see Section 4.5).
2. Possibility to provide a null data base key value when storing a record which has location mode DIRECT (see Section 4.6.3).
3. Explicit declaration of set mode in Schema DDL (see Sections 5.3 and 5.5.2).
4. Concept of indexed sorted sets (see Section 6.10.3).
5. Global search keys (see Section 6.10.3).
6. Hierarchical set selection (see Section 8.6).
7. Complexity of basing set selection on member item values (see Section 8.9).
8. Modification of set selection in sub-schema (see Section 12.7).
9. Dependence of FIND ANY DUPLICATE on randomizing techniques (see Section 15.5.2).
10. Semantics of currency control statements KEEP, FREE, REMONITOR (see Section 17.2).
11. Facilities for checking data base exception conditions with USE declaration (see Section 17.6).
12. Privacy facilities (see Section 18.5).

In addition to this list, the reader is advised to avoid multi-member set types and sorted set types wherever possible. The former complicate the semantics and the latter can have serious effects on execution time.

25.3 Broader Issues

The CODASYL specifications have been subject to a measure of criticism on broader issues such as *data independence* and *basic architecture.*

Some thoughts on the former topic were covered in the discussion on the relationship between the new Data Strategy Language, DSDL, proposed by the Data Base Administration Working Group, and the existing Schema DDL (see Section 19.2).

The issue of data independence boils down to the factors in the data definition of which the programmer can take advantage in his program. If the value of any such factor is changed, then the programmer has to change his program accordingly. Hence, the more such factors enter the picture, the more likely the programmer is to take advantage of them and the more likely it becomes that his program is to be changed when the changes are made to the data definition.

In order to look at this issue objectively, it is necessary to look at these mythical factors and see if there is any positive aspect to them. Do they indeed provide the data administrator and programmer some meaningful power to improve the performance of the total system? This is a question to which it is hard to give a general answer, but what emerges from the discussion is the importance of being able to control trade-offs. Certainly, the data administrator should be able to do this and so, in certain circumstances, should the programmer. This is another way of saying that the system should be flexible enough so that either data independence can be achieved, usually at the expense of performance, or, alternatively, performance should be achievable hopefully at not too much expense in data independence.

The critical phrase in the preceding paragraph is 'factors in the data definition of which the programmer can take advantage in his program'. In the discussion of the DMCL (see Section 19.2), we suggested the following classification of data definition factors:

1. Programmer needs to know.
2. Programmer does not need to know, but could profit from knowing.
3. Programmer does not need to know and cannot profit from knowing.

The concept of a two stage data definition as provided by the Schema DDL, followed by the DSDL, is relevant. Critics have attacked the presence in the Schema DDL of factors such as the following:

1. Set mode
2. Realm declarations and record type to realm assignments
3. Location mode via set
4. Set order

Some of these factors provide an important trade-off to the data administrator. He wants to be able to influence the physical contiguity of records of different types, and the realm concept and location mode via set allow him to do this. In some situations, a decision on the order for the sets of a given type and a decision on the way the sets of that type are represented are also part of the business of tuning the data base. Nevertheless, the fact that the data administrator needs to influence these factors does not imply ipso facto that the programmer must be brought into the act and also allowed his measure of control.

In other words, it is perfectly feasible for the control over certain factors to be available to the data administrator without having to provide analogous manipulation options to the programmer. Such factors, and the erstwhile set mode is a good example, should be included in the DSDL—not in the Schema DDL. If and when the DSDL is formally accepted as part of the CODASYL approach, then many decisions will become much easier.

25.4 Future of the CODASYL Approach

The CODASYL approach to data base management is not perfect. Considerable cleaning up of the specifications is called for and many places where this is called for have been mentioned in this book.

As a basis for a future international standard based on proven technology it is the best candidate. Its structuring facilities fit in more closely with relational theory than do those of other approaches. It offers flexible control to the data administrator who is competent to make intelligent decisions on the data independence versus processing time trade-off. Hopefully, this text will help clarify the approach to a wider number of people and serve to promote a wider understanding of the advantages and problems involved.

References

1. T. W. Olle, 'An analysis of the flaws in the Schema DDL and proposed improvements', in *Data Base Description*. (Ed. B. C. M. Douque and G. M. Nijssen), North-Holland, 1975, pp. 283–298.
2. G. M. Nijssen, Set and CODASYL set or coset. As above, pp. 1–72.
3. W. J. Waghorn, The DDL as an industry standard? As above, pp. 121–168.
4. M. H. Kay, An analysis of the CODASYL DDL for use with a relational sub-schema. As above, pp. 199–214.
5. C. Earnest, Selection of higher level structures in networks. As above, pp. 215–238.
6. T. Gerassimenko, The realm concept as incorporated in the family of database languages developed by CODASYL (for COBOL). As above, pp. 329–338.
7. T. B. Steel, Jr, Data base standardization: a status report. As above, pp. 183–198.

Index

Date Due

AUG 1 2 1980			
RESERVE			
6/7/82			
RESERVE			
SE 17 '82			
6-8-83			
AN 5			
RESERVE			
APR 9 '84			
OFF 6-1 84			
JUN 1 0 '85			
APR 2 1 '85			
OCT 1 3 '86			
OCT 1 0 '88			
JAN 29 '91			
FEB 1 2 '91			
APR 1 5 '94			